F. Vosman & K.-W. Merks (eds.)

Aiming at Happiness

The Moral Teaching in
the Catechism of
the Catholic Church

An Analysis and Commentary

Pharos

Aiming at Happiness

F. Vosman & K.-W. Merks (eds.)

Aiming at Happiness

The Moral Teaching in
the Catechism of
the Catholic Church

An Analysis and Commentary

Pharos

This Volume has been published with the assistance of the Catholic Theological University at Utrecht

BX
1959.5
.U3813
1996

CIP-Gegevens Koninklijke Bibliotheek, Den Haag

© 1996, Kok Pharos Publishing House,
Kampen, the Netherlands
Cover Design by Rob Lucas
ISBN 90 390 0441 2
Translated by Lucy Jansen-Hofland and Henry Jansen from the Dutch Edition

© Nederlandse Editie Gooi en Sticht/Baarn, 1995
Uit op Geluk. De catechismus van de katholieke kerk over goed en kwaad, Uitleg en commentaar onder redactie van K.-W. Merks en F.J.H Vosman, Gooi & Sticht/Baarn, 1995

All rights reserved. No part of this book may be reproduced or transmitted in any form or by any means, electronic or mechanical, including photocopying, recording, or by any information storage and retrieval system, without permission in writing from the publisher.

Table of Contents

Introduction
    KARL-WILHELM MERKS AND FRANS VOSMAN 1

I. The Dignity of the Human Person
    JAN HULSHOF 11

II. In Search of the Happy Life: Happiness and Beatitude
as the End of Human Life and Action
    FRANS VOSMAN 25

III. The Freedom of the Human Person
    RINUS HOUDIJK 57

IV. The Good Tree and the Right Fruits: The Catechism of
the Catholic Church on the Morality of Human Acts (1749-1761)
    JAN JANS 74

V. Passions and Virtues
    PATRICK VANDERMEERSCH 93

VI. Conscience—A Social-Ethical Reading
    FRED VAN IERSEL 113

VII. Sin as the Disruptor of Relationships
    ANNELIES VAN HEIJST 130

VIII. The Theology of Grace
as the Hermeneutics of Salvation and Liberation
    A.J.M. VAN DEN HOOGEN 147

IX. The Human Community
    RONALD JEURISSEN 164

X. The Moral Law
    THEO C.J. BEEMER 182

XI. The Authority of Church Teaching on Matters of Morality
    JOSEPH A. SELLING 194

XII. Scripture and Morality
 KARL-WILHELM MERKS 222

Index of Names 247

Index of Subjects 250

Personalia 256

Introduction

Karl-Wilhelm Merks and Frans Vosman

On 11 October 1992, the thirtieth anniversary of the opening of the Second Vatican Council, Pope John Paul II presented a new world catechism: the *Catechism of the Catholic Church*. This was an occasion where believers were presented with a document that is attributed with high authority.

The Starting Point of the Catechism

In the constitution with which John Paul II introduced the world Catechism (the Apostolic Constitution *Fidei Depositum*) he spoke repeatedly of the need for a "faithful," "sound," explanation showing the "content and wondrous harmony of the catholic faith" and at the same time of a resource that is "suited to the present life of Christians," which can clarify and animate the faith of the contemporary Christian and can give an answer from within the faith to contemporary questions. But, one could ask, are there not enough 'new' catechisms and books of faith published by local bishops?[1] The World Catechism does not want its own account to replace those catechisms.

What was the reason, then, for a *world* Catechism? Ultimately, the Catechism is the fruit of a new attempt at evangelism, for which the pope and the Synod of Bishops had already decided in 1981. The Catechism is meant to be an explanation of the "Catholic doctrine," a "sure and authentic reference text," that can serve as a framework for instruction in the Catholic doctrine and "encourage and assist in the writing of new local catechisms."

---

[1] Such as, for example, the bishops of France, *Catéchisme pour adultes* (Paris, 1991); Italian episcopate, *Signore da chi andremo?* (Rome, 1981); and catechisms by the German bishops, *Katholischer Erwachsenen-Katechismus: Das Glaubensbekenntnis der Kirche* (Bonn, 1985) and vol. 2, *Leben aus dem Glauben* (Bonn, 1985); Belgian bishops, *Geloofsboek* (Tielt, 1987).

What Can be Expected of this Book?

The Catechism consists of four parts (cf. numbers 14-17): the profession of faith (Part One), the sacraments of faith as they are celebrated in the liturgy (Part Two), the life of faith and the meaning of faith for morality (Part Three), and prayer in the Christian life (Part Four). This volume is concerned with the third part, the Catechism's exposition of morality, i.e., the meaning of faith for human acts.

The ecclesiastical tradition has made a link between morality and the happiness of human beings, a link that is also authorized by the Old and New Testaments: Psalm 1:1 begins: "Blessed is the man...." This psalm establishes a link between the contemplation of God's law and human happiness, between good acts and the success of people's projects for their lives. We encounter the same word, "blessed" (Greek: *makarios*) in the Beatitudes of the Sermon on the Mount (Matthew 5:3-12; cf. Luke 6:20-23), which is called the "New Law" (Catechism, 1716-1729). According to Augustine and Thomas Aquinas, the Beatitudes contain the entire teaching of what is important for Christian life ("contains the whole process of forming the life of a Christian" (*ST* I-II. 108.3)).[2] The title of this volume reflects this elementary orientation toward happiness. As such we would like to point out the relative place of morality: life is more than morality, and faith is broader than a doctrine of morality. The title *Aiming at Happiness* is an indication of that toward which the old moral tradition of the Catholic Church directed its moral instruction: happiness, which God desires to give in abundance to mankind, is also the end of all life and actions. For the Catechism as well this idea determines the meaning of morality.

The third part of the Catechism, which deals with morality and is entitled "Life in Christ," is again divided into two sections. The first section is called "Life in the Spirit." This volume will be of help in reading this section. Twelve central subjects of the Catechism are examined, on the basis of which the Catholic view of actions with respect to good and evil is explained. These are: the dignity of human beings, the beatitudes, freedom, the good or evil of a human act, virtues and passions, conscience, sin and grace, the community, the moral law and, finally, the role of holy Scripture in the contemplation of good and evil in actions. The goal set by the authors and editors is to give an *explanation* of each of the key concepts with respect to their precise meaning. They subsequently concerned themselves with *analysis*: how does the Catechism text fit together conceptually and what is implied by the concepts employed? Finally, they give a *critique*: is justice done to the riches of faith? Is the modern understanding of

---

[2] The translation is from Thomas Aquinas, *Summa Theologica*, tr. Fathers of the Dominican Province (London, 1922).

INTRODUCTION 3

human beings made possible?[3] In this way the order of the articles follows the order of the first section of the third part of the Catechism; where it is possible and helpful we have sometimes combined key concepts (virtues and passions) or analyzed as a separate subject (dignity). The second section is called "The Ten Commandments." On the basis of the Decalogue as given in Exodus and Deuteronomy, specific questions of moral acts are illuminated from the perspective of faith and with the help of philosophical distinctions. Another volume with explanations, analysis, and critical commentary will be devoted to this particular morality.

The various authors of this volume—theologians and philosophers—do not express one and the same position regarding moral theology or philosophical ethics. This will certainly become clear in the different analyses of the parts of the Catechism and in the critical comments on the Catechism itself, which results in appealing to the various positions of moral theology. Nevertheless, the authors all share one commitment: even if the critique may sometimes appear somewhat disrespectful, the authors are nonetheless buoyed up by the same commitment from which the Catechism has also arisen: to reconsider the truth of the faith of our time and to explain it in a comprehensible way.

How to Use a Catechism

How does one use something like a catechism today? The catechism used to be an outstanding example of a certain kind of religious education, viewed as instruction in the truths of the faith that one learned from external sources. This idea was based on a strongly objective view of the faith which was directed toward content, and "truths," which could be formulated in a number of principles. The status of the catechism can perhaps best be discerned from the fact that in some countries instruction in the catechism was given by the pastor or curate while instruction in the Bible belonged to the task of the ordinary lay teachers.

For a great number of people today this type of instruction is no longer a convincing model, and this is not simply because many questions and doubts have arisen on the basis of advancing secularization and its accompanying rationalism. The believer's experiences his own role in another way, also giving a new meaning to the old adage of 'faith searching for internal understanding'

---

[3] Compare this with views on the Catechism as a whole (not just the section on morality): T.J. Reese (ed.), *The Universal Catechism Reader: Reflections and Responses* (San Francisco, 1990); the theme issue of *Salesianum* 56 (1990) 1: "Studi sul nuovo Catechismo della Chiesa Cattolica"; on the section on morality, see the theme issue of *Studia Moralia* 31 (1994) 1: "La vie dans le Christ: IIIe Partie du Catéchisme de l'Église Catholique," and various articles in *NRT*.

(*fides quaerens intellectum*). Many contemporary people do not want to learn something from an external source. As modern believers they want their intellect to be addressed. They also want to be respected as far as the awareness of their own dignity, their idea of maturity and responsibility is concerned. Also within their faith they wish to see themselves taken seriously where their faith is concerned, particularly with respect to their convictions of that which belongs to a responsible and just human existence, and with respect to that which is valuable and important to them.

For many believers a critical attitude toward doctrine is not contrary to their faith. This does cause tensions, both where the concept of rationality is shortchanged or narrowed and where in the articulation of the faith no account is taken of this consciousness of one's own dignity and the demand of rationality. The Catechism enters into these tensions, albeit in a more reserved way than as occurs in the moral encyclical *Veritatis Splendor* (1993).

Such tensions are indicated and evaluated in this volume again and again. We assume that the reader, like us, is particularly interested in the issue of how faith can offer clarity and support in a way that is precisely "suited to the present life of Christians," with the characteristics that this life has in our post-Enlightenment culture. We therefore assume that, like the Catechism and ourselves, the reader will not avoid these tensions.

A Catechism for the Entire World?

Other than one might surmise from the image and the reality of the Catholic Church as a centralized world church, a world catechism is not an ordinary matter. In the nearly two millennia that the church has existed, only one other catechism has been published in addition to the *Catechism* with the same authority—the *Catechismus Romanus* of 1566. It was after the Council of Trent (1545-1563) that such a catechism was considered meaningful, and now it is after the Second Vatican Council (1962-1965). In both cases, in the midst of that which was experienced as a deep crisis, it involves a reformulation of the summary of the Catholic faith, through which the Church once again wished to ascertain its identity.

In this respect it would be interesting to compare the *Catechismus Romanus* with the *Catechism*. Points of particular interest in such a comparison could be questions such as: How are the catechisms directed at the situation of their time? Has the expression of the Catholic faith remained the same throughout time? In the time between the sixteenth and the twentieth century, how have the questions developed and changed? It will become apparent then that the catechism is also a product of its age, revealing changes in expression and way of thinking, and that this is something that is to be permitted, even necessary. Finally, although a catechism aims at being a legitimate expression of an eternal content of faith, it will nevertheless express this content for people of a certain period in time. For that reason the question of whether a catechism succeeds in fulfilling this intention or not could be one of the criteria for judging a catechism.[4] Catechisms which deny this claim of relatedness to time misunderstand their own well-defined and, in the eyes of the entire ecclesiastical tradition, limited place. That which obtains for *time* also obtains for *space*. With respect to the Catechism the question is asked more than once as to whether the idea itself of a catechism that is valid for the entire world, a 'world catechism', can be the same as the catechism was after Trent. Has not the ideal of worldwide validity changed fundamentally since that time? The sixteenth century was a period of striking change with regard to the concrete, political, and ideological thinking regarding a (Christian) European superiority and subjection. Now we stand at a point where this global Euro-centrism, developed throughout the ages, is breaking down, to which one of the contributing causes has been a change in the European mentality itself. The meaning of culture and cultures, that is to say, of the necessary and legitimate differences between cultures that appeared on this globe at the same time, has been (re)discovered.

This is the reason behind the question of whether it is still possible in this day and age to write a catechism that is valid for the entire world. The Catechism seems to give a positive answer to this question. It wishes to be seen as a universally valid 'framework catechism', even though it must be further fleshed out, worked out, and concretized by national and regional catechisms. The history of the development of the Catechism, which was submitted to bishops the world over for consultation, would also indicate the global responsibility for the Catechism. The pope calls this contribution a "'symphony' of the faith." As such, the Catechism would not only be a catechism *for* the entire world but also, in a way, a catechism *of* the entire world. There are questions to be posed with respect to this view of global character of the Catechism.[5] In our view, with the realization of a catechism for and of the whole world (if such a thing is possible), one cannot assume that that which is essential to the entire world is said and that the difference in cultures does not essentially add anything to a tradition that itself depends on a limited cultural background. Would the fixed definition of the content of faith need 'only' to be reworded? It is this concept of the ideal, for this is how it is seen, that has been thoroughly investigated. In addition to the representation of the unfolding of faith in time as it is expressed in the term

---

[4] For an informative comparison between the *Catechismus Romanus* and the *Catechism of the Catholic Church*, cf. J. van Laarhoven, "Twee katechismussen: De Catechismus Romanus en de Katechismus van de Katholieke Kerk," in: *TvT* 33 (1993): 371-89.

[5] See the theme issue of *Concilium* 25 (1989) 4: "World Catechism or Inculturation?"

'tradition', the unfolding of the faith in cultures as a key for a valid theological notion of a global character would also have to be (further) reflected upon.

In any case it must be determined just what the worldwide significance of such a document is, and in what ways and to which degree it may be considered as normative in order to obtain as universal in spite of the differences in cultural situations. For this reason and not only for reasons concerned with practical education that the question is asked today whether the idea of a framework catechism for the entire world would not need a reevaluation, given the current cultural plurality, of which the legitimate boundaries cannot be presupposed to be delimited in any way.

We mention this problem here without being able to solve it within the scope of this volume. Yet we believe that it should be included as a question that permanently accompanies the material of the Catechism—all the more so because the problem of the individual nature of cultures in which the Catechism must be 'received', welcomed, and accepted not only presents itself outside of Europe but appears just as much in our own context, the culture within which the Catechism has arisen. There are already questions as to how and whether the world catechism connects with *our* contemporary culture.

The New Catechism and Our Cultural Circle

It may be asked whether the Catechism can still be regarded as 'contemporary' even with regard to Western culture. With regard to ways of thinking and formulation, it seems to be a long way from the way of thinking, speaking, and appraisal of the people of our own culture, as having undergone and received form from the Enlightenment with its characteristics of modernity, rationality, democracy, individualization, and pluralism.

It is a nice anecdotal observation that when the *New Catechism* is mentioned in the Netherlands, it is not the *Catechism of the Catholic Church* that is referred to but the Dutch catechism of 1968. Now this may seem to be a game of names, but such an observation could lead to questioning the actual newness of the Catechism. Newness is not naturally a sign of quality in every case; therefore this question also certainly does not concern that which is new in itself but precisely that renewal that takes into account the changed way of thinking and feeling, the new and differently posed questions of our time which deal with actual problems in current personal and social lives. If the Catechism does not do this, then it will not take root—not in our culture either. Then it cannot fulfil the pretention of constituting the framework for more local contemporary books of faith. This obtains particularly for moral questions which penetrate the daily lives of all. In the answers to these moral questions the direct conscious experience of people and the internal comprehension of presented values and norms play a central role. It is from this that the accessibility or inaccessibility of the ecclesiastical doctrine is actually determined.

To this extent the question of the renewed character of the Catechism, renewal viewed as having entered into the actual cultural situation, is of utmost importance for the acceptance of that which the Catechism wishes to call to mind of the tradition of faith.

The Catechism's Section on Morality

For a Christian, good and just acts, i.e., morality, are inseparably connected with faith. Thus the entire moral section in the Catechism is placed in the middle of (the explanation of the various dimensions of) a (Catholic) believer's self-knowledge: between the confession of faith and the celebration of faith in sacraments and liturgy on the one hand and prayer on the other.

But good and just acts, morality, is also the area in which Christians of various churches meet as well as Christians and non-Christians. Morality is not only something for Christians. According to the traditional doctrine of the Catholic Church, all people are open to the moral dimension of acts and with the correct use of their experiences, insights, and understanding they can all find a good and just order of life and acts. This conviction was expressed in Catholic moral theology because it formulated morality as an ethics of natural law. People can find that which is good even without the Christian faith if they follow their conscience. As far as that is concerned, morality forms an excellent place for living together, for *oikoumenē*.

Both convictions, that faith itself must be paired with a good moral life and that this moral life is mutual for people with and without Christian faith, is expressed in the way in which the moral section is drawn up in the Catechism.

On the one hand the Catechism stresses that its doctrine deals with life from the perspective of faith; on the other hand, it elaborates on the traditional thought of natural law as a model for finding moral truth by linking itself strongly to Neo-scholastic thinking.[6] But the question is whether the Catechism is able to make the general relevance of that which it explains as morality and that which it holds to be normative plausible for all people of this day and age. It is true that, for example, it takes up important themes of contemporary reflection on an anthropological ethical nature with the chapters on the dignity of the human individual and on the human community. But it also holds to models of

---

[6] Cf., for example, M. Vidal, "Die Enzyklika *Veritatis Splendor* und der Weltkatechismus: Die Restauration des Neuthomismus in der katholischen Morallehre," in: D. Mieth (ed.), *Moraltheologie im Abseits? Antwort auf die Enzyklika* Veritatis Splendor (Freiburg/Basel/Vienna, 1994), pp.244-70.

norms and conscience that are difficult to apply to the concepts of people and society in our current culture.

In the section on morality in the Catechism we are clearly dealing with a combination of schemas of moral theology that are not completely reconciled with one another: 'Thomasian' theology (with its supporting ideas of virtues and passions, of grace and Spirit, destiny and happiness) stands next to a Neo-Thomistic theology (with a theory of acts that distinguishes the object of acts, the intention, and the circumstances but does not reflect their connection with the end of acts and life).[7] There is also a view of conscience which could be called modern with respect to the historical period from which the ideas are borrowed.[8]

The Articles in this Volume

As we already mentioned, this volume follows the Catechism's own construction of sections and numbering with a few exceptions. These exceptions are particularly motivated by the cohesion among themes with respect to content which are treated separately in the Catechism. For the rest, in addition to individual interpretation the authors have striven for finding the mutual links between the various chapters as well as making visible the setting of the various themes in the philosophical theological tradition. This clarifies that which is new, that which remains traditional, and the way in which the old and the new are combined into a whole in the Catechism. Explanations are also given as to where and why the Catechism is not, in the eyes of the authors, successful in formulating a new synthesis.

In the first article, entitled "The Dignity of the Human Person" (which begins with the programmatic number 1700 of the Catechism), Jan Hulshof explains what the Catechism means by the term dignity, and when and in which sense this notion was, after some initial suspicion, assumed by the Church.

In the second article, entitled "In Search of the Happy Life" (1716-1729, 1877-1879), Frans Vosman outlines how happiness and the Beatitudes are concepts that fit into Catholic moral instruction. Happiness is the ultimate end of human acts, from which good and evil are examined.

Rinus Houdijk wrote the article "The Freedom of the Human Person." He takes up the idea of freedom as it appears in the Catechism and compares it with

---

[7] M. Vidal, "La Matriz tomistica de la moral general en el Catecismo de la Iglesia Catolica," in: *Studia Moralia* 32 (1994) 1: 21-44.

[8] L. Vereecke, "La conscience morale selon le Catéchisme de l'Église Catholique," in *Studia Moralia* 32 (1994) 1: 61-74.

the concept as it was introduced by the Enlightenment and is elaborated on in the so-called autonomous morality (1730-1748).

Jan Jans, in his article "The Good Tree and the Proper Fruits," deals with the morality of human actions (1749-1761) and demonstrates by means of a theory of action how 'actions' are viewed.

Patrick Vandermeersch illustrates how within philosophical ethics, patristics, and later moral theology, "Passions and Virtues" (in the article with this title) were important in order to know what is morally good and to be able to perform morally good actions. He also indicates how the Catechism deals with these hinge concepts (1762-1775, 1803-1845).

Fred Van Iersel's article, "Conscience: A Social Ethical Reading," goes into the Catechism's concept of conscience (1776-1802), and illustrates the plasticity of the concept of conscience throughout history, looking at the interesting view of Vatican II on conscience as well as the contemporary importance of conscience.

The article "Sin as a Disruptor of Relationships" (1846-1976) was written by Annelies van Heijst. She illustrates the problems to which the use of the term sin gives rise and how the Catechism nevertheless attempts to deal with this concept of faith in order to deal with various contemporary theological re-orientations. As a result, it seems that not only does theology have questions to ask of the Catechism, but that the Catechism also has questions to ask of theology.

In "The Theology of Grace as the Hermeneutics of Salvation and Liberation," Toine Van den Hoogen takes up what the Catechism says about grace in relation to morality (1987-2029). He does this by outlining recent theological thinking on those concepts of faith in particular and drawing attention to the Catechism in this way.

In the article "The Human Community," Ronald Jeurissen deals with the concept of 'community' (1877-1948), which is central to Catholic moral instruction, first explaining what is meant by its 'opposite', the human person. Justice, subsidiarity, and solidarity are explained and finally the *bonum commune* is discussed, with brief references to contemporary communitarianism. This chapter does not constitute a separate section in the traditional structure of morality and it is perhaps for this reason that it has a somewhat unique place in the whole.

In his article "The Moral Law" (1949-1986), Theo Beemer reveals the various meanings of 'moral law' and argues that, because of the content of faith, a distinction must remain between a human positive law, the natural law, and the Law of the Gospel.

Joseph A. Selling's contribution is entitled "The Authority of Church Teaching on Matters of Morality" (2030-2051). Does the Church have the same sort of authority in moral issues, most of which are concrete, as it does in dogmatic issues? Selling looks at its historical development up till the World Catechism. He discusses attentively the terms used in the Catechism and the degree of authority that is intended.

The last article, "The Bible and Morality," is written by Karl Merks. This article is also a link with the following section of the Catechism on the concrete morality in the interpretation of the Ten Commandments (beginning with 2052-2082). Merks goes into the relationship of the Bible and morality (having in mind the whole of the Catechism's section on morality). With this he presents a problem of a fundamental methodological nature, which is closely linked with the mutuality of Christians and non-Christians with regard to morality, which we discussed above. What is the relationship between reason and revelation when insight into moral issues is concerned? What can one expect against the background of holy Scripture, and what need one not expect? How can the sources of our tradition of faith be dealt with in a methodologically responsible and reliable way in our day and age? Thus the commentary on the Catechism ends with a question that extends beyond the range of the Catechism itself, but which, especially today, should be taken into consideration in the writing of a Catechism.

Therefore this volume is not only a commentary on how the Catechism has discharged this task, but is meant to be a stimulation to occupy oneself more deeply with faith at the same time. Being a believing Christian must be possible and still remain attractive to people of this day and age as well.

ONE

The Dignity of the Human Person

Jan Hulshof

The emphasis on "the dignity of the human person" in the Catechism of the Catholic Church is both surprising and intriguing. One needs only to look at the Subject Index of the French edition of 1992 to see that this term (*dignité, dignitas, Würde*) appears remarkably often: forty references to the term are listed. In fact, the word appears more than twice that many times. How is it used?

Traditionally, the word has several meanings. In the first place, 'dignity' has to do with the public, external recognition of someone's function, position, qualities, or merits. In this instance, someone 'has' or 'is invested with' dignity. In Cicero, who uses the word in this social meaning, we find at the same time another more philosophical meaning of the word. 'Dignity' is used here to indicate that which the human being 'is', that which differentiates him from other creatures, an inner and permanent essential characteristic that is unique to the human being as human being. In the Church fathers this word received a special Christian meaning, *dignitas christiana*, which rests on the vocation of the human being to be a child of God.[1]

The Catechism uses the word only once in the first sense (2038). The word is used six times to refer to the Christian vocation of the human being as, for instance, when Sermon 21 of Leo the Great is quoted at the beginning of Part Three: "Christian, recognize your dignity." In most cases by far the word is used to indicate something that is unique to the human being as human being, usually connected with 'person', as in "personal dignity" or the "dignity of the human person" (41 times). In addition, the Catechism speaks twenty-six times of "the dignity of the human being" or "human dignity" or uses the possessive pronoun in conjunction with the term ("our/his dignity").

---

[1] Cf. R.P. Horstmann, "Menschenwürde," in: *Historisches Wörterbuch der Philosophie*, 5 (Basel, 1980), 1124-27; W. Dürig, "Dignitas," in: *Reallexikon für Antike und Christentum*, 3, (Stuttgart, 1950 ff.), 1024-35; J.-P. Wils and D. Mieth (eds), *Ethik ohne Chance? Erkundungen im technologischen Zeitalter* (Tübingen, 1991), pp. 130-57.

The word is conjoined eleven times to the term 'equal' or 'equality' in order to insist on the equal dignity of men and women or the equal dignity of all members of the family. One can find other sporadic references to the dignity of creation, of each being, of body and soul, of all peoples and the dignity of marriage. In the majority of instances, therefore, the word 'dignity' is used in the Catechism to indicate the unique and inalienable status that belongs to the human being as human being and which, for that reason, is a norm for human actions which cannot be transgressed. It is thus not coincidental that the term appears more than seventy times in the third part of the Catechism, which deals with ethics. We come across the term in Part One only some ten times, a few times in Part Two, and only once in Part Four.

This initial overview is somewhat sharpened if we compare the 1992 Catechism with the *Catechismus Romanus*, which was composed at the express wish of Trent and introduced by Pius V in 1566. The word 'dignity' also appears in the Tridentine Catechism, although relatively less and primarily in a different sense. 'Dignity' is used with reference to the sacraments, the priesthood, the ministry, Peter, the Church, the chosen people, Christ, grace, and all those who are obedient to God. Only once do we encounter the expression "dignity of the human person" and then it is used explicitly with respect to the redemption by Christ.[2] The term does not appear at all in the third part of the *Catechismus Romanus*, which deals with ethics.

The Origin

This summary comparison between the *Catechismus Romanus* and the Catechism of 1992 could be faulted for a certain anachronism in its presentation of the question. In the later catechism "the dignity of the human person" does indeed presuppose the context of modern society. But it is certainly not the case that the idea was unknown in the tradition before Trent. Church fathers like Origen and Athanasius were fascinated by the greatness of human beings, created in God's image and likeness. Also, Ambrose's short work, "On the Dignity of Human Existence" is a commentary on Genesis 1:21.[3] In Augustine and other Church fathers human dignity had primarily to do with the soul or the spiritual nature of human beings. "As God by the excellence of His nature surpasses every creature, so does the soul surpass

---

[2] "This one fact that He who is Himself the true and perfect God became human already constitutes a sufficient explanation for the exceptional dignity and excellence of human beings, bestowed on them by divine mercy." (I.4.11).

[3] *De dignitate conditionis humanae libellus*, Migne PL 17, pp. 1015-18.

every corporal creature by the dignity of its nature."[4] In a Christmas oration in the old Roman *sacramentaria* God is invoked as the one who "wonderfully created the dignity of human nature and even more wonderfully restored it."[5] Bernard of Clairvaux speaks of human dignity in his work "On the Knowledge of Human Existence."[6] Thomas Aquinas speaks of the dignity of the person as an autonomous being in a rational nature.[7] He bases his ethics on the conviction that every being participates in the eternal law through the natural law and is thus compelled toward its final goal. For the human being, this occurs in a way that is in accordance with human beings: thus, it is not determined but occurs through reason and freedom. Natural rights, to which human beings can appeal on the basis of natural law, are subsequently not attributed secondarily to human beings *a posteriori* but are intrinsic to human being. For Thomas, therefore, the human being is not a beggar. It is characteristic of the dignity of the human being that she does not receive natural rights only by grace and, likewise, that they are not taken away by sin: "Now the Divine law which is the law of grace does not do away with human law which is the law of natural reason."[8]

In the Renaissance attention shifts to the creativity of human freedom to open up new horizons.[9] In Pico's essay, "On the Dignity of the Human Being," the divine architect says to the human being: "The nature of all other beings is limited and constrained within the bounds of laws prescribed by Us. Thou, constrained by no limits, in accordance with thine own free will, in whose hand we have placed thee, shalt ordain for thyself the limits of they nature."[10]

The ethics of Spanish colonialism gave an in-depth treatment of natural rights that flowed from the dignity of human being as such. Bartolomé de las Casas quotes the words which Montesino used in his Advent sermon of 1514

---

[4] *De Genesis ad litteram* VII, 19, in : Migne PL 34, 364.

[5] Also used as an offertory prayer in the *Missale Romanum* of Trent.

[6] Migne PL 184, 485 ff.

[7] *Summa Theologica*, tr. Fathers of the English Dominican Province (London, 1922) I.29.10 *ad* 2: "And because subsistence in a rational nature is of high dignity, therefore every individual of the rational nature is called a person."

[8] *Summa Theologica* II,IIae.10.10.

[9] B. Facio, *De dignitate ac praestantia hominis* (1447/1448); G. Manetti, *De dignitate et excellentia hominis* (1451); G. Pico della Mirandola, *De dignitate hominis* (1496).

[10] Quoted in Tobias Churton, *The Gnostics* (London, 1987), p.113.

against the *encomenderos* who enslaved the Indians: "Are they not people? Do they not have a rational soul?"[11] De Vitoria, de Soto, Suarez and other theologians developed legal theories in line with Thomas, which make clear that the peoples of America, whether or not they are believers or sinners, can claim rights to property, freedom, and self-government. These are rights that must be honoured by everyone—thus by Christians as well.[12] Thus the dignity of the other is recognized as an inviolable limit.

Alienation

This sort of problem is not encountered in the texts of the Council of Trent, where the emphasis lies on questions of doctrine and Church discipline. Human freedom is addressed only as the religious problem of freedom and grace and not directly as an ethical problem. The Catechism of Trent states very briefly in the first part that the human being, as far as his soul is concerned, is created in God's image and likeness and that God gave him free will.[13] In the third part, which concerns moral doctrine, this insight does not play any role and the Catechism appeals scarcely or not at all to natural rights. Central to the argumentation are the Scriptures and the Church fathers. This is due to the positive theology and the pastoral perspective of this Catechism but perhaps present as well is the influence of what has been called political Augustinianism, the defensive curial theology that merges natural rights into supernatural justice, human rights into divine rights and, chiefly, the rights of the state into those of the Church.[14] The autonomy of human beings and things does not fit into this theology.

Although several theologians discussed Enlightenment ideas, the tension between the new ideas and the Magisterium grew during this period. Kant defined the dignity of the human being no longer from the perspective of

---

[11] Bartolomé de las Casas, *Obras Escogidas*, II (Madrid, 1957 f.), p.176.

[12] Cf. Domingo de Soto, in: *In IV Sent.*, dist. 5: "Faith, as St. Thomas states in II-II.10.4, does not take away the right of unbelievers to property, so that Christians can be in the service of unbelievers. For the divine right that is given with grace does not take away the human right that is given with natural reason. Thus, still less does divine right take away human freedom, so that nobody can be brought into slavery for reasons of religion." Cited in V. Carro, *La teología y los teólogos juristas españoles ante la conquista de América*, II (Madrid, 1944), p.103.

[13] I.2.19.

[14] Cf. H. Arquillière, *L'augustinisme politique*, 4th ed. (Paris, 1934).

transcendental reality but from that of an immanent reality—the subject. One speaks of dignity where one is no longer seen in service to something or someone else but has the opportunity to be herself. As subject, the human being must not "be taken for a bare means, conducive either to his own or to other persons' ends, but must be esteemed an end in himself, that is to say, he is invested with an internal dignity (an absolute worth), in the name of which he extorts reverence for his person, from every other finity (intelligent being) throughout the universe, and is entitled to compare himself with all such, and to deem himself their equal."[15] This is an expression of a latent religio-political calibre.

When the ideas of Locke, Kant and Rousseau were translated politically into the American and French revolutions, the Church's hierarchy had to take a stand. Pius VI and, after him, Gregory XVI and Pius IX engaged in a severe condemnation of the modern civil rights of freedom and equality, and this condemnation was also directed at many Catholics who were able to distinguish between the rights of the human being as such and the ideology of secularism in which they were sometimes wrapped. Even as late as 1910 Pius X condemned the Christian social movement of Marc Sangnier with the accusation that Sangnier sought his inspiration in the conscience, in certain ideas about human dignity, freedom, justice, and brotherhood and not in the directives of the Church's Magisterium. At that time, however, Leo XIII had already set a new direction.

Rapprochement

The expression "dignity of the human being" has been used in the texts of the papal Magisterium since Leo XIII. This was the case initially primarily, though not exclusively so,[16] with respect to social teaching, as is evident from the *Rerum Novarum* of 1891.[17] With Leo XIII, who paved the way for the rebirth of Thomism, the period of political Augustinianism in the Church came to an end. Charity and care are emphasized in the *Rerum Novarum*, but the arguments in the encyclical are based on scholastic legal theory: "The

---

[15] I. Kant, *The Metaphysics of Ethics*, tr. J.W. Semple, 3rd ed. (Edinburgh, 1871), p.251.

[16] See the encyclical *Libertas* of 1888 on the freedom of conscience as a right that the Church demands for itself: "This true freedom, which is in accordance with the dignity of the children of God and which protects in an ultimate way the dignity of the human person, is stronger than all violence and injustice" (64).

[17] See nos. 5, 16, 20, 21, 29, 32.

dignity of the human being, who is treated by God Himself with great respect, may not be violated by anyone without punishment" (32). From this dignity flow the natural rights of the human being and of the primary communities: the right to property, possession, land, the right to life, to the fruits of one's labour, to marry, the right to property for the head of the family, to a sufficient living by means of a just salary, and the right to associate.

It is remarkable that Leo XIII, despite his sympathy for the line of thought of natural law, nevertheless falls back on the positions of Gregory XVI and Pius IX when it concerns modern rights to freedom.[18] Only when the Church itself is threatened by totalitarian powers do we find in Pius XI for the first time a direct plea for the rights of the person in the presence of political power. While he still limits himself in his letters on Italian fascism and Mexican socialism to defending "the rights of the Church and of souls," his 1937 "Mit brennender Sorge" lets the National Socialists know that the principle "Justice is what is useful to the people" ("Recht ist, was dem Volke nützt") is not compatible with the fundamental fact "that the human being as a person possesses rights that he has received from God and must be safeguarded against every assault from the collective"(49).[19] But it is primarily Pius XII, who in his Christmas messages of 1942 and particularly 1944, when the plans for the United Nations were taking shape, sheds light on human dignity as a source of inalienable political rights and duties. Nonetheless, Pius XII is reserved with respect to the Universal Declaration of the Rights of Man, which was published in 1948. This reserve probably has to do with the recognition of the freedom of thought, conscience and religion in article 8, with the implicit acceptance of the right to divorce in article 16 and particularly with the question of whether one can speak of the rights of the human being without mentioning the name of God. It would be fifteen years before Rome would overcome its hesitations.

Reconciliation

The major post-war problems were the international organization of peace, the gulf between East and West and decolonization. John XXIII understood

---

[18] See *Immortale Dei* (1885), no. 51. The 'modern freedoms' are also condemned in *Libertas* (1888), nos. 42-65.

[19] At the same time in *Divini Redemptoris* (1937) communism is reproached for denying to the individual the natural rights that flow from being human and ascribing them to the community (10).

more clearly than any of his predecessors that the Church would have a message for society only if it could come to terms with human freedom, not only in the socio-economic sense but also in cultural, political, and religious respects. *Pacem in Terris* (11 April, 1963) was the spiritual testament of John XXIII. He went ahead with the promulgation of this encyclical, cutting straight through all the Council worries. The two central terms of the document are "freedom" and "human dignity". The pope emphasized how important truth and justice are for society, and not to forget that love is the soul of justice. He goes on to say: "But that too is insufficient, for human society must realize itself in freedom and do this in a way that suits the dignity of the people. Because they have the gift of reason by nature, they bear responsibility for their acts" (35). The encyclical, which refers repeatedly to statements made by Pius XII, places the person at the centre and thus puts a definite end to the misunderstanding that abstractions like 'truth', 'belief' or 'human nature' are bearers of rights. Every human being is a person, equipped by nature with reason and freedom, and therefore a subject of rights and duties, which are inalienable because they emerge directly from his or her nature (9, 145). The encyclical gives a summary of these rights and duties, including the right to worship "according to the correct norm of the conscience" (14). It sees an important step in the Declaration of the United Nations, in which "the dignity of the person is solemnly recognized for all human beings and every human being is given the right to seek the truth freely, to follow the norms of morality, to exercise the duties of justice and to lead a decent existence" (144).

When *Pacem in Terris* was published in April 1963, it was still not entirely clear how and when the Council would address the problems of Church and society. But two things were definite: Church and society would be addressed and the "dignity of the human being" would be the starting point. This is evident from the "Message to the World", eight days after the beginning of the Council, in which the Council fathers declared that they would take up societal questions concerning the dignity of the human being and the community of peoples.[20]

The text that was finally presented to the world in 1965 as the pastoral constitution *Gaudium et Spes* went through six stages, with several versions being produced at each stage.[21] Already in the first phase Fr. Hirschmann S.J. provided a chapter "On the Natural and Supernatural Dignity of the Hu-

---

[20] Cf. H. de Riedmatten, "Histoire de la constitution pastorale," in: J.Y. Calvez, M.D. Chenu et al., *L'Église dans le monde de ce temps* (Paris, 1967).

[21] Cf. C. Moeller, "Die Geschichte der Pastoralkonstitution," in: *LThK: Das Zweite Vatikanische Konzil*, III, 1968, pp. 242-79.

man Person." In contrast to what the title suggests, the text attempts to arrive at a theological anthropology without making any appeal to natural law or natural theology. This view became stronger during the long and complex history of the document's development. In *Gaudium et Spes* the word 'natural right' does not appear and the term 'natural law' only once. In contrast, the concept 'dignity of the human being' became the determinative line of thought, particularly in the first two chapters of the first part and the last three chapters of the second part.

This points to a drastic shift in the paradigms of moral theology. Compared with 'natural rights' the term 'dignity of the human being' has various advantages. It links up better with the biblical view of the human being as created according to God's image and likeness. It does not pose any barrier to those who do not look at human beings and society from this biblical perspective. It takes into consideration the criticism of the concept of natural law made by Protestant and Catholic theologians. It opens the way for a solution to the problem of religious freedom, because it is now concrete persons, rather than abstractions like truth and nature, who are considered to be the bearers of rights. Finally, the term elucidates the legitimate autonomy of secular values. The first draft already pointed out that human beings are created in God's image and likeness, and thereby as God's stewards "are given rule over the works of his hands." The significance of this insight for the relation between the Church and the different cultural sectors does not need further demonstration.[22]

With respect to religious freedom, the Council could have limited itself to a repetition of what *Pacem in Terris* states: "Worshipping God according to the correct norm of one's own conscience and confessing one's own religion in private and public life are also a part of human rights" (14). But not only did the expression "according to the correct norm of one's own conscience" give rise to much discussion, the Council fathers also found that they could not get away with a statement that had not been argued. They would then invite the suspicion that they were arguing for religious freedom out of opportunism without being able to justify it on the basis of the Scriptures and tradition.

Originally, the topics Church, state, and religious tolerance were placed in the ninth chapter of the outline on the Church, but this chapter, which still argued on the basis of the right to truth, was quickly dropped.[23] In the first draft on religious freedom which followed, the phrase 'the dignity of the hu-

---

[22] Moeller, "Die Geschichte," p.244.

[23] P. Pavan, "Erklärung über die Religionsfreiheit, Einleitung," in: *LThK, Das Zweite Vatikanische Konzil*, II, 1967, p.704.

man being' still did not appear, but in the Council hall in November 1963 the reporter, Mgr. De Smedt, explained that the draft connects up with the teaching of *Pacem in Terris* on the dignity of the human being and with the biblical view of the human being as created in God's image.[24] In the second draft (one thinks now of a separate declaration) religious freedom is then based directly on the divine vocation of the human being, but this idea met with theological and practical objections in the discussion held on 23 September 1964. In the third draft religious freedom is thus also directly based on 'the dignity of the human being' and this remains the line up to the definitive text that was accepted at the end of October 1965 and became famous as *Dignitatis Humanae*.

The Council resolved the issue of religious freedom by making some four distinctions. The declaration situates religious freedom on the level of juridical and social relationships and does not take up the metaphysical and moral order, a distinction that, by the way, had already been made in the sixteenth century by the Spanish jurists.[25] Subsequently, religious freedom is formulated as a negative right (free from coercion), which is to be differentiated from the positive duty to seek truth and good. Thirdly, the declaration concentrates on the person as the subject of rights and no longer speaks about the rights of truth, mindful of the words of the sixteenth-century Castellion: "To kill a human being is not to defend the truth but to kill a *human being*."[26] Finally, religious freedom is based directly—secularly, so to speak—on 'human dignity' and not immediately on the theological concept of the divine vocation.

The conclusion is that 'human dignity' plays a key role in the major texts in which the reconciliation between the Church and modern society was settled in the 1960's. When the Catechism of 1992 was prepared, the important question was whether this breakthrough would be honoured.

---

[24] On the history of the text, cf J. Hamer's article in: Y. Congar and J. Hamer (eds), *La liberté religieuse* (Paris, 1967).

[25] Cf. Alonso de Castro, *De justa hereticorum punitione*, II, p.4 (Salamanca, 1547): "Jews, Saracens, and other unbelievers are free to accept the faith or not. I do not mean by this 'free' in relation to obtaining beatitude, otherwise they could obtain eternal life without faith as well as with faith. But I am speaking about 'free' with respect to public human authorities, because they are not subject to the public authorities in this respect, as if they could be forced to accept the Catholic faith." Cited in V. Carro, *La teología*, II, p.89.

[26] Cited by J. Lecler, *Histoire de la tolérance au siècle de la réforme*, I (Paris, 1954), p.324.

Confirmation

During the consultation of 1989 it was particularly the third part of the draft of the Catechism that appeared to meet with much criticism.[27] In the section on fundamental morality many bishops missed an inspiring evangelical vision on the basis of which special moral problems could be treated. Why did the whole first section, including the title, stand under the heading of "the law"? Could no better starting point be found in the Gospel? Why was not more attention paid to the positive and dynamic dimension of moral acting, along the lines of Thomistic teachings on passions, striving abilities, faculties and virtues? Where was the link between the first chapter of the first section, on human dignity, and the following chapters on conscience, freedom, responsibility, virtures and sin with their traditional handbook theology? Why was special ethics dealt with by means of the Ten Commandments and not the five chapters of the second part of *Gaudium et Spes*, in which the various sectors of human life are addressed?

Confronted with this criticism, the editors decided to rewrite the third part on the basis of *Gaudium et Spes*, but this did not prove to be a simple task, because the Pastoral Constitution does not offer a complete survey of moral doctrine, as was the intention of the Catechism. Cardinal Ratzinger finally cut the Gordian knot: the Decalogue was to remain the framework for particular ethics, because as a catechetical guiding principle the Decalogue had enjoyed a long history. The treatment of each commandment would begin with a positive presentation of the virtue in question.

Now that the pattern of *Gaudium et Spes* would not be followed in the second section, the editorial committee found it to be all the more important to rewrite, in any case, the first section of the third part on the basis of *Gaudium et Spes* and particularly to develop the idea of "the dignity of the person" as its supporting foundation. As a result, in the first chapter "The Dignity of the Human Person" it is explained that such dignity has its origin in the fact that the human being is created in to God's image and likeness (article 1) and is directed at happiness in communion with the divine persons (article 2). Everything with which the human being is equipped to realize his vocation, in particular his freedom (article 3) and his conscience (article 6) shares in this fundamental dignity. The second chapter, "The Human Community" elaborates on the insight that the human person is the principle, subject and end of all social institutions (article 1). Respect for the person is the

---

[27] For what follows, cf. J.L. Bruguès, "La morale dans les derniers documents du magistère romain," in: *Documents Épiscopat*, 1994, No. 7, pp. 5 ff.; G. Honoré, "Le Catéchisme de l'Église Catholique," in: *Nouvelle Revue Théologique* 115 (1993): 3-19.

first element of the common good, in particular where the natural rights are concerned, such as the right to act according to one's conscience, the right to protection of privacy and religious freedom. Respect for the person also entails that everyone receives the opportunity to take part personally in social and political life (article 2). Social justice is possible only if the transcendent dignity of the human person is respected as the ultimate goal of society, including all rights that flow from this dignity (article 3). The third chapter is called "God's Salvation: Law and Grace." It is striking that in this context the Catechism holds on to natural law as the 'basis' of the rights and duties of the person (1956), whereas the concept of natural law does not play any role in *Gaudium et Spes*. The final article of this chapter discusses the task of the Church and particularly its Magisterium in the transmission of moral doctrine. Whoever expects an explanation of the dignity of responsible Christians will be disappointed, despite the statement that, for the execution of her task, the Church is dependent on its pastors, the knowledge of theologians and the life experience of every Christian and every person of good will. It is made clear that it is not proper to place personal conscience and human reason over against the moral law or the Magisterium of the Church (2038 f.). After everything that has been said on the dignity of the human being, the Catechism could have gone more extensively into the role of the *sensus fidelium* in the search for concrete moral norms on the understanding that the moral natural law does not fall outside history and is mediated via the subject.[28]

The emphasis on the "dignity of the human person" in the first section sets the tone in the section on particular ethics, especially where the rights to freedom, right to life, social rights and the right to equal treatment are discussed.

In number 2106, within the framework of the first commandment, the Catechism repeats the core of the declaration of *Dignitatis Humanae* on freedom of conscience in religious matters. The dignity of the person is also the source of the family's rights to freedom which are mentioned in the treatment of the fourth commandment in number 2211: the right to have children and to raise them according to one's own moral and religious norms, the right to free profession of faith and religious education, the right to free emigration. Within the framework of the fourth commandment the Catechism also discusses the relations between citizens and the government. The Catechism of Trent had done that already, but it leaves an odd impression two hundred years after the French Revolution. This does not prevent the Catechism from strongly confirming citizen's political rights to freedom (2236 f.).

---

[28] Cf. U. Ruh, *Der Weltkatechismus, Anspruch und Grenzen* (Freiburg, 1993), pp. 102 ff.

The Catechism speaks only in conditional terms of the freedom of speech (1740) and in the explanation of the eighth commandment even the right to the communication of the truth is not seen as absolute (2488).

The rights that have to do with the life and the integrity of the person are strongly emphasized in the Catechism, particularly in view of those who are not in a position to exercise their freedom or are not aware of their dignity. It is as if, particularly in their case, the Catechism wishes to indicate that the dignity of the human person is not exhausted in his right to self-determination and that the meaning of his life transcends the human capacity to ascribe meaning to it. The physical integrity of the human person is central in the explanation of the fifth commandment, where the Catechism speaks of "the inalienable right to life of every innocent human individual" (2273). By using the word "innocent" the text employs a restriction that evokes as many questions as it answers and must be seen in the light of numbers 2266 and 2309 which leave room for the death penalty and legitimate defense. The deliberate killing of a human being (of an "innocent" individual, as the Catechism states again in number 2261), procured abortion, non-therapeutic interference in the development of an embryo and genetic manipulation, euthanasia, dangerous experiments with human beings and last but not least torture are rejected as being "in conflict with the dignity of the human person" (2268, 2270, 2275, 2279, 2295, 2297). In the article on the sixth commandment promiscuity, pornography and prostitution are condemned as attacking the dignity of the human being (2353, 2354, 2355), whereas incest is described as a "scandalous harm done to the physical and moral integrity of the young" (2389).

The Catechism devotes a great deal of attention to the social implications of the dignity of the person. It is a sin against human dignity, according to the Catechism in its treatment of the seventh commandment, when people are degraded in the socio-economic sphere to merchandise or tools (2414). Unemployment is a wound to human dignity (2436). Systems that sacrifice the fundamental rights of persons and groups to the collective organization of production conflict with human dignity (2424). Someone's honour and good name are, so to say, the social witness to human dignity, which are violated by detraction and calumny (2479).

Already in the first section of the third part the right to equal treatment is elucidated in accordance with *Gaudium et Spes*. The equal dignity of all persons forbids every form of discrimination with respect to the fundamental rights of the person on the basis of sex, race, colour, social status, language or religion (1934 f.). Applied to international socio-economic relations, this means that the great gulf between poor and rich societies is unacceptable (1938 f.). In the section on particular ethics the equal dignity of all members of the family is emphasized (2203). The principle finds a peculiar application in number 2377, where artificial insemination, including that of a homologous nature, is rejected with the argument of *Donum Vitae* (1987), i.e. that the primacy of technology in determining the origin and destination of the human person "is in conflict with the dignity and equality to which parents and children together are entitled." We find another application in number 2387 which cites polygamy as being in conflict with the equal dignity of men and women.

After this short overview, can it be said that the vision of the dignity of the human person, as we find it in *Pacem in Terris, Gaudium et Spes* and *Human Dignitatis* is confirmed in the Catechism of 1992?

It is true that *Gaudium et Spes* has a different setting from the Catechism. The Pastoral Constitution is a ground-breaking historic document, directly centring on the reconciliation between Church and modern society. The Catechism is a textbook intended to offer a clear and comprehensive explanation of Catholic doctrine with special attention to the Second Vatican Council. This has the effect of making the Catechism miss the thrust of the Pastoral Constitution. With respect to content, the weight of the catechism is at times distributed unevenly. For example, the Catechism goes extensively and in detail into bio-ethical questions and, by way of contrast, is brief with respect to the destructive effects of racism and sexism in the world of today.

Nevertheless, by having as its starting point "the dignity of the person," the Catechism has taken up a fundamental insight of the Council into the structure of the catechesis. The human person is no longer understood primarily as the addressee of a moral code that is imposed from outside but as the image of God, as the bearer of a matchless and inalienable dignity that permeates her existence from within. The struggle for a society in which every human being is confirmed in his or her value, which offers every human being the necessary material and spiritual living conditions, and in which he or she, free from coercion, can live and love, believe and act, finds a fundamental recognition in this Catechism. With all its failings, it confirms the historic breakthrough of the 1960's and reflects the baptism of the subject in the modern sense of the word and thereby of the modern period itself.[29]

The Challenge

Precisely at the same time when the Church stretched out its hand in the 1960's to conventional society, criticism of this society began to emerge

---

[29] J.L. Bruguès, "La morale," p.7.

from a entirely different corner. In 1961 Ernst Bloch exposed the critical elements of the tradition of natural law in order to show how much the factual structures of conventional society were in conflict with the ideals to which they appealed.[30] In 1964 Herbert Marcuse noted that the ideals of free fulfilment of the personality were important items in the competitive struggle with the East Block countries, whereupon he stated: "The fact that they contradict the society which sells them does not count."[31] Structuralist philosophy then shifted the emphasis: the 'grand narratives' on humanism, human dignity and social justice were replaced by analyses of social, linguistic, ethnological and biological structures, each of which drew a few lines of the grid of the 'book of life' but none of which said anything about the content of the text itself. It became, in addition, difficult to speak of "the dignity of the human person" without addressing the imperious attitude towards nature, which, according to Lévi-Strauss and others, has gone hand in hand with the rise of the subject: "Is it not so that the myth of the exclusive dignity of human nature has led to an initial mutilation of nature, which must irrevocably be followed by further mutilations?"[32] Yet another form of criticism of modern humanism appears in the fundamentalist need to grant priority to 'religion', 'the truth', 'life', or 'the nation' above the subject in the modern sense of the word. All these questions constitute the horizon for those who wish to delve seriously into what the Catechism of 1992 says about "the dignity of the human person." They do not form any reason to let go of this concept, which after a long exile has found a home in the doctrine of the Church. Nonetheless, there is good reason to deal with these questions in such a way that they are incorporated into the process of catechesis, something the Catechism does not really try. That may be a limitation of this book, but at the same time it is a challenge to whoever makes use of it.

---

[30] Ernst Bloch, *Naturrecht und menschliche Würde* (Frankfurt, 1961).

[31] *One-Dimensional Man* (London, 1972 (1964)), pp. 57 f.

[32] Quoted by J.-P. Wils, *Zur Typologie*, p. 131.

TWO

In Search of the Happy Life

Happiness and Beatitude as the End of Human Life and Action

Frans Vosman

Introduction

"Why are we on earth? We are on earth to serve God and to be happy here and in the hereafter through such service." In this way question and answer one of the 1947 Catechism of the Dutch Dioceses brought up the relation between *happiness*, the related religious concept used to reflect on happiness, i.e., *beatitude*, and *action*. This Catechism was intended to be used in introducing children into the faith (and thus not only to the truths of faith). In 1992 the Catechism of the Catholic Church appeared. It is a 'framework catechism', a framework on the basis of which catechisms for children, young people, and adults can be written. It is not an introduction to the faith, as for example the 1987 *Geloofsboek* (Book of Faith) published by the Belgian Bishops and the famous 1966 Dutch Catechism, the so-called New Catechism, were intended to be.[1] In the section on morality in the *Catechism of the Catholic Church* the human desire for happiness, morally good actions and God as the final destiny of life and action are intertwined, thereby giving expression to a very old tradition in which the moral question *par excellence* (what is the good we should do to ourselves and to others?) is involved with the desire for *happiness* (as the highest end of action) and for *God*.[2] I will

---

[1] The bishops of Belgium, *Geloofsboek* (Tielt, 1987); *De nieuwe Katechismus: Geloofsverkondiging voor volwassenen, in opdracht van de bischoppen van Nederland* (Hilversum/Antwerp, 1966).

[2] I refer here to R. Spaemann, *Glück und Wohlwollen: Versuch einer Ethik* (Stuttgart, 1989) and to the more 'Thomasian' A. Plé, *Par devoir ou par plaisir* (Paris, 1980). I distinguish here between *Thomistic*, relying on Thomas Aquinas for erecting a philosophical reflection independent of secular philosophies, strongly emphasizing universal eternal truths, and '*Thomasian*', using his conceptual system to reflect again, theologically and philosophically, on faith seeking understanding in our culture.

remark here right at the beginning that the mutual connections between beatitude, happiness and action have become debatable in the North Atlantic world since the Enlightenment, and more specifically in the late modern period (I will return to this in section 3 where I will discuss the problems associated with the conceptual coordinates of the Catechism). The fact that the 1992 Catechism is a 'framework catechism' and not an introduction to the faith entails that the conceptual coordinates are presented (happiness, good, blessed, community) within which orthodox moral instruction is situated, even though we must carry out the necessary reflection ourselves with respect to confronting our own contemporary mindset (it is only through this process that faith can arise). Such reflection is also necessary regarding the use of the traditions from which the concepts are taken.

Within the context of happiness as a central category for moral action I will explain numbers 1716-1729 "Our Vocation to Beatitude" and numbers 1877-1885 "The Communal Character of the Human Vocation" in the *Catechism of the Catholic Church* and then expound on a number of problems in these sections.[3] These two parts are linked with respect to content, and by looking at them together, I will go counter to the splintering effect that the Catechism's structure has—a splintering which is remarkable, given the systematics for which the writers strove. This splintering, which has already been pointed out by some commentators, originates in the systematics chosen by the Catechism to explain the doctrine of the faith.[4] But it also originates in the fact that different schemas have been employed without being fully reconciled: 'Thomasian' theology (with its supporting ideas of virtues and passions, of grace and the Spirit, destiny, and happiness) stands next to a Neo-Thomistic theology (with a theory of action that distinguishes the object of action, intention and circumstances but does not reflect on their connection to the ultimate end of action and life).[5] Next to both of these is a fully modern understanding of conscience.[6]

---

[3] It thus concerns Paragraph 1 of Part III, Section 1, ch.2, article 1.

[4] See the "Introduction" to this volume. Cf. also U. Gianetto, "Storia della redazione del Catechismo della Chiesa Cattolica. Genere letterario, articolazione, linguaggio, destinatari." in: *Salesianum* 56 (1994): 3-30, who remarks (p.21) that the systematics chosen has this effect.

[5] M. Vidal, "La Matriz tomistica de la moral general en el Catecismo de la Iglesia Catolica," in: *Studia Moralia* 32 (1994): 21-44.

[6] L. Vereecke, "La conscience moral selon le Catéchisme de l'Église Catholique," in: *Studia Moralia* 32 (1994): 61-74.

After this *explanation* and *exposition of the problems* I will try, via an outline of the ethics of Aristotle and Thomas Aquinas, to hold a mirror up to the Catechism. Their premodern conceptual framework can (this is my hypothesis) set up *in clear relief* and *offer a critique* of *the Church's habit of mind with respect to moral theology*, in which the Church understands these concepts in a modern way. We cannot, like Von Münchhausen, extract ourselves from the limitations of our thinking. If we look into the mirror of premodern philosophy and theology, we will then see the peculiarities and limitations of our thought. The Church needs to look into such a mirror itself regarding its proclamation concerning good and evil, so that it can also look at itself critically. After all, doctrine is intended to make Christ knowable and not to serve the conceit of preachers or interpreters. If I make use of Aristotle and Thomas Aquinas, it is because I am attempting to correct the modern articulation of the Roman Catholic tradition, as contained in the World Catechism, on the basis of the heart of that tradition. I will note here that in doing thus I am not implying that we are not confronted with serious problems in our late modern period. We should formulate them, and not just by using the premodern theories of Aristotle and Thomas in a non-critical way. I will not carry out that programme here but will limit myself to showing the contrast, i.e., looking at modernity in the mirror of the premodernity that has accompanied the Catholic tradition. I will continuously attempt to pay proper attention to the actual pluriformity of views on good and evil in late modern society.

Content and Explanation

Beatitudes

Numbers 1716-1719 in the Catechism present in brief the following as the content of the faith:
Every human being has a natural desire to be happy, a desire that has been placed in the human heart by God (1718). God calls us to his own beatitude (1719), i.e., to his fulness. The Catechism brings the Beatitudes as Jesus expressed them to the great crowds of people who came from all directions (Matt. 5:3-12) into the context of happiness and beatitude (being with God). The Beatitudes are a subsection and overture of the so-called Sermon on the Mount: the promise that precedes the *paranesis*.[7] "The beatitudes reveal the

---

[7] Cf. the recent exegetical results, in their relevance for moral theology, in the theme issue (on the Sermon on the Mount) of *Lumière et Vie*, No. 183 (September, 1987).

goal of human existence, the ultimate end of human acts" (1719, cf. 1820). Scripture is thus placed in a more central position in the moral section of the Catechism than had been the tradition in moral theology for a long time.[8] It is also the way in which the human desire for happiness is brought up in the Catechism—with this specific elucidation. In this way the search for happiness is restored to its central importance for moral reflection and this reflection is broadened right from the start, bypassing the approach via legal duties.[9] When, for example, Jesus Christ says: "Blessed are those who mourn, for they will be comforted" (one of the Beatitudes (Matt. 5:4)), this means that those who grieve and mourn for those who were precious and dear to them see before them that which has eluded them, that which they are lacking, the fulfilment of their desire, the concrete good that has departed. In their own reality they see before them that which makes for happiness, that which makes them alive. They see that their past happiness is a part of the great happiness that awaits them. By the power of grace they see their past happiness in deep relief, i.e., that God wants the deceased and the living to live life fully. These Beatitudes also outline the situation of those who are disciples of Jesus, who have set out on the journey of faith and have encountered dangers.[10] To those who live with such an attitude toward and awareness of their reality Jesus makes a promise in the second part of each Beatitude: "they will be comforted;" "they will inherit the earth;" "they will

---

[8] S. Pinckaers, "The Use of Scripture and the Renewal of Moral Theology: The Catechism and Veritatis Splendor," in: *The Thomist* 59 (1995): 1-19; see p. 3; G.J. Hughes, "Our Human Vocation," in: M.J. Walsh (ed.), *Commentary on the Catechism of the Catholic Church* (London, 1994), pp. 336-56, esp. pp. 337, 353. See the critical reflection concerning the use of Scripture in the article by K.-W. Merks in this volume.

[9] *Eudamonia, makarios* (Gr.), *beatitude* and *felicitas* (Lat.) *bonheur* (Fr.) are terms that, viewed historically, have been equated more or less in the tradition with what we call happiness (in older English, 'blessedness'). See Pinckaers, "The Use of Scripture," pp. 4-5. On the shifts in meaning and the change in connotations see D. Runia, *Bios eudaimoon* (Leiden, 1993), pp. 12-13.

[10] K. Demmer, "Das vergeistige Glück. Gedanken zum christlichen Eudämonieverständnis," in: *Gregorianum* 72 (1991): 99-115, esp. p. 102 and nt. 10 on happiness and the Beatitudes. Also, É. Fuchs, "L'Éthique du sermon sur la montagne," in: R. Bélanger, *Actualiser la morale: Mélanges offerts à René Simon* (Paris, 1992), pp. 317-32 on the role of the Sermon on the Mount and the Beatitudes in modern moral theology. See here p. 320: "The Beatitudes define the condition of the disciples. ... The disciples are those who receive and believe the paradoxical promise of happiness in the depth of their distress. They are those who perceive, in their defeat in their search for happiness, a call to receive it as a gift."

be filled;" "they will be shown mercy;" etc. An attitude towards one's own reality and that of others (of loss, poverty, injustice, conflict) is placed within a believing perspective; an ordinary reality (anyone from whatever ideological background can also, in itself, have a similar attitude) is given its own relief in faith. One can also share one's own reality with others or confront oneself with the reality of others. Apart from one's attitude toward one's own reality, there is also one's relation to other(s) that needs to be considered, as in the Beatitudes that mention justice (Matt. 5:6) and compassion (Matt. 5:7). The ascription of meaning in such an attitude, as, for example, in genuine grief, shifts considerably, for the interior aspect of the peculiar meaning of grieving is made clear. The meaning of the goodness of the human being unfolds via what we, "thinking towards God" (P. Schoonenberg), call God's goodness—goodness in itself. The promise applies to those who go and stand before God's reality. It was not for nothing that the theological tradition made a connection with the *virtues* (longlasting attitudes focused on deeds), as the church fathers Ambrose of Milan and John Chrysostom did, or with the *gifts of the Holy Spirit*, as Thomas Aquinas did (see Catechism, 1830-1831). Religion, i.e., making the connection between the anticipated reality intended by God and God, is the heart of the matter. One thus speaks in the spatial images of the kingdom of God, of heaven, of paradise.[11] Our time and space are stored in God. The Beatitudes together indicate what kind of life and what actions (with God as their end) meet God's promise. As a recapitulation of the tradition, that is, in bringing moral questions under the head (*caput*) of the traditional given of beatitude in our current late modern society, this part of the Catechism text is remarkable. Only a few contemporary treatments of moral theology pay any attention to the Beatitudes—they are usually transferred and allotted to the area of spirituality. One of the consequences for moral theology is that the search for happiness from the perspective of faith and the connection between action and happiness from that point of view is scarcely brought up for discussion and even more seldom made central.[12] The Catechism gives a recapitulation

---

[11] The Catechism that was published by order of the Council of Trent, the so-called *Catechismus Romanus*, devoted attention repeatedly to the relation of time and space to beatitude. Cf. *Catechismus Romanus* (edition used: Ratisbonae, 1907), Pars I, caput XIII, qu. IV and V.

[12] I agree with A. Chapelle, "La Vie dans le Christ. Le Catéchisme de l'Église Catholique," in: NRT 115 (1993): 169-85, see p. 175. Exceptions in moral theology include S. Pinckaers, *Les sources de la moral chrétienne* (Fribourg/Paris, 1993); A. Plé, *Par devoir ou par plaisir?* (Paris, 1980); W. Korff, *Wie kann der Mensch glücken? Perspektiven der Ethik* (Munich, 1985); P. Engelhardt (ed.), *Glück und geglücktes Leben. Philosophische und theologische Untersuchungen zur Bestimmung des Le-*

of the tradition *within* its section on morality by placing the scriptural Beatitudes first. It also makes, gnoseologically speaking, a Christocentric approach, an approach that was attempted earlier in the 1947 French national catechism but did not bring about any lasting change with respect to the organization of catechisms.[13] With G. Hughes, however, we must also assert that the recapitulation within the Catechism's section on morality (by the Beatitudes) does not influence the rest of the section.[14] The question raised by Mgr. J. Honoré as to how organic the conceptual scheme of the Catechism is, finds a concrete and practical answer in this section on morality. For that matter, Archbishop Honoré indicated that the central place that the Beatitudes received during the genesis of the Catechism was not undisputed.[15]

Community

We encounter the term beatitude further along in the Catechism, in numbers 1877-1885. The vocation to beatitude is directed at the human being who by

---

benziels (Mainz, 1985).

[13] U. Gianetto, "Storia della redazione," pp. 13-14. For the rest, the entire section in the Catechism on morality is given a recapitulation through the fact that the sacramental life is dealt with before morality. That is, the conception of the Catechism is that moral action and life occurs *within* the life of faith, instead of seeing the sacraments as means for being better able to perform the commandments and prescripts, as done in previous *handbooks on morality* where they were discussed after the commandments. Compared with the "previous world catechism", the *Catechismus Romanus* that was prescribed by the Council of Trent, the place of the sacraments is the same. There too the sacraments preceded morality, which was also viewed as a reflection on the Ten Commandments and the law. The commandments of God were primary, as opposed to His act of creation in which he gave us the desire for happiness.

[14] G.J. Hughes, "Our Human Vocation."

[15] Mgr. J. Honoré, "Le Catéchisme de l'Église Catholique. Genèse et profil," in: NRT 115 (1993): 3-18, esp. pp. 5 and 12. For the outlines and conceptual frameworks of catechisms see J.M. Giménez, *Un Catecismo para la Iglesia Universal: Historia de la iniciativa desde su origen hasta el Sínodo Extraordinario de 1985* (Pamplona, 1987); M. Simon, *Un Catéchisme Universel pour l'Église Catholique: Du concile de Trente á nos jours* (Louvain, 1992); G. Biancardi, "Conoscere il Catechismo della Chiesa Cattolica," in: P. Damu (ed.), *Guida al Catechismo della Chiesa Cattolica: Orientamenti per la conoscenza e l'utilizzazione* (Torino, 1993), pp. 27-102; T.J. Reese (ed.), *The Universal Catechism Reader: Reflections and Responses* (San Francisco, 1990).

nature is a *communal being* (1879). Organized society is indispensable for realizing the human vocation to happiness-in-God (1886). This vocation, however, does not only obtain for the human person, for which she is enabled by society, but obtains also for the human community as such (1877). This is viewed from a theological perspective of grace and the initiatives that proceed from God. Ultimately, being able to live from the perspective of the Beatitudes depends on God's gift of his happiness (1899). With respect to organized society, the Catechism here follows more an Aristotelian-'Thomasian' tradition than modern contract theories.[16] That is, human beings are not viewed as individuals in conflict with one another who enter into society through negotiation and treaty but as simultaneously free and sinful persons, whose capacity for association is placed under grace. Because God wants friendship with us, we can be what we are: *socii*, companions.

Posing Problems

Some things have been said above that require explanation. What is the relation between happiness as it can be seen and experienced by people and 'beatitude' in being with God, which has traditionally been viewed as the end of life and action and the supreme happiness? What do morally good actions and happiness have to do with each other? What does it mean to say that the human being is a communal being and that morally good actions and happiness have to do with community? On all axes problems between (a) beatitude, (b) happiness, and (c) actions arise (thus a <-> b, b <-> c, a <-> c).[17]

For modern Western people who lean towards individualism and to thinking in terms of technical cause and effect and who have difficulty with 'community' and 'destiny' (*causa finalis*) this Catechism cannot be easily grasped. I am pointing out what will be discussed below, i.e., that *causa finalis*, final cause, or the purpose of something or an action, raises an entirely different question than that of the efficient cause, than the question of 'why?'. "For what purpose do we act and live; what is our destiny?" is a different question than that of "how can the fact that we act and that we live be explained; what are the efficient causes lying behind them?"

The line of thought that has been followed and the terms that have been employed, such as "the Beatitudes reveal the goal of human existence, the

---

[16] G.J. Hughes, "Our Human Vocation," p.351.

[17] Cf. P. Engelhardt, "Wer is für das Glück verantwortlich?" in: Engelhardt (ed.), *Glück und geglücktes Leben*, 128-64.

ultimate end of human acts" (1719) come from a philosophical and theological tradition that is foreign to them. Above all, many, including members of the church, wonder whether what is called good does not depend on what each person sees as good: "Every individual has the right—according to a modern axiom—to determine for himself what seems to him to be desirable. This right is even taught as a duty: everyone is himself responsible for the way in which he organizes his life and strives after development,"[18] with all the stress that such a responsibility causes for the individual brings. In any case, happiness does not seem to be tied to something like an end-for-all (who can determine that objectively?), let alone a 'final end' that would consist in being-with-God. The question of who He is is itself quite obscure, let alone that He has a demonstrable role in the good and evil of human actions. Here a few problems related to understanding emerge clearly: problems in connection with belief in God—problems which flow from the modern understanding of the self. These problems are noted as the 'subjectivization' (the individual person who as acting subject places himself central) and 'psychologization' (happiness is viewed as a human psychological state, which can possibly be influenced or manipulated),[19] of the question of what is conducive to happiness. One can recognize here the debate between utilitarianism and emotivism on the one hand and (Neo-)Kantian deontological thought on the other. A specific content is given to 'happiness', namely a state of psychological well-being, in order (in the theory of Mill and Bentham) to function consequently as an objective standard for actions (with a view to maximizing happiness). Kant viewed happiness as understood in this way to be subjectively and egoistically inappropriate for playing a role in establishing norms for good and evil. What is good is determined by the duty that one has recognized and laid upon oneself. Action has to focus on that, and thus effectuates 'well-being', it must not be directed at 'happiness'.[20]

I will mention yet a third problem, i.e., the de-politicization of the question as to what is conducive to happiness, with the help of Ad Peperzak's analysis of the matter. The modern emphasis (and late modern re-em-

---

[18] A. Peperzak, *Zoeken naar zin: Proeven van wijsbegeerte* (Kampen/Kapellen, 1990), p.41.

[19] P. Engelhardt "Wer is für das Glück verantwortlich?" pp.138-42.

[20] I will omit the other gnoseological placing of 'beatitude' and 'action' in Mill, Bentham, and Kant. See P. Engelhart, "Wer ist für das Glück verantwortlich?" pp.143-44 and G. Bien, "Das Glück, die 'erste Freude' und die menschliche Natur. Zur Theorie der Lust bei J. Bentham, J.St. Mill und Aristoteles," in P. Engelhardt, *Glück und geglücktes Leben*, pp.27-75.

phasis) of the "right of everyone to achieve personal well-being in accordance with their own ideas" entails that society is perceived as a collection of people who possess similar rights. All this 'autonomous self-formulation' can, if anarchy is to be avoided, be ordered only by recognizing the autonomy of everyone and at the same time recognizing the necessity of a mutual curtailment of rights. The contract is promoted to the foundation of society. Social relations and the cohesion of society is said to be founded in contractual relations, i.e., the factual correspondence of the choices of the collected individuals. According to Peperzak, "All forms of a connectedness that have not been chosen disappear from the horizon."[21] Being received, being given a promise for nothing (as the ascription of meaning from the past) as well as destiny (the whither of the present) and the fate of the community (the place of the here and now) are thus placed outside the order of thought. These are, after all, forms of connectedness external to the late modern self. I call this 'de-politicization' not because it no longer involves any idea of society but because community is thought to exist only as a project of individuals which must subsequently be realized.[22] The individual can change the project of the community (that which is stipulated via a social contract with respect to what is allowed to be called a 'community'). In addition, community is not something that is given in one way or another ('by nature' or 'willed by God', or by means of another idea that includes the givenness of society) but is something that must be constructed. Community is something that is derived from the individual, without a reality of its own.[23] I am using the term 'politics' in the sense of the ordering of the society of the always social human being. I am thus relying on a premodern idea, preceding our now so usual identification of what is public and private and the separation of the two that dominates the modern idea of politics. In this use of the term politics the public and private realms are not opposed: we are public in our private spheres as well. The raising of a child by a parent is a public action; conversing at home with friends about what really concerns us, such a conversation being constitutive of the bonds of friendship and meaning, is a pub-

---

[21] A. Peperzak, *Zoeken naar zin*, p.43.

[22] K. Held, "Entpolitisierte Verwirklichung des Glücks," in: P. Engelhardt (ed.), *Glück und geglücktes Leben*, pp.77-127.

[23] A closer study is required to compare the poles of tension in which Matthew places the Sermon on the Mount and the Beatitudes, namely legalism and relativism, with the characteristics of late modern culture that have just been outlined: subjectivization, psychologization and de-politicization of happiness. Cf. É. Fuchs, "L'Éthique du sermon sur la montagne," in: R. Bélanger (ed.), *Actualiser la morale*, pp.317-32, esp. 330-31.

lic act as well. We give forms to living together, being witnessed by the other.

In summary, both the connectedness of happiness to God and to the *polis* have become difficult to conceive. This does not mean that, as conceptual coordinates, they should henceforth be abandoned in moral theology, any more than that should be the case with the term *telos* (end, *causa finalis*).[24] Banishing these terms to another field ('God' to dogmatics or spirituality; *polis* to the autonomous, behavioural science of politicology) or to faith ('God' to piety or pietistic experience) is just as disastrous.

The Catechism brings happiness into connection with both God and the community, which, viewed from the perspective of the picture of late modernity that we have just sketched, is at odds with late modernity. The tradition on which the Catechism draws, although difficult to conceive when seen in this way, is extremely relevant. It addresses us with respect to our desire to be happy. In addition, it is extremely critical: it holds up a mirror that completely displays our authenticity as well as our one-sidedness. With the explanation and delineation of problems that follow I will attempt to elucidate the questions that the Catechism poses and the concepts that it employs for them. It should be obvious that I wish to test *the questions themselves* and the conceptuality within which the questions are posed with respect to their relevance. To begin with the latter task: I will elucidate the comprehensive framework in which the Church poses the question of the good in action by going back to its origin: Aristotle's ethics[25] and the moral theology of Thomas Aquinas. I have indicated the purpose of doing this in my introduction.

Aristotle on Good, Happiness, and the End

Given its effect on Western philosophical ethics and Catholic moral theology, the *Ethica Nicomacheia*, in which Aristotle constructed a coherent line of thought on human action with respect to good and evil, is the most important of the three ethical works of this Greek philosopher.[26]

---

[24] See J.-P. Wils, "Transformationen und Rehabilitationen der Teleologie," in: J.-P. Wils, *Verletzte Natur: Ethische Prolegomena* (Frankfurt am Main/etc., 1991), pp. 20-59.

[25] This can be found concisely and accessibly in A. MacIntyre, *A Short History of Ethics*, 12th ed. (London, 1995), pp. 57-83.

[26] The other works are the *Ethica Eudemia* and the *Magna Moralia*, of which the authorship and the editions are still the topic of academic debate.

Like all living beings, people also actively live out their lives. This is done in a characteristically human way, thus with a certain measure of consciousness, rationality and freedom. Even if we do something that another mammal does, for example, eating regularly, we do it as human beings. In addition, we are social beings, existing and only able to exist within the organized *polis*. In the active living out of their lives human beings realize[27] to a greater or less degree their human potentialities, that which is in them with respect to temperament and intent. We strive for an end that is unique to our human activities, which are types of actions. By end, Aristotle means that what has emerged is what could and should emerge (Aristotle's act/potential distinction).[28] Such ends, connected to our striving, can be deduced from the striving itself by means of explanation. We do these things because of an end, for the purpose of attaining something. There can also be other ends, coincidental or unanticipated, to my action, but they do not constitute the end for which I strove—they have nothing to do with the reasons for my undertaking the action. point. If I—to use a modern example—read the newspaper everyday I do that, for example, to keep myself up to date with respect to relevant facts and to acquire insight into relevant developments in the world and around me. In turn, this end can and will refer to still other, higher ends such as, for example, knowledge and insight, so that I can act ably and knowledgeably in the public forum, live with others in public space, and be able to make decisions in concert with my fellow citizens. This daily reading of the newspaper can come to an end through an extended period of strikes by the transporters, but that is not the real end (*telos*, in later influential Latin translations, *finis*) of reading the newspaper. For external reasons I will have lost one of the means for reaching that end. Whenever Aristotle speaks of end, he has *telos* in mind, an end that is realized in combination with, converging with the final end or destiny, the whither (*hou heneka*) of the action. It thus concerns the internal possibility and intent being realized, which in this example is the ability for me with my rational abilities to appropriate knowledge and insight so that I can perform my role

---

[27] Aristotle, *Physica* 192a23, 98b10-199b32. The 'nature' of everything that lives is defined as an intrinsic principle of movement and rest, in which movement presupposes an end determined in advance, to which the movement is directed.

[28] *Ethica Nicomacheia* I.1.1094a; J. Ritter, "Das bürgerliche Leben: Zur aristotelischen Theorie des Glücks," in: C. Mueller-Goldingen, *Schriften zur aristotelischen Ethik* (Hildesheim/etc., 1988), pp. 107-41, esp. 108-09. Originally published in: *Vierteljahresschrift für wissenschaftliche Pädagogik* 32 (1956): 60-94.

in the public forum.[29] That which is good in an act is that which strives after the proper good of that act. An act is good according to the degree that it brings its own good closer. Its good does not lie in the 'product', in the sense of the actual result of the act, but depends on the answer to the question of whether the acting person *knows* what he is doing or if she *has consciously chosen* for the sake of the action itself or if he has performed the act out of a *permanent disposition* (i.e., a virtue).[30] This is how Aristotle answers the question of "what is good to do?" in his *Ethica Nicomacheia*.[31]

The acting person should know what she is doing, i.e., she should use her understanding and with her *reason* identify the goal of her actions. She must pursue the end through her *will*, an element in the line of thought that will become of decisive importance in the Catholic tradition for determining the goodness of an action. The third element is the permanent attitude from which the person acts. For example, by continually acting courageously, one acquires the disposition of courage. Each new action occurs out of this permanent disposition, the virtue of courage. With the words "'since the end, i.e. what is best, is of such and such a nature' ... is not evident except to the good man ...," Aristotle indicates that virtue is the comprehensive category

---

[29] Such a line of thought is called *teleological*. Cf. M. Midgley, "Teleological Theories of Morality," in: G. Parkinson (ed.), *An Encyclopedia of Philosophy* (London, 1988), pp. 541-67. In a strict sense, teleology is to be conceived, i.e., thought from the perspective of the *causa finalis* (R. Spaemann and R. Löw, *Die Frage Wozu? Geschichte und Wiederentdeckung des teleologischen Denkens*, 2nd. ed. (Munich/ Zürich, 1991), p. 61. This is in distinction from the view in which consequences are seen as the end, as in B. Schüller, "Das Geschick eines Wortpaares," in B. Schüller, *Der menschliche Mensch: Aufsätze zur Metaethik und zur Sprache der Moral* (Düsseldorf, 1982), pp. 156-83, who in connection with Broad's distinction between teleology and deontology (correctly) distinguishes teleology from utilitarianism (contra to the now usual identification of the two), but does not ascribe to *telos* its original meaning of *causa finalis*. See J.-P. Wils, "Verletzung und Integrität. Zur Transformation und ästhetischen Rehabilitation der Teleologie," in: J. Schneider *et al.*, *Natur als Erinnerung? Annäherung an eine müde Diva* (Tübingen, 1992), pp. 111-58.

[30] Aristotle, *Ethica Nicomacheia* II.IV.3.1105a.

[31] For extensive source studies see J. Vanier, *Le Bonheur principe et fin de la morale aristotélicienne* (Paris/Bruges, 1965) and J.L. Akrill, *Aristotle on Eudaimonia* (London, 1974). For a survey of current interpretation of Aristotle on this point see G. Lawrence, "Aristotle and the Ideal Life," in: *The Philosophical Review* 102 (1993): 1-34.

of his ethics.[32] It is implied here that a inexperienced person and an outsider to the concrete praxis cannot have a better knowledge than the experienced person of what is at issue here and what good is to be done here and now. More strongly still, it is only the experienced person who has continually applied himself to knowing what the good to be done is can know what good is. This so-called Aristotelian circular argument (only the one who practises the good knows what good is) is not actually a circular argument but holds together a number of poles of tension which are constitutive of ethical actions.

1. The good lies in a personal *mean* (*mesotès*). That which does not constitute a problem for the person who has been accustomed from his youth to actively tackling problems that arise demands great effort by another who has always been anxious and has acted nervously. Courage always lies between two extremes: cowardice and recklessness, but what a concrete and courageous act for a person is depends on that individual's personal abilities. There is room for a personal perfection as well as for the tragic and unchangeable. When I make an effort on the basis of my abilities I can reach my own limit, but not completely change myself. But the latter does not have to occur, and yet I can act in a morally good way. This is not subjectivism but a recognition of the person as public and as a limited human being.

2. At the same time Aristotle's ethics include the idea of *excellence*: that action is very courageous which those who display the virtue of courage in high degree, the courageous, who have experience in dealing with difficult affairs, judge to be so. The experience, that which has proven to be good in practice, receives a place here.[33]

3. Aristotle's ethics is homogeneous i.e., his virtue ethics directs the acting human being to striving after the *completely good*. That, rather than the question of whether something has (just) been permitted, remains the chief question. This comes to expression, as well as elsewhere, in the sustained distinction between the good and the appearance of good. One must have a certain measure of intelligence to be able to choose the right methods for a

---

[32] *Ethica Nicomacheia* VI.XII.1144a34. The translation here comes from Aristotle, *Nicomachean Ethics*, tr. W.D. Ross, rev. J.O. Urmson, in: *The Complete Works of Aristotle*, vol. 2, Bollingen Series LXXI/2, ed. Jonathan Barnes (Princeton: Princeton University Press, 1984), 1144a33-35.

[33] G. Bien, "Die menschlichen Meinungen und das Gute: Die Lösung des Normproblems in der aristotelischen Ethik," in: M. Riedel (ed.), *Rehabilitierung der Praktischen Philosophie*, Vol. 1 (Freiburg, 1972), pp.345-71, esp. p.363. See C. Steel, "Verstandigheid en moraliteit," in: H. Parret (ed.). *In alle redelijkheid* (Amsterdam, 1989), pp.101-15, esp. p.105.

given problem. But this intelligence as such can also be used for bad ends (as we see happen daily in the contemporary variant of this—pragmatism). Nevertheless, neither someone who acts in this way nor his action can be called good, and that judgement is based on good reasons. After all, he or she shows that he or she does know the means but does not have a comprehensive idea of the proper end. We call such a person cunning or limited in perception. He or she has only an idea of an apparent good. Yet Aristotle's ethics is homogeneous in another respect. From the construction of ends toward the final end one looks back at every end and sees the good that lies in it. A partial view in which the satisfaction that a kind of action yields would obtain as a criterion for the good is not sufficient. Also, whenever someone has liberated himself from the appearance of the good and can identify the true good in his actions, it is not that he achieves happiness through striving after that good as an end. Happiness is not an *ergon*: it does emerge, however, within the framework of an action that is directed towards an end in organized society. It is not blind coincidence but something that falls to one's share in a well-specified context, an action directed at the proper end of that action in the *polis*.[34] This ethics opposes the domination of means over ends. But also, the ends and the final end cannot be manufactured and remain in relation to the happiness that occurs, as the inside of the ends.

Medical Practice as an Example:
For example, medical practice has thus its own good, that which is unique and characteristic of acts related to medical practice: helping to heal the sick, helping to lessen pain and staving off death. Those acts performed by the doctor are good insofar as they strive after these goods and to the degree that these goods are pursued.[35] For the moral goodness of the action it is necessary that the doctor holds to these ends in his actions. He must want to strive after them; the good must be a good for

---

[34] *Ethica Nicomacheia* II.1100a31-1101a21.

[35] Aristotle often takes navigation and helmsmanship, politics as the ordering of public life, and medical practice as examples of kinds of action. Medical practice yields more than just an example. Aristotle also often lays emphasis on a close parallel between ethics and medical practice, thus between the kinds of actions that ethics, i.e., reflection on actions from the perspective of good and evil, and the kind of action that medical practice is. Both making someone healthy again and doing moral good requires moderation, the avoidance of two extremes. The parallel lies between the two kinds of action in persistent moderation, striving for the right means or *mesotès*. Cf. W. Jaeger, "Medizin als methodisches Vorbild in der Ethik des Aristoteles," reprinted in: C. Mueller-Goldingen, *Schriften zur aristotelischen Ethik*, 143-60. The parallel between ethics and medicine in the larger context of ancient Greek philosophy is a topic in M.C. Nussbaum, *The Therapy of Desire* (Princeton, NJ, 1994).

him in acting here and now,[36] and he must do it out of the proper attitude. A very able doctor who has great skill and a wide knowledge (knows the means) but believes that killing a patient out of mercy is an end of medical practice is an example of someone who has an idea of apparent good. The good that lies in the kind of actions themselves must be unfolded through the actions—here the staving off of death and the relieving of pain and distress.

Happiness

All striving for limited and more comprehensive ends is done because people believe that their lives will be fulfilled by such ends. "Happiness therefore has to do with [good and with] the highest good, because happiness is the conception in which all people relate themselves to that which seems to be the highest fulfilment of their lives."[37] People use the term happiness in a variety of ways, and not all people are agreed in the meanings they give to it. But they do agree that happiness is the highest: it is the final goal and end of all striving. Everything is complete; everything exists that had to exist; everything is self-sufficient. There is no further striving, no end that is pursued for another more remote end. Aristotle's definition of happiness arises from this: "Happiness, then, is something complete and self-sufficient, and is the end of action."[38] For Aristotle, the highest good is not a metaphysical idea but is and exists merely in the concrete reality of living together in the organized society, in the *polis*. The highest good, happiness, exists in living together, and we participate in it insofar as we can exist freely and acknowledged in the public forum.[39] The good human life is a rational, active life

---

[36] G. Bien, *Die menschlichen Meinungen und das Gute.* p.363.

[37] J. Ritter, "Das bürgerliche Leben," p.112.

[38] *Ethica Nicomacheia* I.V. 1097b20-21. For the translation see W.D. Ross, *Nichomachean Ethics*.

[39] Karl Marx and Hannah Arendt have shown that this inductive view of Aristotle also entailed that he remained a prisoner of the idea that the question concerned free citizens (and not others, slaves) and men (and not women, because they had their existence in the home, *oikos* and not in the *polis*), and therewith confirmed existing relationships. For Aristotle's internal logic on this point see W.W. Fortenbaugh, *Aristotle on Emotion* (London, 1975), ch. 3, "Consequences for Political Theory," pp.45-61, esp. 53-61.

lived on the basis of moral virtue in the well-ordered community.[40] (For that matter, for Aristotle the ordered free society does not coincide with a historical situation, as in, for example, the here and now of the *polis* Athens.)

Friendship

Aristotle speaks in Books VIII and IX of the *Ethica Nicomacheia* about friendship as the foundation for human society, including the society of free citizens in the public forum. As a free citizen, one can consider as good for another what is good from the perspective of friendship. A true friend wishes something as a good for the sake of the other, who is "his alter ego".[41] We cannot maintain a true friendship with many people, but we can put ourselves in the position of friendship and from that perspective consider the goods related to living together in an orderly manner, even if we can and do not wish to maintain a preferential friendship with all. Friendship constitutes the organized community. For Aristotle friendship was the attitude, built up through continuous action, of benevolence for one another, or more precisely, wishing the good for the other for the sake of the other.

Modern Medical Practice as an Example:
To explain these distinctions that Aristotle makes, I will once again return to the field that served as an example above, medical practice, i.e., modern medical practice. Aside from giving an explanation of the distinctions, I will attempt at the same time to clarify what is discussed with respect to morals in modern medical practice.[42] In contemporary medical practice, which must be distinguished from Hippocratic/Aristotelian medical practice, are *technical* actions (what Aristotle would call *technè*, producing actions) and interwoven with these are actions that *are bound to the proper, characteristic ends of medical practice* (what Aristotle would call *poiesis*). Only those who are able to see this *poiesis* in medical practice can say something about the

---

[40] Only the reflective life of philosophy transcends this, because, after all, *theoria* is the highest human ability and activity, where one is well on the way to immortality and divinity. But this activity of reflection is also embedded in the community; this should allow itself to be advised by the wisdom of the philosophers.

[41] *Ethica Nicomacheia* VIII.vii. 1159a. A. Kenny, "Friendship and Self-Love," in: *Aristotle on the Perfect Life* (Oxford, 1992), pp.41-55, cf. p.46. For a indication of the problems see P. van Tongeren "Aristoteles' ethiek van de vriendschap," in: *Algemeen Nederlands Tijdschrift voor Wijsbegeerte* 83 (1991): 273-93.

[42] E. Pellegrino, "The Virtuous Physician and the Ethics of Medicine," in: E.F. Shelp, *Virtue and Medicine* (Dordrecht, 1985), pp.237-55.

moral good or evil of an action.[43] She or he who is an experienced practitioner of medicine is and remains primarily the one who has the capacity for this. Aristotle (and after and with him an important part of the Catholic moral tradition) says it in a much more pregnant way: only those who themselves are experienced in a kind of action like medical practice, who are *phronimos* (Aristotle), *peritus* or belong to the *prudentes* in that field (the Catholic tradition), who have "the eye of the clinician with great experience" (modern medical science), can know with probability what is good to do here and now with respect to an actual patient. The ends that we just mentioned are not principles that must be 'applied' to a concrete instance, but they have to do with practical actions, which concern, according to Aristotle, an peculiar kind of knowledge—practical knowledge and not a theory. There is, namely, no certain knowledge possible with respect to the concrete and contingent, but only probable knowledge. We only know what is good from experience and consultation.

Modern medical actions are for a good part also technical, even highly technical, in nature. That is to say that also with the means and methods that are peculiar to technology (and—as we should add—to biology, to the natural sciences, to mathematics, computer science, etc.) one strives for certainty. That happens by, among other things, working with 'average' statistical values. The uniqueness of *poiesis* and of medical practice in the broad sense is that the doctor often has to deal with uncertainty, with particular situations of a concrete sick man or woman, with 'givens' that are subject to change. In such uncertainties, the doctor must administer a correct, i.e., suitable, therapy or palliative. Medical practice, taken as *poiesis*, requires, in addition to pondering the appropriate means, the identifying the hierarchy of ends. As a medical practitioner, the doctor does not posit the ends, he does not make any hierarchy of ends (at least not as a doctor, possibly as a reflective citizen with other citizens).[44] The ends are already determined: combatting the disease, easing the pain, staving off death. What the doctor does is only to identify, to discover, their hierarchy here and now. There can come a moment that the doctor discovers that the disease cannot be combatted, at the very most she can still only combat the side-effects of the disease. She must still ease the pain and distress.[45] What is concretely good for this person here and now is discovered in the concreteness. It is inventive,

---

[43] R. Sokolowski, "The Art and Science of Medicine," in: E. Pellegrino *et al.* (eds), *Catholic Perspectives on Medical Morals: Foundational Issues* (Dordrecht/etc., 1989), pp.263-75, esp. p.268.

[44] A. Kenny "The Ends of Life," in: A. Kenny, *Aristotle on the Perfect Life*, pp.3-5.

[45] See L. Honnefelder, "Güterabwägung und Folgenabschätzung in der Ethik," in: H.-M. Sass and H. Viefhues (ed.), *Güterabwägung in der Medizin* (Berlin/etc., 1991), pp.44-61, who attempts to reason in an Aristotelian-Thomistic way on goods in medical science. However, the critique can be applied to him that has been indicated by P. Ricœur, *Oneself as Another*, tr. Kathleen Blamey (Chicago/London, 1992), pp.176 and 289-90, nt.83, that a good must be seen as immanent to the praxis and not as a universal 'value' that must be proven in an historical way.

not creative.[46] It is precisely the position of friendship that makes it possible to see this concrete good for the other. All three of the ends cited are subordinate to the final end—happiness. In Aristotelian thought, that is (again viewed concretely) the successful human life. That is the question that remains in all the misery of the incurable, painful disorder: what is a successful life? 'Successful' does not mean successful in the usual sense, i.e., cheerful, glamourous. It means that which this concrete human being can discover (extract) as a completion, the purpose of his or her life.

In actual fact, the ends of medical science change as well, entailed by the fact that that field often changes in nature (for example, prognostic medical science, which has emerged, is concerned with the end of the quality of life). We are all justified in reflecting on the changed ends, and this includes doctors, but they do this not from the prerogative of a medical practitioners but as a citizens.

Just like medical science, ethics, i.e., reflection on human actions with respect to good and evil, recognizes a permanent uncertainty, in which assessment and consultation remain necessary.

The Highest Good

What is now the highest good for human actions, i.e., that which is the most worthy to be striven after? The highest good, Aristotle answers, is happiness (*eudaimonia*),[47] which is also the final end, the *telos*, of all human striving, acting, and living. There are as many ends as there are types of actions; they must be discovered in a hierarchy with respect to one another, contributing to and culminating in the highest good. This requires reflection: which good is being discussed and how does it contribute to the highest good? In addition, there are things that seem to be good: are they in fact good? Are not appearances often deceiving? How do we know that it is truly a good that is at issue? Reflection is also needed regarding that question. But in spite of the inherent uncertainty that accompanies moral considerations, in spite of the fact that we must identify a hierarchy of goods,[48] and the fact that we must continually ask whether it is truly a good that is at issue and not a misconception or deceptive appearance, every type of action has its own good. For the modern reader, who thinks in the framework of nature vs. culture and in the framework of cause and effect according to the model of the natural

---

[46] W. Thys, *De deugd weer in het midden: Van homo moralis naar homo ethicus* (Kapellen, 1989), p. 19.

[47] A. Kenny, "Perfection and Happiness," in: *Aristotle on the Perfect Life*, pp. 16-22; J. Ritter, "Das bürgerliche Leben."

[48] The notion of the hierarchy of goods is further developed in Thomas than in Aristotle. In the latter's *Ethica Nicomacheia* there is, according to many commentators, no coherent analysis of the hierarchy of actions and corresponding ends. See P. Ricœur, *Oneself as Another*, pp. 172-73.

sciences, a significant misunderstanding could arise here. Aristotle does not claim that it is 'nature' used in a biological/physical sense that defines what should always determine what the ends of an action are. Further, next to the *causa finalis*, he also recognizes a connection of cause and effect, the *causa efficiens*, the efficient cause of something. In Aristotle, nature is directed towards an end and thus has a rational and normative character (and this is quite different from the modern idea of 'blind' nature over against meaningful culture).[49] Human nature is not a preprinted blueprint, although it does indicate limitations and the potentialities that can be realized. Mortality is such a limitation and rationality such a potentiality.

Thomas Aquinas: The View of the Good from the Perspective of Friendship

Whoever reads the Catechism on "The Desire for Happiness" (1718-1719) will see Augustine cited there: "We all want to live happily; in the whole human race there is no one who does not assent to this." In *De Trinitate* Augustine spoke of the human desire to reach the destiny for which God had created us. All people are the same in that they strive for an ultimate good, i.e., *beatitudo* (which, despite the ambiguity, is to be translated as 'blessedness').[50] The Catechism thus relies on a patristic articulation of the natural human desire for happiness that propels everyone forward. Combining views and ideas forged by Aristotle, and thoroughly investigated by Thomas Aquinas, with Neoplatonic and Stoic ideas, a view with respect to happiness arose in the ecclesiastical moral tradition.

Thomas Aquinas also, whose theological labour produced the first systematic treatment of moral theology, defined good in action by viewing the action from the perspective of its purpose.[51] Only when we know the end of an action can we say something conclusive about whether it is good or evil. He also makes a *connection between the end of action, the good, and happiness*. Although a number of correspondences and differences between Aristotle's ethics and Thomas' moral theology demand attention, I will limit myself to Thomas' view of the final end of all life and action: happiness.

---

[49] J. Decorte, "De finaliteit van natuur," in: R. te Velde (ed.), *Thomas over goed en kwaad* (Baarn, 1993), pp. 90-106, esp. pp. 93-97.

[50] Augustine, *De Trinitate*, Book XIII, PL 42, 1018. See, for instance, W. Beierwaltes, *Regio beatitudinis: Zur Augustins Begriff des glücklichen Lebens* (Heidelberg, 1981).

[51] H. Kleber, *Glück als Lebensziel: Untersuchungen zur Philosophie des Glücks bei Thomas von Aquin* (Münster, 1988), pp. 95, 98.

Happiness is a lifelong friendship with the good that promises the most for people.[52] God is the *causa finalis*, the destiny or final end, which gives meaning to everything: all things, all living beings, the human being and every morally good human action.[53]

Is Thomas 'merely' Aristotelian or has he, by using Christian insights, broken fresh ground? It is (more generally speaking) misleading to attribute to Aristotle a non-religious, possessive ethics of *poiesis* so as to allow Thomas' Christian ethics, based on creation and grace, to shine. Aristotle also recognizes the tragic element in action, where human freedom and the necessity to act stumble on the impossibility of achieving the good and on that which evades being influenced by actions—that which is not at one's disposal. Aristotle also ascribes a role to the gods in actions. Just as Thomas would do later, Aristotle also thinks inductively: what do people intend when they talk about good and evil and happiness? He honours such ascriptions of meaning, takes them up in order to show their relativity: what people understand by happiness, such as money, honour, or pleasure are goods, but they contribute to a higher good.[54] Despite all these correspondences, Thomas has nonetheless brought about a great change in thought—also by rethinking Aristotle. I will focus this, as I said above, on Thomas' rethinking of friendship and happiness.[55]

Both Aristotle and Thomas view friendship as the recapitulation and integration of all (other) goods.[56] Thomas views friendship as love for the common good. In this he links up (we encountered this Aristotelian line of thought already above) with Aristotle. For Thomas as well, all other goods are seen in relation to friendship (other than in the great scholastics Peter

---

[52] P. Waddell, *The Primacy of Love: An Introduction to the Ethics of Thomas Aquinas* (New York/Mahwah, 1992), p.6.

[53] Thomas Aquinas, *Summa Theologica* (*ST*) I-IIae.1.5 and 6.

[54] *Ethica Nicomacheia*, Book I; cf. Thomas Aquinas *ST* I-IIae.2; 4.8 *ad* 3: "Consequently, friendship is, as it were, concomitant with perfect Happiness;" II-IIae.23.1. All translations of Thomas' *Summa Theologica* are taken from Thomas Aquinas, *Summa Theologica*, tr. Fathers of the English Dominican Province (London, 1922).

[55] H. Kleber, *Glück als Lebensziel*, pp.35 ff., 72, 93, as well as elsewhere.

[56] See S. Pinckaers, *Le renouveau de la morale* (Turnhout, 1964), pp.31-43, 256-63; resumed in S. Pinckaers, *Les sources de la moral chrétienne: Sa méthode, son contenu, son histoire*, 3rd. ed., (Paris, 1993), pp.438-40.

Lombard and Thomas' teacher, Albert the Great).[57] But is the friendship between humans, in which some form of equality must be present, suitable for referring to the other fundamental relation, i.e., the relationship between God and humans? Can one presume any equality between Him and us? On this point Thomas rethought the Aristotelian concept of friendship (*philia*; *amicitiae*) thoroughly.[58] "Nevertheless, according to Thomas, friendship between God and people is possible. Although both parties are very unequal, they do have something in common. That is, God has something that he shares with people: he wills that people share in his eternal blessedness, an endless and blessed life."[59] God's will to bestow blessedness is the basis on which friendship between Him and people can arise. From a human perspective, *beatitudo* consists in accepting the highest good, i.e., loving God. This love (*caritas*) has the structure of friendship. It is love characterized by benevolence for the other (*benevolentia*, not a desire for what one can possibly receive from the friend); we possess the internal space to wish him well.[60] Aside from this benevolence, however, equality and mutuality are also of importance for friendship (*mutua amatio*). This (and only this) friendship, with these characteristics, is suited to connecting a theological interpretation of love with it. This mutual benevolence is based on some kind of communication: "... since there is a communication between man and God, inasmuch as He communicates His happiness to us, some kind of friendship must needs be based on this same communication ...."[61] In other words, the mutuality of the friendship of people and God exists on the basis of the initiative of God to allow us to share in his blessedness.

---

[57] This is the thesis found in S. Pinckaers and, by means of its resumption, in B. Bujo, *Die Begründung des sittlichen: Zur Frage des Eudämonismus bei Thomas von Aquin* (Paderborn, 1984), ch.2 on *amicitia* and ch.3 on *amor amiticiae*. Cf. R. Guindon, *Béatitude et Théologie moral chez saint Thomas d'Aquin: Origines, Interprétation* (Ottawa, 1956), pp.31-39 on Lombard's Augustinian position with respect to *eudaimonia* and pp.114-27 on Albert, who introduced Aristotle's *Ethics* (at least the parts known to him) into theology and placed the notion of *eudaimonia* central in 'moral theology' but did not yet integrate Aristotle's reflections on friendship into the concept of *eudaimonia*.

[58] Thomas Aquinas, *ST* II-II.23.

[59] H. Woldring, *Vriendschap door de eeuwen heen* (Baarn, 1994), pp.89-90.

[60] E. Schockenhoff, *Bonum hominis: Die anthropologischen und theologischen Grundlagen der Tugendethik des Thomas von Aquin* (Mainz, 1987), pp.493-98 on the uniqueness of the position of friendship love.

[61] *ST* II-II.23.1.

Friendship is thus a model for the association of human beings with God and an adequate indication of our admission to happiness, after and because Thomas rethought the characteristics of (the Aristotelian concept of) friendship in taking God's offer as its foundation.[62] *Autarkeia*, the independence which for Aristotle was the hallmark of *eudaimonia*, is thus theologically recast. Dignity based on one's independence of what others do or could cause is replaced by dignity based on reception. Respect, *re-spicere* (to look upon) from the viewpoint of the Catholic faith is not atomistic but begins from being accepted by God, and on that basis we receive one another. Happiness is identical with blessedness (in the sense of wholeness, holiness, the achievement of the highest good).[63] The destiny of human life is union with God. This union has the character of friendship and indeed—and this is precisely the point of contrast with our late modern culture)—*in a political sense*. It does not concern here a modern concept of politics as party politics. The context is the ordering of society. Our friendship with one another goes back to the friendship of God with people. His friendship also precedes our human friendships. Both relations (of God with us and us with one another) are public relations. In the friendship that God willed to begin with us he introduces an order into his involvement with us and we subsequently order ourselves in that way. Here Thomas uses Paul's idea of *koinōnia* (1 Cor. 1:9), the community initiated by God (as a processing of the Aristotelian concept of *koinōnia*). God longs for friendship with human beings, to be in their company. The good that He wishes for them is that they see Him and enjoy His presence. Thomas does not speak here figuratively or metaphorically (and certainly not 'piously') but remains strictly within the conceptual coordinates of political friendship. It concerns an ordering of human relationships through taking up the moral position of friendship and regarding the good for the other, the other as a part of the whole, from that perspective. This occurs on the basis of a preceding order offered by God. Only by doing the good do we see God; only through God's incarnation, Jesus Christ, do we know what is completely good.[64] From that perspective, as it were, one looks back on all the other things that are considered to be good in our life. They receive their ordering and their direction from this union, this friend-

---

[62] E. Schockenhoff, *Bonum hominis*, pp. 501-72, esp. p. 527.

[63] Aristotle, *Ethica Nicomacheia* VII and VIII; Thomas Aquinas, *Summa Theologica* II-IIae.23.3; *Questio Disputata De Virtutibus in Communi* 2.2.

[64] Thomas discusses this in *ST* I-IIae.69 and in his commentary on Matthew 5 (the Sermon on the Mount, where the Beatitudes are found), the Catena aurea in Matthaeum 071 CMT, cp. 5 (R. Busa, (ed.), S. Thomas Aquinatis, Opera omnia, 5. Commentaria in scripturas (Stuttgart, 1980), p. 153.

ship with God. In this life it consists in the loving contemplation of God, in a still incomplete form. People can be happy if they direct themselves to the final end.

Thomas' thought thus moves from the God-human relation to the relationships between people and the relationship of a human being to him- or herself. The ultimate decisive change in perspective in Thomas' line of thought is that the relation that someone starts with another and the relation that he or she has with him- or herself is viewed as taken up in the friendship of God with people. So-called natural love for oneself is also taken up into this, through which the person loves herself as the dwelling-place of God.[65] The human person begins to see herself as a gift of God and the others as gifts as well. This stipulation is taken up in designating the substance of actions. According to Robert Sokolowski in his attempt to clarify the substance and morality of an action over against the subjectivization of good and evil:

> The substance of a moral action lies therefore not in a thought or in an intention or in an act of willing, but in thoughtful behavior, in an embodied performance which, as good or as bad for another, is done or averted as the agent's good or bad. It is the thoughtful form that makes the performance moral, but of course the form needs the performance as its embodiment and expression.[66]

Actual, thoughtful behaviour is the point here. A murder is an evil, if we remember that through that action another is robbed of the foundational good—life. The intention alone does not make it into an evil (even as a good intention cannot make something into a good). In view of the various worldviews, however, we need at least an idea that life is a good or that people have the right to live (or some such fundamental notion). Without such an idea the ending of someone's life is not to be seen as murder. Faith dovetails into such a qualifying idea through our remembering that life is not only a founding good for the other but also given to him or her as a gift, as space in which to arrive at happiness. All these are radical qualifications of the good that life is and all these qualities of life are cut off by murder. The evil does not lie in a preceding intention or consideration but in the action, as the good also always lies in the public action itself ('public' here refers to an action in which the actor enters into a relation with another or himself as another). The example of murder may also have made clear that, without the

---

[65] Thomas Aquinas, *ST* II-IIae.25.4; 26; 27.4.

[66] R. Sokolowski, "What is Moral Action?" in: R. Sokolowski, *Pictures, Quotations and Distinctions* (Notre Dame/London, 1992), pp.261-76. See p.267.

radical ascriptions of meaning from the perspective of faith, we still have an ascription of meaning at our disposal which we share with those of other worldviews: life is a fundamental good.

The Discovery of What Good is

Just as I did by employing Aristotelian distinctions, I will now, using views borrowed from Thomas in relation to happiness, friendship and what a good is, give a further explanation of the Catechism (1717; cf. 1820). How are we to understand the Catechism when it says, "[The Beatitudes] shed light on the actions and attitudes characteristic of the Christian life"? I will first remind my readers that this is expressed within the larger denominator of "Life in Christ," a teaching concerning the moral nature of the human being (his 'dignity') and "moral decisions" (1696) which seeks its "first and last point of reference" (1698) in Jesus Christ. Thus the text strives to be Christocentric.

We strive for all kinds of things that are goods—justice, for example, as well as premoral[67] concerns such as health. In themselves such matters and relations have great value: everyone, whether or not they are believers, can strive for such matters and relationships that are good in themselves. In that striving action we are equal, we encounter one another in action, in the necessity to act, no matter what our faith is. It is also possible that we can also agree in what we consider to be a good. For example, as people with very different attitudes to life and views, we can call one and the same relationship just and we can all call something a good worth striving for, such as every member of our community or someone who wishes to join our community having a right to food and shelter. We can also understand such a good as Christians, if we, with a few intermediary steps, view it from the perspective of the final end—friendship with God. The just relation remains one and the same good: when we achieve it it is a good in itself. We can also misunderstand the good and, acting accordingly, fall short with respect to the good, even quite seriously. We have created an unjust relationship that in itself is an evil, with the privation of being. Evil is the privation of the good. To be good in actions is to bring being to fulness. If we view that which we

---

[67] M. Rhonheimer, *Praktische Vernunft und Vernünftigkeit der Praxis: Handlungstheorie bei Thomas von Aquin in ihrer Entstehung aus dem Problemkontext der aristotelische Ethik* (Berlin, 1994), pp. 125-26, criticizes the distinctions between moral/non-moral, premoral/moral, originating in the long-term German discussion in moral theology, inasfar as one can speak of a good merely from the perspective of practical reason. However, the fact remains that some goods like justice can only be realized through actions, while other goods like health are also pregiven and cannot be (completely) taken up into the domain of actions.

call good from the perspective of the friendship with God and therewith take up a (believing) position that we do not share with all, good and evil do not change in themselves. Christians who give their hearts to God or, better, give them to him as gifts as a response to His gifts, do not see *per se* better than or differently from others that a good is involved. Together with someone of an entirely different worldview, a Christian can perceive that there is a specific good in an action here and now, such as, for example, that justice must be done. Christians *possibly* see the good in a different way ("... the eye being cleansed by the gift of understanding ..." as Thomas says[68]) and in a different hierarchy of goods. The community of believers will, for instance, see human life as a good that is characterized by and understood from the idea of its being a gift. Christians will attempt to view the continuing uncertainty of our human life from the viewpoint that it is a gift. As such, life is a good—also when we are very ill, either in body or mind. We may hardly or not at all experience it as a good, for pain and distress overshadow the good. Nevertheless, we can judge human life to be a good, just as we can and must call the pain and distress, as well the death that comes, to be evil. We can never call the evil of death a good, with which the other, real evil of pain and distress may be fought. What remains to us, i.e., the actual reduced human life, remains a good: we must not destroy it. We can fight pain and distress within the boundaries which must be retraced time and again. The faith that sheds light on this does not establish what is a good or an evil. All of us, Christians and non-Christians, can distinguish between good and evil in actions by means of practical reason. Faith does shed illumination on the fact that human life is living in a community (in this case of the reduced possibilities, for example, caring for the comatose patient, i.e., clothing, washing, etc.) and *how* life can be seen as God intended it and as we have come to understand it through Jesus Christ.

As far as this is concerned, Thomas's "moral theology" is ultimately Christocentric—Christocentric in a well-defined sense which is not to be misunderstood. God shows himself to be the highest good in the incarnation: Christ is the apex of what God wishes to disclose of himself. The revelation in Christ does not replace the potentialities that we, ordinary people, already have for arriving at the good in freedom. Every attempt to read a *Glaubensethik* into Thomas, in which the unique free potentialities already bestowed on human beings are slighted seems to me incorrect: 'Christ as centre' then places the given of faith of Christ as the highpoint of God's self-communication in competition with God's other work: he propels us, his image, already by his grace in the direction of his love since he gave us freedom in time and

---

[68] Thomas Aquinas, *ST* I-IIae.69.2 *ad* 3.

space. "But it belongs to the essence of goodness to communicate itself to others .... Hence it belongs to the essence of the highest good to communicate itself in the highest manner to the creature."[69] We see what good is through the light that faith in Jesus Christ sheds on our human reason. God is a God who gives life, perfect life. When death comes, he will also be there to take human life into his hand and shelter it in his bosom: the fulness of happiness (*Catechism*, 214, 655). By way of clarification, there is no condemnatory language here concerning the human being who has fallen into distress with respect to his experience, his feeling life to be something painful, frightening, or even terrible. Neither is it said here that someone must feel something different or—just as absurd and disrespectful—that someone would feel differently if he or she would hold different ideas—to the contrary.

Assessment from the Position of Friendship

Whenever happiness is discussed here it concerns an assessment from an objective position: that which can be called worthy of striving for from the external position of friendship, that which I should grant someone in benevolence so that it may go well—very well—with her or him. This does not imply any judgement about someone's feeling; to the contrary, it implies that I view his or her experience and ascription of meaning directly *with* him or her. Only then can there be a foundation for indicating concretely what he or she has seen as a good in his or her own life story and what I as a friend wish for him or her.[70] It is from this position which I take up as friend with respect to myself that I can assess what attracts me. I then view my own good from the broader perspective of the common good. Can I, for example, see the use of alcoholic drink as a good? It may attract me—that much is clear—but is it a good? Insofar as it can make me feel good, make me forget my worries, and promise the pleasure of good company, it can seem to be a good. If I view it from the perspective of friendship to myself, I can consider all of that to be a good. But there is still a clear contrast: feeling good is not in every case the highest good; accepting what I actually strive for and what I shun in my concerns is certainly a higher good than forgetting them; the pleasure of good company will be enhanced by making myself known to my friends and they to me, that they accept me as I am and I them. From

---

[69] Thomas Aquinas, *ST* III.1.1, resp.

[70] D. Runia, *Bios eudaimoon*, pp. 12, 23, plays objective and subjective off against each other by positing "established and universally accepted" over against "feeling," a conceptual figuration that is set up falsely in many variations, including Roman Catholic moral theology and the teaching of Roman Catholic moral doctrine.

the perspective of such contrasts, the glass that I raise with my friends is a good for me, but a limited good. From the viewpoint of friendship to myself, the glass can also be an evil, if it, for example, is the fifth glass, that I drink alone at home, because it allows me to close my eyes to reality.

By taking the position of friendship with respect to myself and the other and looking at what attracts and repulses I can identify what good is. Whenever I concur with my will and strive for it in my actions the good is realized (the *dilectio*). Also whenever the possibilities (to go where one wills, to speak with one another, to share a meal together, to communicate with one another in whatever way through word, gesture, or touch) in our lives decrease, it remains a human life until the end. Decreasing capacities and death are, indeed, 'natural', in the precise sense that they will surely come but are not therefore a good. Whenever we reconcile ourselves to the idea that life is like that, as human beings and possibly also as Christians we ascribe a meaning to what in fact presents itself in life, without naturalizing pain, disease or death and calling them 'normal'. We can reconcile ourselves to a certain degree with the evil of decreasing communication, pain and death; we face the facts and accept them, but we do so with the understanding that life is beautiful and good and in the hope that a richer life can still be given. The tradition of faith places this in the framework of grace and the contrary of grace, i.e., sin as the refusal of the community of love with disease and death as the punishment for original sin (*Catechism*, 385-390).

Faith and the Good

The believing community will also *possibly* see a different hierarchy of goods from those of a different worldview. Watching over one another (i.e., continuing to see the good for the other with an unceasing respect, helping her as much as possible with respect to opportunities, caring, etc.) is more highly esteemed than independence (in the sense of the ability to manage for oneself). Independence is not to be judged as being of little account. But there is something higher. I have used the term *possibly* twice now. Those of other worldviews can concur even entirely or to a large extent with what the church holds as good. We can see that in the practical societal or political acts that occur, as, for example, in the fact that some humanists do not consider the ability to manage for oneself to be the highest good any more than Catholics do. The church places such a good (concretized in the examples of raising children to be independent in viewing, judging and acting, or advancing, with a never ceasing respect, the individuality of older people, their own place and their own story) in the light of remembrance and expectation. It is a good that the believing community has been able to see in the light of faith because of the tradition. We know it because of the experiences and the insights of our believing predecessors.

The Beatitudes Again

The previous 'world Catechism', the sixteenth-century *Catechismus Romanus*, already clarified the point that whenever it is said that life is always a good, it is a qualified view of life that was in mind: physical human life is a condition for experiencing all other goods. Happiness excludes every evil.[71] Complete happiness, *beatitudo*, is life with God, which encompasses our life in its earthly relationships. Looking back from that perspective to our experience that life can be horrible and degrading, we must not call that injustice and suffering good but continue to call it what it is: evil. Physical human life as such, however, is still a good. It is a completely different question as to whether we may and can confront ourselves with that which is horrible, degrading, unjust rather than—out of the inability to do such—denying the horrible and allowing an apparent good, a *bonum apparens*, to take its place.

If I now connect this interpretation, derived from Thomas, of a good, a *bonum*, with the Beatitudes such as "Blessed are the peacemakers, for they will be called the children of God" (Matt. 5:9), I arrive at the following: those who strive for peace and make peace in the human relationships of internal struggle and war strive in this for something that appears good to them. They do not themselves invent the good of peace, but it addresses them as something good and they pursue it. Such a peace comes into existence and continues to exist on the basis of justice: everyone receives his due. Peace is thus a political idea, concerned with the just ordering of society. A good in such a framework will make full human life possible. For the believer (the disciples to whom the promising beatitudes are spoken), the understanding of the good as 'getting one's due' and as 'full life' are under the claim of faith. By reflecting from the moral position of friendship on what will bring someone his or her due and reflecting on what God wills for his friends (John 13:5-17; 15:12-17) they identify what good is. The believer who understands and acts accordingly will be blessed. This is not given as a consequence but as a promise. Such an understanding and acting also contains happiness. It is not an experiential result that is striven for directly (even though it can be a result). The order is rather that it radiates from the *understanding* of God's love on the concrete good that is identified here and now. This not merely a different or an extra consideration but a *change in the identification* of the good. This is continually an identification within a societal order, looking at communal existence from the position of friendship, and is thus political in nature.

---

[71] *Catechismus Romanus*, Pars I, Caput XIII. qu. IV.III: "Vita est magnum bonum"; IV. "Felicitas malum nullum admittit. Omne bonum concludit."

The Catechism leaves aside this political ordering when it speaks about the Beatitudes. What has indeed been said elsewhere about God's friendship with human beings (277, 374, 396, 1468) obtains here as well. But the splintering of this basic idea in the Catechism is of such a nature that this theologoumenon is not brought into discussion at a crucial moment of the explanation of the Catholic faith: Jesus Christ's promise to those who wish to believe and wish to seek the good in the beatitudes.[72]

Conclusion: Action, Community, Happiness

Numbers 1877 and 1889 speak of the "vocation of humanity" and of the inspiration to "a life of self-giving." It would be a mistake to understand these terms in a modern and moralistic way, as if we, if we 'truly' believe, must primarily do a lot. Believing and continuous, good action do not relate to each other like understanding a task and performing it. By way of conclusion, I will draw attention to four matters on the basis of the preceding insight into Aristotle's and Thomas' theories of the good, viewed from the perspective of friendship.

1. *In action itself that which good is proclaimed*; the insight in what is concretely good is not deduced from a prior metaphysics, ontological insight, not even when the reflection of faith is presented in the form of metaphysics or ontology. In action, for example, the treatment of citizen by an official in the Social Services and vice versa, what respect entails comes to the fore.

2. *Hidden in action lies an occasion for faith.* I will tilt the perspective now and look within the triangle of faith-good/evil-actions, from the axis of good/ evil/actions to faith. By discovering what is good and what is evil one can get a better view of what the special perspective of faith on reality is. For example, the discovering of evil can lead one to see that that must be seen as sin, within the coordinates of grace and reconciliation. Or, to remain with

---

[72] One commentator on the new World Catechism, G.J. Hughes, concludes that the section on morality is "in many respects a very traditional document," and as far as the conceptual scheme is concerned and sometimes the details follows the moral systematics of Thomas Aquinas. Cf. G.J.Hughes, "Our Human Vocation," p.353. The secretary of the Editorial Team of the Catechism, Mgr. C. Schönborn, "Les Critères de rédaction du Catéchisme de l'Église catholique," in: NRT 115 (1993): 161-68, esp. p.167, witnesses to the supportive character of Thomas' moral theology: "This plan of the 'fundamental moral' is not only inspired by *Gaudium et Spes*, but above all by the *Summa Theologica* of St. Thomas Aquinas." In this case this is not so (in my view, unfortunately) at this crucial moment. See S. Pinckaers, "The Use of Scripture."

the example just above, of the citizen and the official, showing respect and being respected, treating someone in a social role, as *socius*, can be the occasion for taking the perspective of faith. The human experience of justice being done and being received can be an occasion for comprehending what God's order could mean: living in just relationships and being received generously. This same experience can make it self-evident that one does justice and receives another. But it can also mean that by gaining space for justice (a *bonum arduum*, an attractive good but difficult to achieve) I desire all the more that justice is done to me. The experience in action with justice and disgraceful injustice, i.e., the actual turning to the good brings me to understanding what goodness is and that and how God is actually good. This can bring one to a purer lament and request in prayer. It brings me to the significance of God's law, to understanding the given direction.[73] By understanding in practice what is good and what is evil, what appropriate honour and objectionable humiliation is, our belief as to who God is becomes clearer. In action we are on the road of faith, which does not go from faith via deduction to good actions but from insight in actions with respect to good and evil to an understanding of what faith is. Faith must be told to us, held before us, and lived before us. Next to this, however, there is the possibility of faith in the discovery of good and evil via one's own life story. In other words, even though faith must be revealed (we cannot arrive at it ourselves) in the life story of a human person there is a point of contact for faith. But the reverse is also true: even though I am sympathetic to happiness, because of what I have done and what I have undergone, for happiness-in-relief, thus for belief, I must be nudged. And I can still reject it. Nonetheless, my own conceptions of happiness and my own striving for happiness are and remain the point of contact for the proclamation of faith. This constitutes all the more reason to criticize the tendency in which 'true' happiness is marked off from 'the people of today' who are said to be 'hedonistic'. One finds a point of contact for discovering what counts as happiness in the conceptions of happiness (of 'getting a kick', of the great Chance, of large amounts of money) of the inner-city young people who frequent gambling establishments and in their experience there (what it means to be admired, to make themselves insensible, to find themselves part of a group). They also live with a concrete idea of how what they find attractive fits into a 'happy' life, just as the middle-class person struggles for a larger house, the monk in his abbey and the religious organization that offers heroin prostitutes a place of refuge. For all of them it obtains that he or she must pursue what is apparently good or a real good. (Who in fact comes closest to the intrinsic good actions like

---

[73] Cf. É. Fuchs, "L'Éthique du sermon sur la montagne," p. 321 on the great and unique significance of the idea of law in connection with the Beatitudes.

giving water to the thirsty and feeding the hungry is a matter still to be investigated).

3. The *Beatitudes* are *not* to be understood as *inspiration* for the *individual* person nor simply as an impetus for the will. I am now looking at actions from the perspective of the axis of faith and good/evil to action. The Beatitudes are directed to the disciples whom Jesus has just called and to the people. They indicate what awaits those who listen to his words and act accordingly. In the words, however, an "objective reality has already begun."[74] This imitation does not consist in a great and powerful willing-to-do-good. *Whoever imitates does this because he/she has come into contact with what is good and with the promise in relation to the destiny of this life.* Something is not good because I find it good myself or experience it as pleasant; something is not good because God says it or commands it. I call something good because I recognize and endorse as good that which attracts me. As I can be a friend or enemy to another, I can also be a friend or enemy to myself.[75] The human being acts according to the analogy of God's action with respect to the human being. By doing the good continually, persistently and with eagerness, (thus confirming the virtue in me) I build up an analogy with God's friendship for human beings.[76]

4. Those addressed by the Beatitudes are to be viewed as *social beings who live together within an order of justice*. It was not for nothing that I took the example just above of a social relationship (official/citizen). I could place other social relationships next to it: activist/powerful, citizen/politician, doctor/patient, worker/capitalist. I would add parent/child and life-partner/life-partner as well: *insofar as these relationships also have a public form.* The parent raises the child to be a *socius*. The life-partner, in all possible variations, stands up for his/her partner as a person in the public forum. With these examples I want to illuminate the sociality of the human being as a given and as destiny. It is this understanding of the human being which does not receive much coverage in the Catechism (1877-1885). The natural given of sociality does appear, but not the moral aspect of this sociality. The perspective of faith arises when the human being is discussed as one who gov-

---

[74] K. Demmer, "Das vergeistige Glück," p. 103. See also R. Guindon, *Béatitude et théologie morale chez Saint Thomas d'Aquin: Origines, interprétation* (Ottawa, 1956), p. 325: "*the* Beatitudes are a foretaste of *the* Beatitude."

[75] G. Savognone, "L'Amicizia nel pensiero di S. Tommaso d'Aquino," in: *Sapienza* 34 (1981): 431-41; R. Sokolowski, "What is Moral Action," pp. 261-76, 315-17, p. 269.

[76] In connection with the differences between *amor, amicitia, dialectio* and *caritas* in Thomas see E. Schockenhoff, *Bonum hominus*, pp. 490 ff.

erns with God (1884). The apolitical view of happiness and beatitude that the Catechism actually employs means that the critical potential of the preservation of the premodern idea of politics in the tradition of the church (see the closing paragraph of section 3 of this paper) is not used. In any case, it does not have any effect in the discovery of what is truly good, through the light of faith. A connection between God's *gubernatio* (His governing with a view to the order of society) and human sociality and their political nature is unfortunately lacking. If an introduction to the life of faith is ever to be written on the basis of the World Catechism, a clear explanation of the connection between God's *gubernatio* and the political being of the human is necessary.

THREE

The Freedom of the Human Person

Rinus Houdijk

Overview of the Teaching of the Catechism

Already before the discussion of human freedom (1730-1748) the Catechism indicated the place ascribed to human freedom. As a rational being, the human being is in a position to recognize the order established by the *Creator* and to direct herself, by means of her will, at the truly good. For this human beings have been given the gift of freedom, so that they can choose freely for or against the law that makes itself heard in their conscience (1704-1706). One can see immediately the place granted to freedom: it is the condition that makes the observation of the commandments (which is the crucial point) possible. Albert Keller S.J. defended the thesis once in an interesting philosophical essay that, viewed formally, the moral life of the human being can be directed at nothing else but the exercise of freedom. To enter into relationships is only defensible, viewed ethically, insofar as it serves freedom. This thesis is all the more provoking if one understands it against the background of a current notion according to which freedom receives the character of a responsible experience of freedom only when it is subject to moral relationships. In 'morality' this notion makes one think immediately of a limitation of freedom: morality states that what freedom wishes to do it may not. It is not for nothing that the commandments, as in the Decalogue, are primarily *prohibitions* and original sin is said, after all, to consist in that an authority (God) says, 'you must', whereas the free human being answers, 'I do not wish to'. It is in this internal dilemma, then, that the unending struggle between good and evil takes place. In this understanding the affirmation of freedom is indeed needed and indispensable (otherwise, one cannot speak of morality at all and human beings, like animals, would be entirely determined), but this freedom appears to have no other purpose than to subjugate oneself under moral obligation and thereby to lose itself. As a current phrase has it: 'not freedom from but freedom to'.[1]

This characteristic, described by Keller in such a striking way, is entirely applicable to the concept of freedom advocated in the Catechism. The article in question (3) stakes indeed a great deal by ascribing to human beings the dignity of controlling his actions (with a reference to Irenaeus) and by quoting Sirach 15:14: "God willed that man should be 'left in the hand of his own counsel'" (1730). The Catechism immediately indicates, however, the proper purpose of this freedom, i.e., to seek the *Creator* (1730)—only then is true ('veritable') freedom possible (1733). How is this worked out further?

The first paragraph is devoted to the theme of freedom and responsibility. Freedom is the power, rooted in reason and will, to perform well-considered actions. Here free will is characterized by self-determination, it displays its capacity to grow in truth and goodness, and it attains its perfection when it is directed toward God (1731). Human freedom implies the possibility of choosing between good and evil, in which the characteristic property of proper human acts consists (1732). One becomes free to the degree that one does good. There is no genuine, true freedom unless one does good. To choose wrongly is a misuse of freedom and leads to sin (1733). Through their freedom human beings are also responsible for their actions to the extent to which these actions are voluntary (1734). Imputability and responsibility for an act can be lessened and even nullified by ignorance, inadvertence, duress, fear, habit, inordinate attachments, and other psychological or social factors (1735). But every act which is directly voluntary can be imputed to the actor (cf. Genesis 3:13). An act can also be indirectly voluntary, i.e., in case of reprehensible negligence or omission (1736). The bad effect of an action is imputable only if it is foreseeable and if it could have been avoided (1737); it is not imputable when it is not intended as the end or means of the action (1737). On the basis of the natural law, society must recognize each human being as a free and responsible being, and personal freedom must be respected, especially in moral and religious matters. This right must be recognized and protected by the civil authorities within the limits of the common good and public order (1738).

The second paragraph is devoted to the theme of human freedom in the economy of salvation. Human freedom is marked from the outset by sin, which the whole of human history attests. Human beings sinned freely (1739). Freedom is threatened in may ways, such as when freedom is under-

---

[1] A. Keller, "Freiheit und Bindung: Ausdruck verantwortlichen Handelns," in: J. Gründel (ed.), *Leben aus christlicher Verantwortung: Ein Grundkurs der Moral*, 1 Grundlegungen (Düsseldorf, 1991), pp. 41-62. In connection with what we have just discussed see pp. 42-43.

stood as being able to do everything and as including one's own self-interest. It is also threatened whenever the economic, social, political, and cultural conditions for a just exercise of freedom are disregarded. By deviating from the moral law, human beings violate their own freedom, disrupt their solidarity with their equals (English translation: "neighbourly fellowship") and rebel against God (1740). Christ has redeemed us by his cross: "For freedom Christ has set us free" (Gal. 5:1). In Christ we have communion with the "truth that makes us free" (John 8:32). The Holy Spirit has been given to us, and where the Spirit is, there is freedom (1741). The grace of Christ is not in competition with our freedom when this freedom accords with the sense of the true and the good that God has put in the human heart (1742).

Surveying the whole of Article 3 on freedom, one must assert that, proportionally, much and detailed attention is paid especially to the voluntariness and imputability of human deeds (1735-1737), a fact which, in my view, reflects the accent on the observation of law. Aside from the practical interest in freedom as the voluntariness of actions, the theoretical perspective on freedom, via the continuing accent on 'genuine' and 'true' freedom, is paradoxically enough, as it were, directed at the nullification of freedom. After all, freedom is scarcely an independent concept with a consistency of its own but from the outset is intended to merge and dissolve into the more fixed and definite reality of complete truth and goodness (of which, the continuous presupposition runs, the Magisterium is the authentic interpreter). One cannot escape the idea that the whole article has something unreal about it. The treatment of the theme follows well-known (Neo-)Scholastic paths; nowhere is it noted that since the Enlightenment and the French revolution the theme of freedom has become a central concept for the self-understanding of human beings and society in the West—unless one is to understand the Catechism's accentuation of God's (the 'Creator') fixed and pre-given order as an implicit defence against the, in its view, threatening modern understanding of freedom.

The Postmodern Context

In itself, however, the affirmation of human free will is still of great importance, precisely also when the *postmodern* view of time is taken into account. It is characteristic of this view that the 'humanism of the human being' which was dominant in the Enlightenment is no longer self-evident, as has been expressed by philosophers such as Michel Foucault. It can no longer be straightforwardly assumed that the human being is a proud, self-constituting subject. The subject, rather, is developed in a network of knowledge (as power), relations and institutions and within that network must win his freedom. History is also no longer simply a history of progress, into which the human being only has to insert himself in order to realize his freedom. History has become an impenetrable and chaotic spectacle within which it is not easy to discern any direction and to take up one's position. It is therefore of particular current significance to defend the free will of the human being.

In addition, there also exists at this time what has been introduced as a permanent objection to human freedom since the rise of the exact sciences, i.e., the *determinations* of physiological, biological, social, etc. nature, which are said to relativize human freedom to a great extent and even to destroy it. Two points with respect to this are important for ethical reflection. On the one hand, these determining factors need to be recognized and identified as closely as possible. On the other hand, one must not lapse into theories that *reduce* human freedom to these determinations. It is crucial to develop an idea of human freedom which does not have an *absolute* freedom in mind but a *conditioned* freedom.

The Technological Seduction

A quite challenging question is invoked in the modern and postmodern periods by technological knowledge and capacity and the technological utopia inherent to it, also in reference to human freedom. Is it conceivable that technology could replace the freedom of human beings by an entirely systematic control of human behaviour, and could that not also be seen as very desirable, given the fact that human history appears to be a succession of evil and failure?

B.F. Skinner has outlined a way 'beyond freedom', as the only way out of the impasse in which in his view the appeal to the autonomy of the human being and to the moral freedom of human beings ends time and again, as history shows. It is better to rule out human freedom and to replace it by an efficient technology of behaviour, through which the progress of the human being and humanity can be achieved without fail.[2]

One can and must, of course, register objections of an immanent-ethical nature to such plans, objections which amount to the fact that at the same time that one dispenses with the (postulated) progress of human beings one also dispenses with the human being herself as freedom. For me, however, such theories make clear first and foremost how *inescapable* freedom, which in itself represents a non-negotiable value, is at the same time for human be-

---

[2] B.F. Skinner, *Beyond Freedom and Dignity* (New York, 1971). Cf. R. Burggraeve, *De bijbel geeft te denken* (Louvain/Amersfoort, 1991), p.226.

ings, for at the foundation of such technological projects free decisions are present as well.

The Worries of Theologians

Where, as it were, the underside of freedom threatens to be undermined by forms of determinism, there exists a specific threat to freedom on the top, i.e., in forms of theological thinking about grace and freedom. In the course of the centuries theologians have been greatly concerned to give reflection on the relationship of human beings to God and the relationship of freedom and grace a proper direction.

The problems consists in that the ecclesial theological tradition adheres on the one hand to the fact that the human being, also after the Fall, possesses a real freedom of choice, in which the human being is considered to be responsible and accountable for his actions in principle, whereas on the other hand, the theological tradition states that human freedom has been affected adversely by concupiscence and in that sense is a fundamentally weakened freedom. Added to this is the belief that, according to the theological tradition, human beings are not able of themselves to do good and God thus comes to our aid with his free and edifying grace (the unbaptized or unbelieving person can also do good, but in that case God has already given this person his 'antecedent grace'). This theological view thus says not only that grace is necessary as a condition for the possibility of freedom but also that good human actions emerging in freedom are nothing else than realized in and through grace, whereas this action is at the same time the highest realization of my human freedom. This is what constitutes the worries of the theologians: how is one to understand that the supreme realization of human freedom comes into being simultaneously with the supreme salvific action of God to human beings. Thus a genuine theological struggle with respect to directions could develop since the Council of Trent concerning the relationship of freedom and grace.

Viewed from our contemporary perspective, one cannot escape the impression that in this struggle God and the human person are nevertheless seen as actors who deprive each other of their respective terrain. In the meantime, modern theologians have shown that God and the human person are not in competition with each other in creation and salvation. God and people *do not compete* (P. Schoonenberg); God's activity entails precisely that human freedom is optimally realized (K. Rahner).

For that matter, this cooperation between God and people entails that God has the primacy (once more: *while* human freedom comes to its highest realization). For modern human beings as well, with the prevailing notion of the autonomous subject, it will be difficult to conceive of this relationship, because it could lapse easily into a modern version of the idea of 'synergism', that is, that the actors contribute equally to the action. God's activity comprehends the whole activity of human beings, which nevertheless comes into its own right.

It is also good for the ethical perspective, I think, to accentuate the gracious embrace of God who supports our lives entirely. It makes clear that the moral life of human beings does not only consist of commandment and law but also, more fundamentally, in God's embrace which makes it possible for us to do good and finds enjoyment in us. It concerns here "the fruit of the Spirit" (Galations 5:22). Fortunately, we are not left with the strict and overwhelming ethical demand under which we should collapse. The supporting power of God's embrace keeps us going.

Viewing the history of theology generally, one can assert that since Augustine and his struggle with Pelagius there have been two main lines that have monopolized Western Christianity. The first line consists in the accent on the capacity for free self-determination which is considered to be characteristic of human beings (*liber est causa sui*). This is intended to say that the human being, without being absolutely determined, in principle is in a position to make a free decision ('willingly, knowingly') on the basis of a rational judgement. But this line is immediately joined by a second line, which consists in the accent on the *actual* lack of freedom of human beings since the Fall, which is situated in our susceptibility to weakness, covetousness, and sin. The struggle between Augustine and Pelagius seems to me to come down fundamentally to a difference in the assessment of the human condition. Should the human being be seen, more pessimistically, as a being inclined toward evil who cannot survive without the light of revelation and the discipline of the church? Or can the human being be seen, more optimistically, as a weak and sinful being but one who is able of herself to move in the direction of truth and goodness? It appears to me that the sober Augustinian line is dominant for the most part in the Western history of theology, even in the Middle Ages with his discovery of the self-adjusting existence of the human being and of the 'earthly realities'. The justified indignation of Luther and the Reformation concerning the excesses of the religious practices designed to earn salvific merit in the Catholic Church have had the result that the accent came to lie very strongly on the Augustinian view in the Reformation: salvation lies in election and grace, not in one's own merit and free choice. Has Western Christianity repressed Pelagius too much?

Freedom and Modernity

In theology and in social ethics the concept of freedom and the other basic values (equality, solidarity, etc.) are often discussed all too abstractly, separated from their social context. If that does occur, then one's eyes are opened for the confiscation of 'freedom' for socially integrative aims and for use by existing power complexes. In contrast, freedom can also be viewed 'progressively', in which case freedom refers to emancipation, the broadening of the social conditions for the self-development of all citizens but also to being free from dependence and uncertainty in economic crises or in cases of sickness or accidents.

We can follow this two-track content of the concept of freedom even further if we look at the history of the word 'freedom', as J. Moltmann describes it. In the first place, freedom has the meaning of domination, for 'freedom' appeared originally to be associated with a society of slave owners. In such a society only the lord is 'free'—the slaves, women, and children, over whom he is lord are not free. But whoever understands freedom as lordship can be free only at the cost of others. His freedom means oppression for others; his wealth makes others poor. Therefore, for the powerful their freedom always implies a 'security problem'. The same concept of freedom that was present in feudal societies is preserved in the 'bourgeois society' of the Modern Period. The common background seems to be already indicated by the world 'lord'-ship: a patriarchal society in which power is in the hands of the man. If a woman becomes free in this sense of the word, then she is able to hold her own and has become 'her own master'. For modern society freedom is understood primarily in this sense: being master of one's self, self-determination, being able to do and permit what one wishes. That means freedom for the individual: everyone is free. But it also means that no one has a share in another. In the ideal case there would be a society of free but lonely individuals.

The etymology, according to Moltmann, however, also indicates another meaning of freedom. That person is free who is *gastfrei* (hospitable), i.e., generous, affectionate, open, good-humoured, and loving. In this case freedom points toward community instead of lordship. Someone is free whenever she is valued and recognized by others and whenever she values and recognizes others. In the mutual openness to and participation in the lives of others the individuals are lifted above the limits of their individuality. That is the social side of freedom: love and solidarity. And this makes one free. That also means that a freedom understood in this way includes the removal of dependence relationships in actual society as well as the removal of relationships of exploitation with respect to others and nature.[3]

The move to the foreground of the 'liberal' components of the concept of freedom above the social components in Western society shows that freedom is not only a positive achievement but at the same time constitutes a problem. H. Krings speaks of the "price of freedom" in modern Western states. Freedom has its price when it concerns the foundation of freedom: an *a priori* metaphysics of permanent principles and normativity no longer needs to be sought in an argumentative discussion within a multiplicity of worldviews. This freedom also has its price if it concerns the social certainty of existence. The so-called fundamental social rights cannot be viewed simply as the continuation of the so-called rights to freedom—tensions will appear. Such tension is evident in, on the one hand, preservation of the social state and, on the other, the staving off of totalitarianism in the welfare state. Finally, the price of Western freedom also consists in the liberalist idea of freedom. Political freedom can not exist in a minimalization of the justice system in order to advance the freedom of individuals. This is so already because of the actual complexity of contemporary society in which the individual existence is developed already in all kinds of social connections. But it is primarily the moral content of the idea of freedom itself that exposes the shortcomings of the liberalist concept of freedom. The guaranteeing of freedom in the private sphere over against the superior power of the state and society is a legitimate concern, but this private freedom belongs to the fruits of the legal order and is not its foundation. For the content of the idea of freedom consists in the confirmation of the freedom of every individual, the recognition of her value as a person. In that sense the idea of freedom must be principially seen as a communicative idea of freedom, with which an individualistic concept of freedom is defeated.[4]

An approach such as that of Krings, although in itself correct and directive, remains, however, still too much of a speculative matter. Theological ethics will want to connect these speculative insights to a practical criticism, in which the reflection on freedom is connected to both a philosophy of the

---

[3] J. Moltmann, *Menschenwürde: Recht und Freiheit* (Stuttgart/Berlin, 1979), pp. 88 ff.

[4] H. Krings, "Der Preis der Freiheit," in: A. Paus (ed.), *Werte, Rechte, Normen* (Kevelaer, etc., 1979), pp. 11-27, 24 ff.

Other (E. Levinas) and Critical Theory (M. Horkheimer) in which the social and societal conditions of freedom are thematized.[5]

The Catholic Church and the Modern History of Freedom

It is sufficiently known that the Catholic Church in the Modern Period has from the outset had difficulty in taking part in the transfer from feudal social relationships to the bourgeois and democratic relationships of modern Western society which have developed since the French Revolution. The manuals on church history and the monographs concerned attest again and again to this. They differ substantially only with respect to their assessment of this fact. Some appraise the resistance of the church to the Enlightenment as an principial attitude that, for the sake of the truth, cannot be given up, while others see it as a rearguard action that has no prospects and will not be won. Most occupy a moderate middle position between these two extremes.

If we take as an example the church's attitude to freedom of conscience, we can see that the encyclical *Mirari Vos* of 1832 (Gregory XVI) called freedom of conscience an "absurd error or rather a delirium." The question is how such a position should be understood. From the perspective of surprise and lack of understanding that such a statement could evoke for contemporary self-understanding, including that of many Catholics, one could try to remove the sting from such a statement by saying that the church is only defending itself against a modern individualist misuse of the freedom of the subject (R. Aubert). But that is an evasion. If one would present the text of *Mirari Vos* today, one could, with all due respect, do nothing else than be bewildered at the continuous vituperation, indictment, insinuation, and condemnation of modern thinking and the new understanding of life (which of course is not the only one), and it is completely painful to have to listen to the continuous injured tone which sometimes even descends to the level of jeering. This offensive response of the church in both vocabulary and content indicate that very fundamental matters are at stake in the view of the church: it is a question of life or death (in the understanding of the official church). I agree with J. Hulshof when he states: "The ordering of ecclesiastical and

---

[5] For a Jewish critique of the concept of freedom see G.H. ter Schegget, *Volmacht in onmacht: Over de roeping van de christelijke gemeente in de politiek* (Baarn, 1988).

secular authority given by God was at stake."[6] In my view, this statement is correct but does not constitute an occasion for asking once again for understanding for the church afterwards. It is better to state that the church experiences the 'shock of modernity' precisely on the issue of the modern principle of freedom, through which it feels its existence to be fundamentally threatened. And it is better to consider that there is no other way than to leap the hurdle in terms of a (without doubt critical) dialogue on the basis of a self-understanding of the church as "an institution of socially critical freedom" (J.B. Metz), instead of evading it by using terms of bitter accusation and condemnation.[7]

One could object that these general statements should not be connected to only a single text from 1832, were it not that in my view the principially antagonistic understanding continues to exist, even though the vocabulary is more moderate and the tone somewhat milder. An exception to this can be found in the few decades around the Second Vatican Council (1962-1965), the period between Pius XII and John Paul II, and in particular in Vatican II itself, which moved in the direction of a recognition of the principle of freedom. The Declaration on Religious Liberty attests to this. One can do nothing else but hope that the steps taken there will prove in the long run to be directive for the further development of the church.

Religious Freedom

The considerations drawn from history and political theory by E.-W. Böckenförde[8] show that in our society only a long and difficult historical

---

[6] J. Hulshof, "Christenen en de vrijheid van anderen: Mensenrechten als hermeneutisch probleem in de katholieke traditie," in *Tijdschrift voor Theologie* 32 (1992): 31-56, 34. Cf. K. Hilpert, *Die Menschenrechte: Geschichte, Theologie, Aktualität* (Düsseldorf, 1991), pp. 138 ff.

[7] An alternative can, of course, also be to play up the irreconcilable opposition—which is what *Opus Dei* does.

[8] E.-W. Böckenförde, *Staat, Gesellschaft, Kirche*, Christlicher Glaube in moderner Gesellschaft, vol. 15, (Freiburg/Basel/Vienna, 1982); Böckenförde, "Einleitung zur Textausgabe der 'Erklärung über die Religionsfreiheit'," in: H. Lutz (ed.), *Zur Geschichte der Toleranz und Religionsfreiheit*, Wege der Forschung, vol. CCXLVI (Darmstadt, 1977), pp. 401-21. I am following Böckenförde's historical interpretations extensively here, but I do not follow in entirety his (in critique of the recent 'political theology') theological reflections on an "a-political political" position of the church with respect to social questions, a way of speaking that he finds so praise-

process has led to religion being separated from the state's power of decision. He correctly puts the emphasis on the liberating character of that process. Not only was thereby a political solution found for the many and long-lasting religious wars but it also broke with the conviction, which had been accepted till the Modern Period, that the state was fundamentally obliged to confess and protect (true) religion. In the meantime there is no longer any institutional connection between the state and a specific religion or worldview. The state as such no longer 'has' or 'represents' a religion. The universality of the state, its spiritual and normative foundation, is no longer institutionally guaranteed by a (privatized) religion but is determined solely on the basis of its secular aims. On the other hand, each religion or worldview is now free, precisely because of religious freedom, to manifest itself actively in society, but now no longer from a position of an 'official' religion but as a cultural activity and influence. The 'modern' situation of the separation between church and state (*actual* interrelationships do, of course, still exist) is an achievement that cannot be undone, including if, for example, churches should try to preserve or win back as much 'institutional Christianity' as possible.

These developments on the part of the state are answered by a true reversal that has occurred on the part of the church, which is described by Böckenförde as follows. Until Vatican II the church had continually rejected religious freedom in principle for two reasons. The first reason was that the church adhered to the principle that truth has priority above personal freedom and that errors had no right to exist over against the truth. The second reason was that faith was viewed as a kind of legal obligation, so that abandoning faith and church could be conceived as an act of unfaithfulness and a violation of the legal system. Though this attitude slackened somewhat, the church adhered to this attitude fundamentally until quite recently. The position was still defended by Cardinal Ottaviani in 1960 that the state is obligated to prohibit error and to defend the true religion. Toleration of error can be permitted only with a view to the general welfare on very serious grounds. And this was not the view of a peculiar outsider, but a view that lay entirely in the line of the statements issued by the nineteenth-century popes Pius IX and Leo XIII, who, for the modern period as well, held to the idea of a 'Catholic state' and the duties of the state with respect to true religion, who rejected religious freedom as a natural right and spoke of the toleration of other religions as a permitted evil under certain circumstances. Characteristic for this 'old' view is, according to Böckenförde, that it is not the human being as person who is the subject of rights but the abstract term

---

worthy in the 'social teaching' of the present pope.

'the truth'. Rights do not come to the human being as human being but only insofar as he is in religious and moral truth. Socially and politically this view resulted in intolerance, over against both 'unfaithfulness' to the faith as well as 'false' beliefs.

Vatican II broke with this tradition *in principle*. This Council placed the problem of toleration in an entirely different schema in its Declaration on Religious Liberty, seeing it now on the basis of the juridical recognition of the freedom of the human person. The Declaration not only 'tolerates' someone's worldview but comes to the full recognition of everyone's "right to religious freedom" and understands this as an unconditional right of the human person. It is no longer the objective truth of someone's religious conviction that is at issue nor his subjective attitude with respect to the truth, but the freedom of the person as such. According to Böckenförde a principial step is made from 'the right of the truth' to 'the right of the person'.

How fundamental this change is is evident from the fact that the Declaration (6) deprives the possibly existing privileged position of the church in a Catholic state of its *principial* justification. Böckenförde establishes that the 'Catholic state' is therefore no longer a *catholic* desideratum. Alongside this principial recognition of religious freedom the Declaration nonetheless adheres explicitly to the truth claims of the Catholic faith (1-2). These two concerns are not in contradiction with each other. At least, the Declaration distinguishes here clearly between the juridical order on the one hand and the moral order on the other. The obligation to seek the truth is a moral obligation, whereas religious freedom is matter of *law*. Although they are connected to each other, they are, however, to be distinguished with respect to content and aim: the right is concerned with the mutual relations among people and in relation to the state in a just society, whereas morality concerns the authentic and good life. With this distinction, the 'old' view of the 'right of the truth' can be given a (limited) place: in the moral order error has no 'right' over against the truth, but this must not be transferred to the sphere of law. The fault of the 'old' view lies in this identification of the sphere of morality and the sphere of law.

Böckenförde emphasizes strongly (and I think correctly) that what the Declaration teaches about religious freedom is the *opposite* of the doctrine of the nineteenth-century popes. In the Declaration of Vatican II it concerns a true rejection and nullification of the 'old' teaching and does not persist in a harmonizing interpretation (J.C. Murray, R. Aubert). For the papal statements in the nineteenth century were directed not only at a laical/liberalist misunderstanding of religious freedom but at the same time denied absolutely and unconditionally the right to freedom of religion (and thereby also made no distinction between the moral order and the legal order). One can thus speak of historicity with respect to official ecclesiastical statements.

In line with these considerations by Böckenförde, K. Rahner also emphasized that in the Declaration on Religious Liberty there was a new self-understanding of the church, a self-understanding from within and not simply under pressure from without (the process of secularization). This new self-understanding was reached at the Second Vatican Council only after serious resistance by 'conservative' groups. If since Vatican II the church no longer claims secular methods of power as far as the faith was concerned, if the rights of the 'erring' conscience are also recognized, if the autonomous order of the secular state is accepted, then the church commits itself to that from within. Advancing the truth of Christianity and the church by political means must, since Vatican II, be condemned in the name of the Catholic self-understanding itself.[9]

Now, in the 1990's, however, reality compels one to note that adherents of the aforementioned 'conservative' groups are once again dominant in the ecclesiastical centre of power. It should therefore not be wondered at that in the official works issued under the pontificate of John Paul II the theme is heard once more that truth is prior to freedom (see section 9 below). The renewal implemented by the Second Vatican Council finds itself at present in an institutional sleep, until history reaches a time when it will awaken once again.

Autonomy and Theology

The much used and ambiguous word autonomy is not understood here primarily as determining one's own life in the sense of being one's self, self-determination or one's own choice (of conscience) but in the moral meaning following Kant: morality is based in the human being himself as a rational being and not in something outside him, whether that be nature or God or whatever authority. It is of great importance to see that from the Kantian origin of this concept, there can be no discussion at all of 'subjectivism', as if morality could be referred to the actual preferences or arbitrary choices of an individual. The issue here is precisely that the subject finds the *foundation* of his moral actions in the imperative of his own human reason through which he *becomes obligated*.

In the seventies there appeared within Catholic moral theology the school of the so-called 'autonomous morality', whose founders in particular were A. Auer with his book *Autonome Moral und christlicher Glaube* (1971)

---

[9] K. Rahner, *Über die bleibende Bedeutung des Zweiten Vatikanischen Konzils* (Munich, 1979), pp. 6 f.

and F. Böckle with his *Fundamentalmoral* (1977).[10] The starting point of the school of 'autonomous morality', in line with Kantian thought, is that ethics in principle is the area of autonomous human reason, which is itself competent to make ethical judgements, without being in principle dependent on something external to it (the 'ethical thesis'). This means that ethics cannot in principle be based on the content of faith or a religious authority. In relation to the Magisterium this is an extremely sensitive point: ethical competence does not lie ultimately and originally with the Magisterium but with human reason itself (the 'Magisterium thesis'). If the Magisterium intervenes in ethical issues, the validity of this will be a matter for human reason to judge. The ethical statements of the Magisterium are also dependent on the validity of arguments presented.

One can easily see that this school thus wishes to withdraw from Neo-Scholasticism, which possessed a quasi-official position in Catholic theology and which, in the eyes of this school, was characterized by a 'heteronomous morality of commandment'. One must also see, however, that this school clearly diverged from Kant on the point that human reason was viewed as open to God from within (Auer) and was understood as an autonomy based in God (Böckle: 'theonomous autonomy'). It remains, nevertheless, that the demands of human decency can be known equally by Christians and non-Christians. In that sense faith does not bring any new insights with respect to content in the area of morality (the 'theological thesis'), even though faith can be of great significance for morality in its integrating, criticizing, and motivating capacity with respect to the morality that is lived.

In the meantime, the concept of autonomy, "a troublesome latecomer to ethics" (H.M. Kuitert), up to the present is part of a broad discussion in philosophical and theological ethics, in which the status and scope of the concept is at issue. Even though, in my eyes, there is no going back beyond the recognition of autonomy for ethics and moral theology, there are still problems. It must, however, first be stated beforehand without reserve that a democratic society can only have at its disposal a secular moral foundation

---

[10] A. Auer, *Autonome Moral und christlicher Glaube, mit einem Nachtrag zur Rezeption der Autonomievorstellung in der katholisch-theologischen Ethik*, 2nd ed. (originally published 1971), (Düsseldorf, 1984); F. Böckle, *Fundamentalmoral* (Munich, 1977). An excellent discussion of this school, also in relation to Neo-Scholasticism, can be found in V. MacNamara, *Faith and Ethics: Recent Roman Catholicism* (Dublin/Washington, D.C., 1985).

that has come into existence on the basis of consensus and not one that is dominated by a confession or worldview.[11]

I myself see two problems. The first problem relates to the contextuality of an autonomous morality or a rational ethics, and linked to this is that Western freedom, as we saw above, has its price. I mean that autonomy and rationality, for that matter deviating from Kant himself, actually lands in the terrain of liberalism which is, in addition, coloured primarily by an individualistic and utilitarian view of the human being. The second problem consists in that no *intellectual* contribution to ethics is attributed to faith, church, and theology (only a 'motivating' and 'integrating' contribution). In my opinion, this is connected to the view that there is no consideration given to the fact that human reason is always imbedded in a worldview and that this imbedding of human reason in a worldview influences this reason itself in what reason *sees* and *knows*. In this sense faith, church, and theology can see or know or tell something that is relevant for moral *insight*. But it would be wrong if one would wish to read what is said here as reintroducing the idea of religious *authority*. The concern here is that faith does not enter in as an authority or a 'continuous tradition' as such but as a *view* of humanity.

I have already said it: moral theology can no longer go back to a time before autonomy. Which autonomy? D. Mieth had defined autonomy well as the methodical independence of the ethical reason (formally) and as the objective of identity of the human person (materially), in accordance with the guidelines *secundum rationem agere* and *secundum personam agere*.[12]

Some Recent Vatican Documents

In the 1980s the Congregation for the Doctrine of the Faith devoted a few instructions to (Latin American) liberation theology, with which it has been, as it were, at war up to the present: the instruction "Libertatis nuntius" on liberation theology (1984) and the instruction on Christian freedom and liber-

---

[11] Cf. A.W. Musschenga, B. Voorzanger and A. Soeteman (eds), *Morality, Worldview, and Law: The Idea of a Universal Morality and its Critics* (Assen/Maastricht, 1992).

[12] D. Mieth, "Autonomie," in: Peter Eicher (ed.), *Neues Handbuch theologischer Grundbegriffe*, vol. 1, rev. exp. ed., (Munich, 1991), pp. 139-48, 148.

ation "Libertatis conscientia" (1986).[13] The motto is again "the truth shall make you free" (John 8:32). In the light of the foregoing we can see completely the impact of this motto for us. Characteristic for these texts is that freedom is not described positively in itself, as including the value of the human person and as the foundation of human rights, but the texts go immediately over to an defence against misunderstandings.[14] In the modern history of freedom 'serious ambiguities' are noted; ultimately morality and God will be experienced as a hindrance to freedom and liberation. The root of modern tragedies lies precisely in that. Because morality and God are no longer accepted, their representative, the church, is also no longer accepted; people will think that the hierarchical structure of the church is in conflict with the principle of equality.

Over against these lapses primarily two insights are advanced. It is said, with the modern understanding of freedom in mind, that freedom is often spontaneously thought to mean that one can do what one wills, independent of an external will. One must, however, learn to see that one is free only through respecting the moral order. Against liberation theology it is said that the true Christian understanding of freedom cannot consist primarily in a social or political liberation, for Christian liberation is primarily soteriological and ethical, and it is precisely the poor who understand that.

The encyclical *Veritatis Splendor* (1993) has the same motto and the same character as the documents mentioned above when it discusses freedom—the primacy of the truth is brought into the foreground elaborately and positively (VS, 31 ff.). The lapses of freedom are made much of and nowhere is the understanding apparent that the absolutization of the truth can also be a lapse in which the truth can be totalitarian. The second chapter of the encyclical also includes a discussion of the school of 'autonomous morality'. Viewed formally, it strikes one that no discussion is conducted here with the actual representatives of this schools and their writings but that the discussion is broached by the of course pejorative definitions of autonomy formulated by the encyclical itself, which are then attributed to the represent-

---

[13] Congregation for the Doctrine of the Faith, Instruction "Libertatis nuntius" on liberation theology in: *Origins* 14 (13 September 1984): Instruction on Certain Aspects of the "Theology of Liberation"; Congregation for the Doctrine of the Faith, Instruction on Christian freedom and liberation, "Libertatis conscientia" (22 March, 1986) in: *Origins* 15 (17 April 1986): 713-28: Instruction on Christian Freedom and Liberation."

[14] Cf. B. Fraling, "Freiheit und Gesetz: Gedanken zur Enzyklika Veritatis splendor," in: D. Mieth (ed.), *Moraltheologie im Abseits? Antwort auf die Enzyklika "Veritatis splendor"* [Quaestiones Disputae, 153] (Freiburg/Basel/Vienna, 1994), pp. 129-43.

atives mentioned. With respect to content: if autonomy is defined as turning away from God (and thus also from the church)—that which for that matter has not been done by any of the theologians intended—then the condemnation is already contained in the definition itself.

Conclusion

A theological reflection on human freedom cannot be concluded without paying attention to the intriguing and disturbing passage on freedom in F.M. Dostoyevsky's novel *The Brothers Karamazov* (Book V, ch. 5). The church, in the form of the Grand Inquisitor, has to be able ultimately to solve the problem of human freedom. If Jesus would return to earth, he would arouse the feeling of true freedom in people, would again raise human beings into revolt. The church, however, has taught people to lay down their freedom voluntarily at the feet of the Grand Inquisitor—they are satisfied. They believe themselves to be actually free after they have relinquished their true freedom. People would rather have that "terrible burden of free choice" removed and the Great Inquisitor magnanimously assumes this burden from the people.

Dostoyevsky foresaw that in the twentieth century the temptation to yield human freedom to totalitarian systems in the form of political, ecclesiastical, religious and economic systems of totality again and again would triumph. In the context of this reflection critical attention must fall on the Catholic Church particularly: is it really an institution that promotes freedom, and will the members of the church be satisfied with nothing less than the true freedom of Jesus?

FOUR

The Good Tree and the Right Fruits

The Catechism of the Catholic Church on the Morality of Human Acts (1749-1761)

Jan Jans

Introduction

"Human acts, that is, acts that are freely chosen in consequence of a judgement of conscience, can be morally evaluated. They are either good or evil" (1749). This statement contains two powerful assertions: that human acts *can* be evaluated, and that they are evaluated as good or evil. The immediate response to this is the question of how one arrives at such a judgement. The answer to this is to be found by means of a theory of action, that is, a theory in which the various elements that determine the nature of a moral act are brought into relation with each other. The first part of this article is about the Catechism's theory of action. In the second part I will present a theory of action that attempts to resolve apparent difficulties. By way of introduction I will first describe a case that I used for many years in a completion course for nurses, and which was reproduced in a recent publication on nursing ethics.

"A nurse in the maternity ward is appointed to purchase disposable diapers. There is a choice of three products: product A is an expensive but quality product, product B has a balanced price/quality ratio, and product C is inexpensive but does not meet the requirements. As a critical observer, we find that product B (the best buy) is purchased. With this knowledge of the matter, we spontaneously judge this nurse favourably: he has acted rightly. Now we learn that a representative of the firm that makes product C had tried to bribe this nurse. The firm offered a rather large sum of money if their product was purchased. This offer was rejected. Through this knowledge our judgement is refined: this person is not only capable of choosing the right product, but is also apparently motivated enough to choose for quality in spite of a tempting offer with the purchase of something else. On this basis we decide that we are dealing with someone who is good. This means that he has acted out of a good disposition. Later, however, we learn that the nurse rejected the offer of C not out of moral integrity but in the hope that the manufacturer of A would offer a higher bribe. In the light of this knowledge our judgement alters once again: the factual act remains morally right, but the motivation behind acting in this way and not in another way appears to rest on a dubious disposition."[1]

The Morality of Human Acts

For those who are somewhat familiar with the various key categories that were developed in Catholic moral theology for judging human actions, the approach of the Catechism is immediately recognizable as the neo-scholastic doctrine of the *fontes moralitatis*, the 'sources of morality'. A comparison between the universal ethics of the Catechism and the encyclical *Veritatis Splendor* even causes the Spanish moral theologian to conclude that a Neo-Thomist restoration is undoubtedly involved.[2] With regard to numbers 1749-1761, Vidal refers approvingly to Albert Chapelle, "someone who was close to the writing of the text," who restricted himself to the comment that the Catechism only posits a act of recollection here and thus presents the traditional doctrine without adding anything new.[3] For some this makes clear what the doctrine of the Church is and how by means of it one can arrive at a judgement on the goodness and badness of human acts. This is precisely what the Catechism wishes to propose. However, for others who look at this doctrine more critically from a moral-historical perspective, there are all sorts of questions as to the meaning of the terms used as well as to the usefulness of the model as a theory of action of moral theology. It seems, for example, with respect to the technical terminology used—*finis operis* ('object'); *finis operantis* ('intention'); *circumstantiae* ('circumstances')—that the rigorous precision for which the theory strives is plagued by inconsistency

---

[1] A. van der Arend and C. Gastmans, *Ethisch zorg verlenen: Handboek voor de verpleegkundige beroepen* (Nijkerk, 1993), pp. 29-30.

[2] M. Vidal, "Die Enzyklika 'Veritatis Splendor' und der Weltkatechismus: Die Restauration des Neuthomismus in der katholischen Morallehre," in: D. Mieth (ed.) *Moraltheologie im Abseits? Antwort auf die Enzyklika "Veritatis Splendor,"* Quaest. disp. 153 (Freiburg im Breisgau, Basel, Vienna, 1994), pp. 244-70; cf. J. Wissink, *Hanteert Veritatis splendor een neothomisme?* in: H.W.M. Rikhof and F.J.H. Vosman (eds.), *De schittering van de waarheid: Theologische reflecties bij de encycliek Veritatis splendor* (Zoetermeer, 1994), pp. 78-95.

[3] M. Vidal, "Die Enzyklika 'Veritatis Splendor' und der Weltkatechismus: Die Restauration des Neuthomismus in der katholischen Morallehre," p. 253.

when the aim of the acting person is also included in the circumstances. And the questions about the model as a *theory* of moral actions go even deeper when it is apparent that it developed from concrete pastoral needs related to confession where the confessor, on the basis of questions directed at the intention, the means used, and relevant circumstances, attempted to determine the guilt of the confessant.[4] I do not wish to continue with or go deeper into such questions and critique here, but at least they bring me to the conclusion of regarding a purely historical reference—'restoration' or 'recollection'—as being of little help to those who consider the doctrine of the Catechism to be meaningful for this day and age. Therefore, if the Catechism suggests that a judgement on "good acts and evil acts" (1755-1756) can be reached on the basis of "the sources of morality" (1750-1754), it is necessary to make a precise analysis of what exactly is in the text. In a certain sense, as will become apparent, the authors of the Catechism make this easy for us; after the actual explanation there follows a summary, entitled "In Brief" (1757-1761). Paying attention to the formulation used there and paying particular attention to that which is *not* summarized is in my opinion a hermeneutic key for understanding the Catechism's theory of action.

The Sources of Morality

Numbers 1750-1754, entitled "The Sources of Morality," are divided as follows: number 1750 cites the 'sources'; number 1751 deals with the object; number 1752 treats the intention; number 1753 takes up the relation between intention and act; number 1754 looks at the circumstances. In order to make my analysis easier to read, I will systematically cite the number concerned.

1750
"The morality of human acts depends on:
-the object chosen;
-the end in view or the intention;
-the circumstances of the action.
The object, the intention, and the circumstances make up the 'sources,' or constitutive elements, of the morality of human acts."

---

[4] Cf. G. Stanke, *Die Lehre von den "Quellen der Moralität": Darstellung und Diskussion der neuscholastischen Aussagen und neueren Ansätze*, Studien zur Geschichte der katholischen Moraltheologie 26, (Regensburg, 1984), pp.18-81; and J.A. Selling, "'*Veritatis Splendor*' and the Sources of Morality," in: *Louvain Studies* 19 (1994): 3-17.

As will become evident, the chosen order of object, intention, circumstances is not without significance. And although the possibility of a hierarchy between the three sources remains open, it seems unlikely given the qualification "constitutive," that the Catechism would support a theory of action that arrives at a moral judgement on the basis of one or two of the three elements. Thus the summary in number 1757 is remarkable: "The object, the intention, and the circumstances make up the three 'sources' of the morality of human acts."

1751

"The *object* chosen is a good toward which the will deliberately directs itself. It is the matter of a human act. The object chosen morally specifies the act of the will, insofar as reason recognizes and judges it to be or not to be in conformity with the true good. Objective norms of morality express the rational order of good and evil, attested to by [1749] conscience."

The emphasis placed on the *object* may not cause one to lose sight of the fact that the text constantly and thus emphatically speaks of the object *chosen*, which apparently is part of a human act, namely its "matter." This matter is chosen by the will in a conscious activity because it is viewed as a good. What is the significance of this object for morality? According to the text, there is a criterion for this: the choice made can be put to the test for being or not being in agreement with the *truly* good—a test that is carried out by reason. The result determines the morality—good or evil—of the act of the will. In turn, the activity of reason is determined by the rational order of the good and the evil—an order that according to the text is expressed by the objective rules of morality. I conclude from this that these rules concern the object. If the will follows these rules, then the will chooses a truly good object and the act of will is good. If the will does not follow these rules, it goes against the rational order and opts for an object that cannot endure the test: such an act of the will is evil. Conscience—assigned the function of 'judgement' in number 1749—is only the confirmation of this. In number 1758 the whole is summarized as follows: "The object chosen morally specifies the act of willing accordingly as reason recognizes and judges it good or evil."

1752

"In contrast to the object, the *intention* resides in the acting subject. Because it lies at the voluntary source of an action and determines it by its end, intention [2520] is an element essential to the moral evaluation of an action. The end is the first goal of the intention and indicates the purpose pursued in the action. The intention is a movement of the will toward the end: it is concerned with the goal of the activity. It aims at the good anticipated from the action undertaken. Intention is not limited to directing individual actions, but can guide several actions toward one and the same purpose; it can orient one's whole life toward its [1731] ultimate end. For example, a service done with the end of helping one's neighbour can at the same time be inspired by the love of God as the ultimate end of all our actions. One and the same action can also be inspired by several intentions, such as performing a service in order to obtain a favor or to boast about it."

Whoever wishes to grasp the core ideas of this long paragraph by looking at the summary of the Catechism itself is in for a surprise: this "element essential to the moral evaluation of an action" does not reappear in a separate paragraph. In my opinion this means that the importance of whatever is said about the intention in the presented theory of action is at least subordinate to the importance of the object, and can even be excluded for a certain number of actions.

In the explanation itself it is remarkable that the Catechism begins by formulating the intention as "in contrast to the object." In connection with the "objective norms of morality" in number 1751 (which had bearing on the object) and the affirmation that the intention "resides in the acting subject" in number 1752, this can lead to a division between objective and subjective morality. The result of this becomes clear when the Catechism emphatically deals with the asymmetric relation between intention and act in number 1753. In number 1752 I further believe it to be important that there appears to be a double reasoning as to why the intention is an "essential" element: it "lies at the voluntary source of an action" and "determines it by its end." On the basis of its voluntary source the intention is apparently "a movement of the will toward the end". If I then ask what the relation of the intention and object is here, already knowing that the object is "a good toward which the will deliberately directs itself," then I believe that this relation must be characterized as the means of attaining an end. In my own words, the will directs itself toward an end (the intention) and selects a means to that end (the object, excluding cases where the object itself would be the end). The further specification of the intention, particularly expressions such as "first goal," "goal of the activity," "the good anticipated," "directing individual actions," "guide several actions toward one and the same purpose," and "orient one's whole life toward its ultimate end" are results of this. This is also apparent from the two examples that the Catechism itself gives.

1753
"A good intention (for example, that of helping one's neighbor) does not make behavior that is intrinsically disordered, such as lying and calumny

[2479], good or just. The end does not justify the means. Thus the condemnation of an innocent person cannot be justified as a legitimate means of saving the nation [596]. On the other hand, an added bad intention (such as vainglory) makes an act evil that, in and of itself, can be good (such as almsgiving)" [cf. Matt. 6:2-4].

My interpretation of the previous statements is complicated by the paragraph just cited which declares that the relation between intention and *act* is emphatically formulated as a relation between end and means. A new category also apparent in the explanation, namely, "behavior that is intrinsically disordered," and "an act that, in and of itself, can be good" respectively. In the analysis I restrict myself to two points here. I will return to the difficulty we encountered (the relation act-object-intention) after I conclude my discussion.

First, there is the question of whether the examples mentioned, particularly with the terms used, illustrate the central affirmation that "the end does not justify the means." Both "lying" and "calumny," as well as "almsgiving" are words charged with moral values that are more than "means." Thus the examples given are tautologically obvious, but this does not give us any more information about the precise relation between a so-called "good intention" and "behavior that is intrinsically disordered," and an "added bad intention" and "an act that, in and of itself, can be good" respectively.

This brings me to the second point, namely the asymmetry in the significance of the intention within the Catechism's theory of action. Up until now the intention was not classified as good/bad, except for a suggestion in number 1752: "It [the intention] aims at the good anticipated from the action undertaken." But here in number 1753 the intention receives a moral qualification: it is called good or bad. In contrast with the moral classification of the object, however, no criterion is given for this. An asymmetry *does* appear in the application: that which in itself is disordered cannot become "good or just" by means of a good intention; "in contrast," that which in itself can be good becomes evil by means of an "added bad intention." This difference could be explained by the difference in what could be called 'intrinsic nature': according to the Catechism certain behaviours *are* in themselves disordered, while other acts in and of themselves *can* be good. The badness is ontological, whereas the goodness is still conditional. Thus in the Catechism's line of thought an "added" bad intention suffices to makes this last sort of action evil. However, this again gives rise to the question of the relation between the intention and the act. From the Catechism's statement which first posited that "intention is an element essential to the moral evaluation of an action" (1752), it now appears that when we speak of "behavior that is intrinsically disordered" the (good) intention plays no role, whereas when we speak of an "act that, in and of itself, can be good" such a (bad) intention receives the specification of "added." Or, even if the intention plays a role in the moral judgement, according to the Catechism's theory of action it is only appended.

The direction in which the Catechism is going is also evident in the summary in number 1759: "'An evil action cannot be justified by reference to a good intention' (cf. St. Thomas Aquinas, *Dec. praec.* 6). The end does not justify the means."

1754

"The *circumstances*, including the consequences, are secondary elements of a moral act. They contribute to increasing or diminishing the moral goodness or evil of human acts (for example, the amount of a theft). They can also diminish or increase [1735] the agent's responsibility (such as acting out of a fear of death). Circumstances of themselves cannot change the moral quality of acts themselves; they can make neither good nor right an action that is in itself evil."

We should first note that the authors of the Catechism apparently had no problem with the contrast between what they wrote about the circumstances as one of the "constitutive elements" of morality in number 1750 and the affirmation in the first sentence in number 1754 (which in my view is not compatible) that "the circumstances are secondary elements." That the authors had in mind something similar to the second statement is obvious from the fact that this number, just as was the case in number 1752 concerning the intention, does not appear in their own summary. However, there does appear to be a parallel between the meaning of the intention and the circumstances: both are, as far as importance is concerned, appended. The elaboration of this is interesting, particularly the fact that the circumstances seem to have a dual influence. The first influence is the "increasing or diminishing moral goodness or evil of human acts;" the second is to "diminish or increase the agent's responsibility." Excluding the question of whether or not the examples used are edifying (is "the amount of a theft" not part of the objective means?; is "acting out of a fear of death" not part of the subjective end?), a much more important question is left untouched by the Catechism's theory of action, namely, what the relation is between the moral goodness and evil of human acts and the agent's responsibility—both of which according to the text can be influenced to a certain degree by the circumstances. That the circumstances do not acquire any real moral significance by this (i.e, also for the good), however, is immediately apparent from the following sentence, which repeats the asymmetry indicated earlier with respect to the intention. If the moral quality of acts is fixed, then this particularly means that "they [the circumstances] can make neither good nor right an action that is in itself evil."

Good Acts and Evil Acts

The Catechism applies the preceding theory of action in the next two paragraphs in order to come to a verdict about good and evil acts. Number 1755 contains the criteria for morally good as well as morally evil acts. Number 1756 explains the significance of the intention, the circumstances, and the object.

1755
"A *morally good* act requires the goodness of the object, of the end, and of the circumstances together. An evil end corrupts the action, even if the object is good in itself (such as praying and fasting 'in order to be seen by men').
The *object of the choice* can by itself vitiate an act in its entirety. There are some concrete acts—such as fornication—that it is always wrong to choose, because choosing them entails a disorder of the will, that is, a moral evil."

The first conclusion at which the Catechism arrives is that a morally good act can arise only in one way, but that the act can be corrupted in two different ways. It appears that with regard to goodness the text follows the classic adage *bonum ex integra causa*. This being said, it remains (just as in the case mentioned above) unclear of what the criterion for the goodness of the intention and circumstances might consist. At least, one could deduce from this that whenever human actions are judged, the object, the end, and the circumstances do play a role. However, the two following descriptions of morally evil actions restrict this, first to the relation between end and object, and next to the object alone.

The first affirmation with relation to a corrupted action appears to be a repetition of what we already read in number 1753, but upon closer examination this is not the case, because there is a shift in the use of various terms. In number 1755 we read: "An evil end corrupts the action, even if the object is good in itself"; in number 1753 we read: "an added bad intention makes an act evil that, in and of itself, can be good." The result is the same in both cases—a corrupted or evil action—but the first case sees the "object" as "good in itself" and the second "the act". Are we to conclude from this that for the Catechism "object" and "act" are one and the same? The second affirmation in number 1755 bases moral judgement on "the object of the choice" alone. But if this can corrupt "an act in its entirety," then "object" and "act" cannot be one and the same unless, morally speaking, for certain 'concrete behaviors', i.e., 'acts', the selected object is of such a nature that it in itself already corrupts the act, as will be stated in number 1756. But then what is the significance of the very last sentence of number 1755 in which the reason why one may never choose certain concrete behaviours is that because "choosing them entails a disorder of the will, that is, a moral evil"? If here the relation between the "object of the choice" and "choosing them" is a "disorder of the *will*" here, then at the same time the intention becomes involved (cf. 1752)—a position that was rejected in the preceding sentence.

1756
"It is therefore an error to judge the morality of human acts by considering only the intention that inspires them or the circumstances (environment, social pressure, duress or emergency, etc.) which supply their context. There are acts which, in and of themselves, independently of circumstances and intentions, are always gravely illicit by reason of their object; such as blasphemy and perjury, murder and adultery. One may not [1789] do evil so that good may result from it."

Again, just as in number 1752, it is in my opinion striking that the Catechism evokes an antithesis between the preceding while once again opening the discussion on the significance of the intention (and the circumstances). Is this merely the negative counterpart of the first line of number 1755? Or, to put it more generally, if the object, the intention, and the circumstances are the "constitutive elements of the morality of human acts" (1750), then it is evident that "*only* looking for the intention", or "for the circumstances" is an inadequate approach which approximates subjectivism or consequentialism. In my opinion, the sentence serves as an introduction to a repetition of the last affirmation of number 1755, but now supplemented with a specification of the role of the circumstances and the intention in connection with those acts that become corrupted by the object of the choice. There is no trace any more of any "contrast" (1752) to the intention or of the "secondary" (1754) of the circumstances for those "acts which, in and of themselves, are always gravely illicit by reason of their object"; they are as such precisely "*independent* of the circumstances and intentions". If one takes number 1750 seriously, as well as the affirmation in number 1752 that the "intention is an element essential to the moral evaluation of an action," one can only conclude with a paraphrase of the first sentence of number 1756: it is erroneous to judge the morality of human acts by considering only the object.

The Catechism's summary reproduces three sentences of the preceding paragraphs as follows: "A morally good act requires the goodness of its object, of its end, and of its circumstances together" (1760). "There are concrete acts that it is always wrong to choose, because their choice entails a disorder of the will, i.e., a moral evil. One may not do evil so that good may result from it" (1761).

The Catechism's Theory of Action

From the preceding analysis it seems to me that the Catechism's theory of action is burdened with a lack of clarity and inconsistencies. Generally these are concerned with the difference between the formulated starting point "the object, the intention, and the circumstances make up the 'sources' or constitutive elements, of the morality of human acts" (1750, confirmed in no. 1752 with respect to the intention), and the actual manner in which the Catechism comes to its conclusions without allowing the circumstances and/or intention to play a role or even excluding them in a positive way (1756). As I have already mentioned above, I find it significant that it is precisely the passages that concern the intention and the circumstances that do not appear in the summary of the text.

More specifically, the text is characterized by a multiple sense of the central notion "object". Number 1751 posits the object as "the matter of a human act." Thus here the object is determined to be a part of the act. From number 1752 I derived that the relation between object and intention is seen as that between means and end. In number 1753, however, it was shown that the Catechism views means and end as the relation between act and intention. From my discussion of number 1755 the question was raised as to whether object and act are therefore one and the same, and how this can be compatible with the choice for an act that is a disorder of the will without again reintroducing the meaning of the intention. Finally, according to number 1756, the object is in a position to designate acts "in and of themselves" as always immoral. In the extension of my analysis of number 1756 one could possibly accuse the Catechism's theory of action of (a form of) objectivism, but what this would accomplish remains unclear 'in itself' because the notion "object" is itself unclear.

This lack of clarity is confirmed by an analysis of the examples that the Catechism gives and to which I have only indirectly referred in the preceding sections. The following examples of "actions," "behaviour," or "(human) acts" respectively are given: "a service done" (1752); "lying," "calumny," "condemnation of an innocent person," "almsgiving" (1753); "theft" (1754); "praying and fasting," "fornication" (1755); "blasphemy and perjury, murder and adultery" (1756). What is the object or "the matter of the human act" (1751) in these acts that allows the act to be judged as in itself disorderly or good? On the basis of the statement in number 1756, that there are acts that can be judged morally independently of circumstances and intentions, there remains only—if morality is determined by object, intention, and circumstances—the conclusion that in a number of cases act and object coincide, which paradoxically leaves the doctrine of the "three sources" hanging. Whoever objects to this by saying that the terms used are synthetic categories and thus do not have the nature of a "matter" but rather contain a reference to intention and circumstances only confirms that the meaning of "object" is unclear and, as such, undermines the whole of the Catechism's theory of action.

To round off the first part of this article I would like to conclude by citing the critical reaction of Richard McCormick, and then present Hans-Günter Gruber's reflections as a transition to the second part.

Richard McCormick[5] reacts to the manner in which the encyclical *Veritatis Splendor* presents the object of the action and comes to certain conclusions with regard to intrinsically evil actions.[6] According to *Veritatis Splendor* there is a category of actions that, because of their object, are intrinsically immoral, that is, their object is of such a nature that the action is morally evil regardless of their circumstances and the agent's intention. With a reference to Bruno Schüller McCormick comments first of all that, analytically, this sort of statement is obviously correct if the object itself is already characterized as morally evil. But that is not the problem. The real question is what the criteria are for labelling 'the' object of an action as morally evil.

---

[5] R.A. McCormick, "Killing the Patient," in: *The Tablet* (30 October 1993): 1410-1411; repr. in: John Wilkins (ed.), *Understanding "Veritatis Splendor"* (London, 1994), pp. 14-20. My rendering of McCormick's position is taken from: J. Jans, "Moraaltheologisch crisismanagement: Achtergronden en implicaties van de encycliek "'Veritatis Splendor'," in: *Tijdschrift voor Theologie* 34 (1994): 49-66, p.57.

[6] For the relation between the Catechism and *Veritatis splendor*, cf. *VS* 5: "It seemed fitting for [the encyclical] to be preceded by the Catechism of the Catholic Church, which contains a complete and systematic exposition of Christian moral teaching." For the importance of the doctrine of intrinsically evil acts, see *VS* 115: "Each of us knows how important is the teaching which represents the central theme of this encyclical and which is today restated with the authority of the successor of Peter. Each of us can see the seriousness of what is involved, not only for individuals but also for the whole of society, with the reaffirmation of the universality and immutability of the moral commandments, particularly those which prohibit always and without exception intrinsically evil acts."

McCormick illustrates this with the famous distinction between falsehood as an ethical act in protecting a secret and falsehood as an immoral act in cheating someone who has a right to the truth. In both cases the goal of the agent is part of the object, and one can eventually say of the second case that it is intrinsically immoral or, summarized in a synthetic term, a lie. With another example he clarifies the significance of the context of a moral action: "When masturbation occurs in the context of sperm testing, there are many theologians who believe that this context enters the very object or meaning of the act. In other words, they regard it as an act different from self-pleasuring, much as they would think killing in self-defence is a different act from killing during a robbery." Hans-Günter Gruber[7] characterizes the Catechism's theory of action as an example of objectivistic ethics of law. This yields, as is evident from the Catechism itself, unambiguous and clear norms that are expressed in the objective regulations of morality. But how do people deal with conflict situations with the help of such a theory of action? Gruber contrasts the Catechism with traditional moral theology which was aware of the possibility of conflict and developed the doctrine of "the act of double effect" and that of "the lesser evil" for dealing with such situations. But it appears that both these notions as a theory are missing from the Catechism, although mention is made of "(double) effect" in numbers 1737 and 2263. This leads Gruber to conclude that the Catechism simplifies the moral issue in a precarious way by reducing the actual complexity to an issue of universal normativity. Moreover, he claims that this model leads to an "externalizing of morality" by which the moral subject arrives at a legalistic attitude. This fits in with that which I observed in the analysis of number 1754—that the Catechism's theory of action barely touches upon the relation between the morality of human acts and the agent's responsibility.

The Morality of Human Acts

Dissatisfaction with an object-oriented normative moral theology has led a number of (moral) theologians to petition for a renewed consideration of the constituents of the morality of human actions. Looking back today at this 'renewal of morality'[8] one is able to outline a few lines of force as a result of

---

[7] H.-G. Gruber, "Haltung oder Handlung? Zur Bestimmung des Sittlichen im Spannungsfeld von subjektiven und objektiven Gehalten," in: *Theologie der Gegenwart* 36 (1993): 287-300, pp.289-92.

[8] Cf. S. Pinckaers, *Le renouveau de la morale: Etudes pour une morale fidèle à ses sources et à sa mission présente* (Tournai, 1964), 269 pp.

this: a reworking of the traditional sources, especially through an intense study of Thomas himself in his own historical context (in contrast to the coloured reading of the sixteenth-century as well as nineteenth-century Thomistic Renaissance), the relation between person and act by relating motivation, intention, action, and circumstances with one another, and having an eye for the multiplicity of concrete actions that prompt categories of judgement more differentiated than that of good/evil. Because a complete overview is outside the scope of this article, I will limit myself to presenting the 'revisionist' theory of action in general, following the line of Louis Janssens.[9]

The Unity of Human Actions

The 'traditional' doctrine of the sources of morality led to a division between objective and subjective morality. Because of this a gap arose between a moral order beyond persons, given to them and prescribed through objective norms, and the acting person himself, who had to conform to this order via his conscience as the subjective norm of morality. This gap was visible in expressions such as 'objectively grave sin' but 'subjectively light guilt'. In an attempt to rise above this dichotomy Janssens, in his fundamental study *Ontic Evil and Moral Evil*,[10] ties in with the way in which Thomas Aquinas in *De Actibus Humanis* (*ST*, IaIIae.6-21) connects the structure and morality of human actions with the agent. Janssens shares this starting point: only actions that arise from the will—regarded as *appetitus rationalis* and thus as the specifically human characterization—of the person are *human* actions, and this obtains for internal as well as external actions. In contrast to Neo-Scholasticism which arrived at a separation between object (*finis operis*) and intention (*finis operantis*), Janssens stresses that Thomas—who was familiar with the concepts *finis operis* and *finis operantis*—only mentioned these concepts in order to posit that a *finis operis* was always transformed into a *finis*

---

[9] For an explanation of the discussion and its background, cf. B. Hoose, *Proportionalism: The American Debate and Its European Roots* (Washington, 1987), 159 pp.

[10] L. Janssens, "Ontic Evil and Moral Evil," in: *Louvain Studies* 4 (1972-1973): 115-56; repr. in C. E. Curran and R. A. McCormick (eds.), *Moral Norms and Catholic Tradition*, Readings in Moral Theology, Vol. 1 (New York, 1979), pp. 40-93. The first four essays in this collection are just as many cornerstones in the 'revisionist' moral theology: P. Knauer, "The Hermeneutic Function of the Principle of Double Effect," pp. 1-39; L. Janssens, "Ontic Evil and Moral Evil," pp. 40-93; J. Fuchs, "The Absoluteness of Moral Terms," pp. 94-137; and B. Schüller, "Direct Killing/Indirect Killing," pp. 138-57, respectively.

operantis because an 'end' in the moral sense only exists in that a subject strives for it.

Next, there is the question of how the agent's will directs itself toward the end. Thomas distinguished between the willing of an end in itself, and the *actus compositus*, particularly the willing of an end *and* the means necessary for attaining it. These external actions, however, cannot be separated from the willing of the end: the human act is a unity of which according to Thomas the action of the will forms the formal element and the external action forms the material element. It is precisely through this relation of formal and material that the action of the will determines the concrete reality of the entire act. This structure of the human act then also directs reflection on its morality.

The first moral question that arises according to this approach is that of the morality of the end, 'the object of the will'. This end is a moral good if it corresponds to the natural disposition that is specifically human—namely, reason. Whether people direct themselves toward the moral good as the end of their acts depends, in Thomas' view, on their virtuousness. In other words, someone who is virtuous strives for the morally good because he/she holds this dear and wants it as an end for the sake of the good itself. The following question deals with the morality of the external action—the means. Given Thomas' starting point that the human act is a unity, it follows that the morality of the means cannot be determined separately. Following his own theory of action Thomas then arrives at the following statement: the morality of the human act is formally dependent on the end and materially dependent on the object of the external action. A concrete judgement will therefore always be prompted by an evaluation of the formal element. Thomas sees two possibilities here: the end can either be good or evil.

If the end goes against reason (that is to say, against the insight of meaning acquired by conscience) it is morally evil. This evil end, as the formal element of the entire act, corrupts the whole of the action. Or, in terms of the intention, a bad intention taints the whole action because the intention is the will for the end as the very reason for the entire action.[11] Conversely, if the end corresponds to reason, then the entire action is morally good on the condition that the external action also conforms to the requirements of reason. After all, not every external action is capable of becoming the mater-

---

[11] The difference from the Catechism's theory of action is particularly clear on this point because Thomas himself gives the example from which number 1753 concludes: "An added bad intention makes an act evil that, in and of itself, can be good." For Thomas, however, the intention is not added but is precisely the starting point of the moral judgement of the entire action. Cf. *ST*, IaIIae.19.7 *ad* 2. It is remarkable that this reference is missing in the Catechism.

ial element of a formally good end, and yet the intrinsic cohesion between form and matter requires that the latter is suitable for 'receiving' the former and thus effectively realizing the end of the will. According to Janssens, Thomas used yet another method to determine the relation between intention and external action. If the former is the end of the agent and the latter is the means thereto, then the external action is only a 'means' in the true sense of the word if it is itself in proportion to this end—that is to say, if it is suitable for attaining this end through its effects. Human reason is the criterion here just as in the determination of the morality of the end: the means used shares in moral goodness if it, according to reason, is in proportion to the good end.[12] Stated negatively, according to reason there can be no contradiction between the end and the means in the *whole* of the action. The conclusion then is that the means is also relative with regard to the end and that for determining this relation reason must establish the proportion between end and the means also by way of the effects.

'Evil' in Human Acts

It is an everyday experience that our actions entail not only those effects than the ones for which we strive. A classic example is the main and side effects of a medication. The terms used already indicate that the already mentioned relation between end and means is indeed proportional: the end sought is healing, and the means are appropriate if and as long as the side-effects are proportional to this end, that is, that the intended effect does not cause more damage in terms of health than if the means were not used. If this proportion is not there, then we are no longer speaking of a 'medication' but a 'poison'.

In the initial stages of the revision of moral theology Peter Knauer argued in his thought-provoking study, *The Hermeneutic Function of the Principle of Double Effect*,[13] that the principle of the act with double effect is the

---

[12] The significance of Thomas for this so-called proportionalism is elaborated on later by L. Janssens. Cf. "Saint Thomas Aquinas and the Question of Proportionality," in: Louvain Studies 9 (1982-1983): 26-46; "Perspectives and Implications of some Arguments of Saint Thomas," in: *Ephemerides Theologicae Lovanienses* 63 (1987): 354-60; "Teleology and Proportionality: Thoughts about the Encyclical Veritatis Splendor," in: J.A. Selling and J. Jans (eds.), *The Splendor of Accuracy: An Examination of the Assertions made by Veritatis Splendor* (Kampen, 1994), pp. 99-113.

[13] Cf. nt. 10. It is no coincidence that Knauer, who wrote the first version of his study in Louvain, refers to Janssens, in particular to an article from 1947: "Daden met meerdere gevolgen," in: *Collectanea Mechliniensia* 32 (1947): 621-33. For an elaboration of his way of thinking in dialogue with the critics of 'revisionism' in

fundamental principle of the whole of morality because it answers the question of when the causation or admission of an evil is a moral evil. His proposition is that *every* act exists in the tension between the good end sought and unwanted evil effects. Given that people act out of the value of an end, an action is entirely good in a moral sense when a proportionate relation exists between these effects. It is morally evil when this relation does not exist: the action is then in conflict with the value of the end.

Janssens takes up the problem of this ambiguity by using the distinction between ontic and moral evil.[14] Thomas' formulation of the problem of when the killing of a human being (an evil) can be justified (and therefore is not a moral evil) brings him to the conclusion that a distinction must be made in our concrete actions between 'ontic' evil (killing) and 'moral' evil (murder), a distinction that should not make us lose sight of the fact that the two kinds of evil are also connected. Janssens considers it essential for a theory of action to perceive that every concrete action, composed of end and means, is characterized by ambiguity because ontic evil—that which restricts and harms us as human beings—is constantly present in our actions. The reasons he gives for this are human temporality, the fact that all actions are related to the characteristics and limitations of our material dealings with things and with one another, and our human sinfulness. What are the impli-

---

moral theology, cf. P. Knauer, "A Good End Does Not Justify an Evil Means—Even in a Teleological Ethics," in: J.A. Selling (ed.), *Personalist Morals: Essays in Honor of Professor Louis Janssens*, Bibliotheca Ephemeridum Theologicarum Lovaniensium 83, (Louvain, 1988), pp. 71-85.

[14] In later writings Janssens usually uses the terms premoral values and disvalues: "there are realities in and outside of us that, by virtue of their own characteristics, arouse in our experience a positive reaction in this sense that we rejoice over them and greet them as valuable and thus as worthy of consideration (*prosequenda*), as in, for example, life, physical and mental health, desire and happiness, friendship, the cultural values of science, technology, art, etc. We call them *premoral values* (classically: *bona physica*). ... There are also realities in and outside of us that, by virtue of their nature, are experienced by us in a negative way as regrettable, obstructing and thus as something to avoid and resist (*vitanda*), as, for example, hunger and thirst, pain and suffering, sickness and death, mutilation, mental disturbances, ignorance, erring, violence, exclusion from our social environment, etc. We call them *premoral disvalues* (classically: *mala physica*)." In: "De zedelijke normen," J. Ghoos (ed.), *Ethische vragen voor onze tijd: Hulde aan Mgr. Victor Heylen* (Antwerp/ Amsterdam, 1977), pp. 40-41; "Norms and Priorities in a Love Ethics," in: *Louvain Studies* 6 (1976-1977): 207-38; "Normen en prioriteiten in een ethiek van de liefde," in *Sacerdos* 46 (1978-79): 15-31, 129-50; "Ontisch goed en kwaad—Pre-morele waarden en onwaarden," in: *Sacerdos* 54 (1987): 347-66; "Ontic Good and Evil—Premoral Values and Disvalues," in: *Louvain Studies* 12 (1987): 62-82.

cations of this for the morality of human actions? When and to what degree is it justifiable to permit or cause ontic evil?

In continuation of his Thomistic explanation on human action and the related structure of morality, Janssens points out four requirements for being able to speak of true proportionality. First, if ontic evil is the actual end, that is, the object of the act of the will, then the entire action is morally evil. Secondly, if one sees the entire action from the point of view of reason, it may not exhibit any contradiction between the means used and the morally good end. Thus the presence of ontic evil is in itself inadequate in order to be able to come to a judgement of moral evil; the moral significance of this evil is not implied in its existence, but in the relation to the end sought. Or, in other words, the morality of the means does not depend on the relation between ontic good and evil *in* the means (that would be a kind of objectivism again) but on the proportion between this means and the good end sought. A moral judgement is possible only on the whole of the human act. Thirdly, it is our moral duty to restrict the ontic evil in our actions as much as possible. Janssens sees in this the core of a dynamic morality that strives for that which is humanly desirable and thus makes an effort at opposing that which restricts people (ontic evil—premoral disvalues) as well as promoting that which is good for their development (ontic good—premoral values). And it does this each time in accordance with the historical possibilities. Fourthly, in striving for a good end and in the consideration with regard to the means thereof, this end must be placed within the whole of the meaning of human life. Only from this broad perspective does one acquire an idea of the place and rank of the separate ends and their relative value.

Good/Evil—Right/Wrong

From the above the 'revisionist' theory of action draws the conclusion that a moral judgement requires a different terminology in order to be congruent with the reality of human actions. As far as the *intention* is concerned this leads to the use of the notions of morally good and morally evil. Only here can one speak of good or evil 'in itself', particularly in the orientation of the will to a recognized value or disvalue (an ontic good or evil). Depending on the degree to which one ties the relation between the intention of the person and her being-a-person itself (for example, in a virtue ethics or in the form of the fundamental option), one can, on this basis, determine that moral good and evil refer to the person herself. For a judgement of the *realization* of our intention one uses the terms morally right and wrong, depending on whether the means—in the light of the results—are/were not appropriate for realizing the good intention.

In a strictly logical way, one could formulate the following combinations: morally good and morally right; morally good and morally wrong; morally evil and morally right; morally evil and morally wrong.[15] But does this not shortchange the unity of the human act, which is determined through the subject and composed of the intention as formal component and the external action as material component?[16] If the root of human morality lies in the intention, then morality is in a strict sense determined by its goodness or badness. In a broader sense morality is then the realization of the good intention in an appropriate, thus right, external action. But one cannot rule out that the intention directs itself toward an apparent good (the innocently erring conscience), and that as a result the person who attempts to realize this intention causes actual disvalues, or that one with a good intention actually makes a mistake in the choice of the means (the absence of the required proportion). According to this theory of action, one cannot speak of moral evil in either case: the acting person is morally good, his action is wrong. Viewed from the dynamics between end and means, however, the third logical combination—morally evil and morally right—is actually possible at first glance (a crime syndicate that organizes first-aid assistance after an earthquake) but makes little actual sense, for insofar as the agent consciously realizes the actual values for third parties, he/she does this in the broader perspective of an intentional moral evil (getting the population into their grasp). Finally, the fourth combination represents intrinsic immorality: intentionally implementing evil while being aware of the effects. These are the Catechism's examples, but there they are presented as determined by their object alone: adultery, murder, perjury, blasphemy, greed, theft, condemning an innocent person, calumny, lies.

Conclusion

The theory of action of the 'revisionist' model starts from the moral subject herself and in this way links personal responsibility with the whole of the action: the intention, the means, and the effects. A moral interpretation of

---

[15] Cf. B. Schüller, *Die Begründung sittlicher Urteile: Typen ethischer Argumentation in der Moraltheologie*, 2nd enlarged ed. (Düsseldorf, 1980), p. 141.

[16] Cf. K. Demmer, "Das Selbstverständnis der Moraltheologie," in: W. Ernst (ed.), *Grundlagen und Probleme der heutigen Moraltheologie* (Würzburg, 1989): 9-25, p. 17: "... moral truth is of a complex nature. Originally, it does appeal to the goodness of humans, therefore to their disposition. But goodness of disposition carries responsibility for the rightness of the action."

these components exists only through their involvement with one another and as such with the subject. The Catechism's theory of action introduces a subordination, separation, and even opposition between the 'sources' it cites. By stressing the object, the intention appears decisive only in the event that it is evil, and responsibility is classified under the effects. In finally wanting to determine actions as moral by looking at the 'object' alone, this theory of action becomes mired in the unavoidable complexity of human actions which are nevertheless the source of ethics and moral theology itself.

FIVE

Passions and Virtues

Patrick Vandermeersch

Passions and virtues are separated by conscience, as is suggested by the consecutive order of articles 5 through 7 in the Catechism's structure. In itself this order already offers material for quite some commentary. However, the editors of this volume have chosen to deal with the passions together with the virtues, and to attach to it a short treatment of the turbulent debate between the Magisterium and psychoanalysis. Conscience has been treated in a separate chapter. Given the place that discussions on conscience have taken in the history of moral theology, this is a valid choice. Should one attempt to investigate the problem more deeply, however, one soon notices that every attempt to analyze the problems in a coherent way founders. The unique nature of Catholic ethics appears to lie in the specificity of its historical stratification rather than in its inner consistency. Just as geological formations support the earth's crust so the Catholic nature of morality is supported by layers that are derived from various cultures and philosophical systems. It is still not clear how they are related to one another, nor exactly how Catholic practice is rooted in them. This explains the fact that a number of words such as 'passions' and 'virtues' promptly evoke a number of emotional associations and a sense of familiarity but that they do not immediately refer to a clear, well-structured and deliberated system.

Therefore, the only way to attain more clarity on the way in which Catholic ethics has been built up consists of archeological excavations and the separation of the layers of which the Catholic legacy consists. Only then can one determine whether in the long run there is a hidden logic in what at first glance was united primarily by the whimsical course of history. Thus, on the one hand, we cannot avoid duplicating a number of aspects that are treated in the chapter on conscience. On the other hand, it will become evident that the passions and virtues are not, as one might think at first, counterparts of each other.

Not a Biblical but a Philosophical Starting Point

Nevertheless, one matter is clear from the start: Catholic ethics did not arise from a systemization of biblical statements but from an appropriation of reflections of philosophical ethics.

This may surprise people today, particularly those who, in contrast to the over-moralizing Christianity of the last centuries, wish to base their belief and actions in something like the direct biblical source. However, we may not forget that the Bible does not immediately present us with the very first Christians. The letters from Paul, the oldest texts, date from the fifties of the first century, but the oldest gospel (Mark), is usually dated around the year 70. For the rest, that which we call the 'Bible' rests on a selection or 'canon' that for the most part dates from the second century. Thus, assuming a biblical starting point means in fact assuming the complex religious historical and ecclesiastical developments from the years 50 to 150 as a norm for one's actions. If anyone should attempt, nonetheless, to arrive at original Christianity by means of the texts he or she will perhaps find even less of a foundation for ethics. In the first place, the first Christians expected to see the end of time. Such an expectation directed toward the last days does not stimulate the construction of an ethical system or the pursuance of a 'better world'. In Christianity, therefore, there was apparently no well thought-out ethical system oriented toward the betterment of the world. Living morally simply meant that one attempted to prove through one's pious conduct that one was worthy to see the Lord. With the end of time approaching, it was not easy to take the responsibilities of daily life seriously, as is apparent from, among other things, Paul's exhortations that time was short and that it was probably no longer worth the trouble to marry, but this did not mean that one could spend one's days in complete idleness.[1]

When it became apparent that the last days were not at hand after all, more attention was given to the way in which a Christian should direct his or her daily life in order to be a true Christian in that area as well. In the gospels, which were written then, increasingly more room was made for the implications of the Christian way of life for this world. The first text in which a Christian way of life is outlined is the *Didaché* or *The Teaching of the Twelve Apostles*—a second-century text that only just missed being included in the collection of what was selected as the 'Bible'. The concept of the Christian way of life outlined there consists of withdrawing from everything, not standing up for oneself, and being as modest as possible with respect to one's own desires, The continually recurring form of address "My

---

[1] See 1 Cor. 7:25-35, 2 Thess. 2:6-15.

child," directly expresses the overpowering fatherly tone of this *Teaching*. It clearly stems from a time in which the Christians secluded themselves in small, relatively closed groups which expressly isolated themselves from their surrounding society, not wishing to participate in public life in any way.

It is only when this isolation was broken and Christianity, as a religion, began to belong to the existing society that Christians started to reflect on and formulate their own philosophy of life, also with respect to ethics. This resulted in an absorption of the major philosophical traditions of the Greek-Roman world by the Church fathers, primarily those traditions that supported the same missionary universalism and paid as much attention to all layers of the population as Christianity did. Thus Stoicism and Platonism had a great influence on the Christianity of the first centuries. Aristotelianism would leave its mark later as well, but that would not occur until the Middle Ages. These are the two central pillars of Catholic ethics, which can also be found in the Catechism: a view of the *passions* that originated in Platonism and Stoicism, and a teaching on the *virtues* that, with regard to concept goes back to Aristotle primarily, but was adapted by Thomas Aquinas to the belief in creation as total view that coordinated everything.[2]

The Passions

What is a passion? It is the position that is assumed in no. 1767, i.e., that the passions themselves are neither good nor evil must catch our attention more than the Catechism's laconic definition in no. 1763, which defines passions as the "emotions or movements of the sensitive appetite that incline us to act or not to act in regard to something felt or imagined to good or evil". The fact that this is expressed so emphatically points to the ambivalence of the Christian attitude to passions right from the start. It often seemed (and seems) that passions were to be viewed as evil. The fact that 'passions and virtues' are presented as binomial in the title of this essay is witness to this even today. 'Passions' are almost synonymous with 'vices', and virtues appear to be the opposite of passions. However, as we will see later, this is not

---

[2] The catechism has chosen to translate the Latin term *passio* with 'passion'. The term is indeed more flexible than that of 'passion' as 'suffering', for which we had opted in a first version of this text. The connotation of passivity, i.e., 'that which one undergoes', has been abandoned. Sometimes the one translation is advantageous and sometimes the other. In order to be consistent with the text of the Catechism, we have used 'passion', except in cases where it is not suitable, as in the *apatheia* or apathy of the Stoics.

the case. The ambivalence in the evaluation of the passions derived from an antithesis that we already find in the two philosophical systems from which Christianity has drawn: Stoicism and Platonism.

In Stoicism it is clear that the passions belong to the all too human characteristics that must be repressed as much as possible. The goal of life consists of achieving *apatheia*, the state of apathy. According to the Stoic worldview, the order of the cosmos was established forever by the fate of a divine will. Any changes that occurred were only a temporary shift within an cycle of eternal return of the very same things. Therefore it was no use—and also areligious—to think that one could change anything. Thus Stoic apathy was also a religion. This did not mean that the Stoics were not concerned with their fellow humans or affairs of the state, although these concerns could be a source of sorrow. On the contrary, they were socially engaged and in their universalism felt themselves to be citizens of the world who, for example, felt that non-Romans should not be treated any differently than Romans, an attitude that was quite new. Their ideal of *apatheia* led them to place justice foremost in their social concern and not love, since that inevitably brings us to sympathy and preference.

Conversely, love, and with it *eros*, was central in Platonism. In Plato's *Symposium* and his *Phaedrus* we find the proposition that the goal of philosophy consists of sublimating the erotic to contemplation, which assumes in the first instance the development of an erotic link between student and teacher. This link, however, should not have physical sexual gratification as its ultimate goal. According to Plato, one must gradually shift one's fascination with beautiful bodies to a fascination toward more abstract forms of beauty, until one arrives at a spiritualized philosophical contemplation. Thus, according to Platonism, the erotic had to become spiritualized, a notion that naturally presupposes a certain ascesis. In actual practice, therefore, the Platonic model of the erotic, which assumed a form that was directed at higher levels or a 'sublimated' form, could also represent a Stoic conception.

Thus although Platonism and Stoicism appear to be far apart, when viewed as separate systems, we nevertheless find a mixture of Stoic and Platonic elements in the practice of Christian spirituality. It was from this that the previously mentioned ambivalent attitude with regard to passion arose. This is expressed very clearly in the early Christian spirituality of chastity and the monastic order—a phenomenon that must have been surprising to a non-informed observer.

As soon as Christianity was established as an accepted religion and was no longer threatened by persecution so that martyrdom, which was the supreme sign of dedication to Christ, was therefore no longer attainable, Christians sought an ideal to replace it and soon found it: chastity. We may think this a strange substitute, and the logic that was employed cannot be grasped immediately. Nevertheless, the texts are very explicit: whoever dedicates himself to Christ as a chaste person engages in a battle that was at least the equal of martyrdom. While the martyr suffered pain for only a short time, the chaste person must battle against sexual desire for his—or, primarily initially, her—whole life long. It was a prerequisite that she (and later he as well) does not become insensitive to desire, like the Stoics, but allows it to come to full strength in order to be able to say 'no' with heroic courage.

In the account of this ideal there is a definite allusion to Plato. When Methodius of Olympus wrote the first major Christian treatise on chastity, he even called it *Symposium*. In spite of this definite allusion, there are nevertheless certain essential differences in the spiritual path of Christian chastity that can be observed. First of all, the erotic used by Plato as his starting point is of a homoerotic nature. It sustains a process of identification. This is not the case with Christian chastity.[3] Plato further assumes a sexual desire that is directed toward a real person, but which must subsequently be transformed on an abstract level into a libido no longer directed toward the human body. Something analogous can be seen in the later great mystics, but the first and more general Christian texts on chastity got no further than the very expressive depictions of erotic representations of a love relation between the chaste person and Christ. Applying the texts of the Songs of Solomon to Christ, the chaste person hears coming from his the latter's mouth: "You have robbed me of my sense with one glance of your eyes, with one bead of your string! How much better your breasts taste than wine, and the smell of your clothes is better than all spices! I find honey and milk under your tongue, and the smell of your clothes is like of the smell of Lebanon!"[4] The emphasis does not lie on a transposition of these images toward a more abstract level, but on the battle that must be fought in order to remain faithful to the eroticized and idealized human image of Christ and not to succumb to sexual desires directed toward an earthly human being.

---

[3] One could raise the point that this is the case with male chastity—particularly when one identifies oneself with the suffering Christ. This view, however, calls attention to the fact that the chaste man often regards his soul as female. Here we encounter a central point in M. Foucault's thinking which, due to his untimely death, he was unable to work out further. On pp. 251-78 in his book *L'usage des plaisirs* (Paris, 1984) he refers to the fact that Christianity replaced homosexual love with heterosexual love as the driving force of spirituality. This claim requires not only historical investigation but also a closer psychological analysis of the mechanisms of identification and attachment involved.

[4] Methodius of Olympus, "The Banquet of the Ten Virgins; or, Concerning Chastity," in: *The Writings of Methodius*, A. Roberts and J. Donaldson (eds.), Ante-Nicene Christian Library, vol. 14. (Edinburgh, 1869), p. 59.

We find this notion of battle, which clearly distinguishes the spirituality of chastity from Stoicism, again in a more elaborate form in monastic spirituality, which through Evagrius Ponticus (d. 399) and John Cassian (d. 435) would greatly influence the West and lead to the doctrine of the cardinal sins. In this (now chiefly male) monastic spirituality the erotic is no longer present in the same simplistic way as was the case with virgins. It is indeed said that the male monks must feel themselves in their soul to the 'bride of Christ', but this does not harbour any overt homosexual or transsexual images. On the contrary, the monk must, as a eunuch, set aside his sexuality. Thus spirituality no longer arises out of a process of abstraction that makes uses of sexual images. In this monastic spirituality sexuality is increasingly equated with 'impurity', and this is one of the central vices or passions against which one must fight.

A list was made of these vices, in the conviction that there was a set order in which they must be fought. A certain vice may serve a positive function in the struggle against another. Pride, for example, can be useful as a stimulant to become holy, or to put a stop to greed or avarice. Thus the teaching on vices contains a whole psychology, and the fact that this was reflected upon thoroughly is evident from, among other things, the differences of opinion on the moment in which one may suppress one's aggression: if this was done too quickly, there was the danger of falling into the vice of *acedia* or apathy, and this melancholic state of mind hindered further progress toward the spiritual goal.

In the West the view of John Cassian, who introduced the monastic order from the East, has been predominant. He posited the following series of eight vices: gluttony, impurity, avarice, anger, despair, sloth (*acedia*), idleness, and pride. Gregory the Great would appropriate the list, discarding sloth (*acedia*) and adding envy.[5] Pride is removed from the list as a separate vice in order to function as a general name for all vices. For the rest the term vice is now substituted by that of 'sin' and the order is changed. Thus one now arrives at the classic list of the 'seven cardinal sins', of which, however, the order has been changed and which in this Catechism is also different from the one to which the author refers. Here we find this list, for unexplainable reasons, not as the logical conclusion to the section on passions but later, with the sins, under number 1866. There it reads as follows: pride, avarice, envy, wrath, lust, gluttony, and sloth. As an alternative to

---

[5] "Radix quippe cuncti mali superbia est, de qua, Scriptura attestante, dicitur: 'Initium omnis peccati est superbia' (Eccli. X, 15). Primae autem ejus soboles, septem nimirum principalia vitia, de hac virulente radice proferuntur, scilicet inanis gloria, invidia, ira, tristitia, avaritia, ventris ingluvies, luxuria" (Gregory the Great, *Moralia*, 31, 87, PL LXVII, 621 a).

sloth we find added "or acedia". In the Dutch version the almost untranslatable term, *acedia*, was replaced by *lauwheid* ('halfheartedness' or 'tepidity') so as to arrive at the original meaning of what in the course of history came to be called 'sloth' and sometimes 'laziness'.[6] By transplanting monastic spirituality, which stemmed from the desert, to the ordinary believers who lived in cities and villages, melancholy simply became equated with laziness in daily work in the rise toward contemplation.

That it seemed to present no problem in replacing one cardinal sin by another and in changing the set order of the sins follows from the fading of the psychological insights that were contained in these views about a battle against the vices. What did remain and steadily increased in importance was the practice that the monks had connected with this doctrine: that of confession. During his apprenticeship a monk had to learn to bare all of his thoughts, without any fear or reluctance, to an older monk and then subject himself completely to his judgement. This practice, initially intended for monks, stood at the beginning of an institution of confession that was eventually transferred to ordinary people. This is an important turning point with far-reaching psychological consequences. There was already a tension in monastic spirituality. Whereas reflection on vices or cardinal sins was intended to teach a monk to know himself so that he, with psychological understanding, could bring about a happy conclusion to his spiritual journey, confession to an older monk meant that he subjected himself completely to the guidance and judgement of another.

By the time this form of spiritual guidance, particularly under the influence of Irish monks, would be practised among ordinary believers, forming the institution of confession, very little of the psychological insights of the doctrine of the vices remained. 'Confession' reigned, and the task of the confessor shifted from giving self-insight to imposing penance as payment for the evil done. In order to help the father confessor, who was often not very educated, as well as to prevent dishonest competition between parish priests and regular clergy—who were all too eager to have people come and confess in *their* Church so that they could earn their penance and discounts on their penance (indulgences)—standard rates were prescribed for every type of sin. The father confessor became the one who had the power to close a transaction in which it was determined exactly which rate would suffice to have a sin. In this 'rated penance', which took root in the seventh century, the psychological insights that were linked to the original teaching on vices had disappeared completely. Discussions on the gravity of sins concerned the

---

[6] Like the English version, the French text does not attempt to translate the untranslatable. The list of the seven deadly sins there reads: "Ce sont l'orgeuil, l'avarice, l'envie, la colère, l'impureté, la gourmandise, la paresse ou acédia."

equality of the penance to be done, and this is where we sometimes find things that are strange to us. Thus Pope Gregory's attempt in 731 to make the rates uniform established that a cleric who had committed murder was given ten years' penance, but a lay person only received five (or even less in extenuating circumstances), while a bishop who committed adultery had to do twelve years' penance.

Does this mean that the psychological analysis is completely gone? Not at all, but it is now directed toward something else, namely, the subjective ability to appraise the gravity of a sin. The straightforward and uniform rates would not stop the bidding and the resulting process of inflation, but people would adhere to confession as an institute all the more. With the Fourth Lateran Council (1215) it was decided that every believer should confess at least his serious sins or 'mortal sins' every year, and it was also urged that believers go to confession much more than this minimum. The campaign was a success, because up until thirty years ago weekly confession for faithful believers was very usual. After Trent new guide books for the father confessor were published to determine what was a venial sin and what was a mortal sin, and in this consideration more attention was paid to the issue of whether one had 'knowingly' and 'willingly' consented to the sin. Here it was not only sins that had actually been committed that were in view. It was argued that there were also 'internal' sins: evil thoughts, bad intentions that had not been enacted, and the sensual pleasure taken in sultry ideas (*delectationes morosae*) that one had cherished too dearly or for too long. These sins could also be mortal sins, and it was therefore important that one confess them to the father confessor. One might think that one had returned to the old monastic spirituality, were it not for the fact that the framework within which the judgement now occurs was not the psychology of spiritual ascent but that of the evaluation of the motives for feeling guilty.

'Guilt feeling' is the key term that was introduced by the practice of confession in the ethical experience of the good Catholic. Sexuality in particular was the subject of the experience of guilt, and even more so as the second half of the nineteenth century approached and outside of the Church sexuality was relegated to the private areas of life in order to fulfil a new, complex, and very ambiguous role in the social life and the individual psyche. It is then also understandable that psychoanalysis already held an attraction at the end of the 1930's for Catholic theologians who wished to break through the constriction of the official Roman doctrine and propagate a *théologie nouvelle*, a new theology. One may ask whether the way in which the heated debate at the time, which centred on guilt feelings did not hinder ethical reflection as well as reflection of the possible contribution of psychoanalysis in full. Yet before we take up this, we must discuss the other theme given in the title—the virtues. The foregoing has already prepared us for the understanding that 'living virtuously' gradually came to mean 'living obediently', whereas that was not what it meant initially at all.

But before we go on to discuss the virtues, let us take one last look at the text of the Catechism on the passions. Of the complex history that we sketched above almost nothing can be found except for the summary that we find, not in the exposition itself, but under number 1772—in the 'In Brief' formulations. The cardinal sins are found much later, as already mentioned, under number 1866. But what about love and hate, which we have not yet encountered in the lists of passions mentioned? The Catechism has added them to the list of passions to accommodate modern sensitivities, aware of the power of love and hate as psychological motives. Furthermore, with a cosmetic reference to Thomas Aquinas one could give this adaptation the polished appearance of tradition in that Thomas posits as a starting point of his doctrine of virtues the fact that people by nature are attracted by good and repulsed by bad. This brings us to the doctrine of virtues which, in contrast to what the Catechism suggests with these cosmetics, has not in any way developed as a counterpart to the doctrine of the passions and sins.

The Virtues

In the history of Catholic moral theology the virtues are not the opposite of the vices. Reflection on both simultaneously has not occurred. In the Catechism separates the vices and virtues by article on conscience. In this the Catechism mirrors the course of history. First, there is the spirituality elaborated on by the monks which begins with the notion that holiness is the result of the struggle against the vices. Good comes of itself into the picture once the roots of evil have been torn out. This view is subsequently applied to every believer via confession, where that which is evil, rather than which is good, is articulated. It is only after this that we come to the Middle Ages' scholastics, which will reflect on the virtues in themselves, that is, they will examine how the positive potentialities of human nature must be developed.

We are therefore dealing with a more recent layer in the history of moral theology here, although the material of which this layer is composed is of a much earlier period. Here too the philosophy of classical antiquity has been consulted. The inheritance of Platonism and Stoicism can still be found in the list of a number of central virtues, the so-called 'cardinal virtues', which we will be discussing: prudence, justice, strength, and temperance. Yet with regard to what a virtue actually is, it is Aristotle who has been most influential in moral theology.

Thus Aristotle's influence is late. Platonism and Stoicism were much more important in the first centuries of Christianity. After Augustine's death in 430, few important new developments are to be found in theology for seven centuries, and we are very poorly informed for a great portion of this period. In the Middle Ages a new impulse arose for theological reflection in the cathedral schools and the universities that developed from them. Aristotle's texts were introduced to the West by the Arabs, and his philosophy then became the cornerstone on which new and great theological syntheses were built.[7] The pre-eminent author who is impossible to leave out of Catholic theology is Thomas Aquinas (1224/5-1274).

Thomas' starting point is God's creation and he makes of the doctrine of creation a major framework within which he places moral theology. The creation is one large and directed whole, and people experience this in their own beings. In contrast to Augustine and later the Reformation, Thomas assigns only a secondary place to the Fall, and in his opinion it did not fundamentally affect human potentialities, especially the human mind. Thus a person may trust the urge he feels to actualize the various potentialities with which he is born. They are engraved in his heart through God's plan of creation. In order to respond to God's plan, a person must actively fulfil these capabilities, and in this self-realization she will attain the ultimate form of happiness that awaits him: the contemplation of God.

Within this framework of the belief in creation that he introduced, Thomas then uses Aristotle's *Ethica Nicomacheia* in order to indicate how people can follow this path to self-realization and ultimate happiness. It is here that we find the virtues. Aristotle, who begins his volume by positing that the ultimate goal of life is happiness, immediately adds that no mathematical formula exists to tell people what they must do to attain this. The only instruction given is to follow the 'proper mean', which means: avoid extremes. In other words, while it is not possible to formulate positively how one must act precisely, on the other hand it *is* clear what is wrong. One of the examples that Aristotle gives and which may seem unusual from the Christian point of view is that of aggression. Whoever continually reacts explosively and acts aggressively is wrong, but the other extreme, someone who never defends himself and simply accepts everything, is just as wrong.[8] Thus the secret is to cultivate, through practice, an attitude by which one avoids extremes and ultimately, through intuition and reflex, seeks the proper mean. This attitude, which one appropriates through training and practice, is what Aristotle calls a virtue.

---

[7] For the most part Plato's texts will not be rediscovered until the Renaissance (the *Symposium* was rediscovered relatively late in that period). See P.B. Cliteur and W. van Dooren (eds.), *Geschiedenis van het humanisme* (Boom, 1991), p.115.

[8] *Ethica Nicomacheia*, book IV, chapter 5.

Thus a virtue is an attitude that one cultivates by the continual repetition of certain deeds. Whoever pauses to think about this definition immediately notices how different it is from what many people think of today when they hear the word 'virtue' and where living virtuously coincides with obedience and passivity. Aristotle specifies the active character of virtue. He argues that people do not acquire any virtue without conscious reflection and insight. Furthermore, people must enjoy practising a virtue for, let us not forget, that virtue serves the development of human potentialities, the ultimate goal of which is happiness. It should be clear: a virtuous person does not emerge through drill and naivety is the opposite of a virtue.

According to Aristotle, the ultimate goal of life—and this is also the reason why one must cultivate virtues—is happiness, and this can be found in the realization of the highest potentiality that one possesses: one's rational ability. Knowing and penetrating reality, thus living philosophically, is the ultimate happiness. Thomas Aquinas also appropriates this notion for his belief in creation. Given the fact that people are created and that the drive to know is linked to the highest human ability, reason, there is nothing else but that one must be able to realize this drive. Otherwise, creation is poorly assembled. The drive to know is thereby fully realized only if it can attain the ultimate why, the final cause—God. It is because of this that, according to Thomas, we must be able to know God, and that the ultimate goal of life and ultimate happiness lies in the contemplation of God.

It is outside the scope of this article to go more deeply into the content of this *visio beatifica* or beatific contemplation. We will restrict ourselves to the remark that if, according to Thomas, this contemplation of God is reserved for the hereafter, this does not mean that he does not consider the question of whether there should also be a place reserved in heaven for other human potentialities and forms of happiness: possessions, friendship, physical enjoyment, etc. For a more in-depth discussion we must relinquish the subject to dogmatics, indicating the importance that Catholicism has continued to attach to 'natural theology', namely, to the fact that people can arrive at the knowledge of God outside of revelation as well. The primacy that is attributed to reason does play a role in our discussion of the 'divine virtues' below.

But, going on to the central place that is attributed to human reason, I would first like to make a comment on 'natural law' that has played such an important role in ethics since Thomas and especially in sexual ethics. When they hear the term, many think immediately of conformity to the biological order of nature and thereby of reproduction as the norm for sexuality. However, this is not the meaning that Thomas gives to the term. 'Nature', which is the issue here, has the same reference as in 'natural theology'. Just as Thomas is convinced that people are capable of knowing God through their own rational nature, so they can also, by means of their reason, distinguish what is good and what is evil. This must not be dictated to them by external sources.[9] However, it is indeed the case that Thomas, as a person of the Middle Ages for whom the order of the cosmos could not help but mirror the eternal wisdom of God, could not imagine that the purpose of sexuality would *not* be reproduction. But the argument, therefore, is that people must organize their lives according to that which they can understand rationally and not at all that they must blindly subject themselves to biological laws.

Cardinal and Divine Virtues

The fact that Thomas borrows his reflections on virtue from Aristotle with respect to content does not mean that the list of virtues in the latter's *Ethica Nicomacheia* will also constitute the standard list of Catholic ethics from now on. Nor is there a reversion to the list of vices which, in the form of the seven cardinal sins, had become a standard series in order to link them to the virtues as their opposites. What does return is the number seven, the result of combining four central virtues of universal human nature, the so-called 'cardinal virtues', and three virtues which typically express the believer's perspective on life, the 'divine virtues'.

The cardinal virtues originally come from Plato's *Republic*,[10] where he summarizes four virtues that are important for the continuation of a state: wisdom, courage, temperance, and justice. The Stoics appropriated these and popularized them, after which they were Christianized by St. Ambrose of Milan (d. 397).[11] Thomas appropriates these four, although he—here again in line with Aristotle—replaces 'wisdom', which is directed too much to contemplation, with the practically oriented 'prudence'.

If these cardinal virtues do not belong to the ready-made knowledge of the ordinary believer, the divine virtues, in contrast, are better known because they belong to the prayer formulas that people have learned to rattle off by heart. They can be found under the so-called 'acts': the act of faith,

---

[9] This obtains at least for the important affairs in life. For less important affairs Thomas is aware that human conventions and laws are necessary, and possibly even a push by revelation is required, to which a minor role is acknowledged in the matter of ethics. Thomas does *not* make any appeal to the Fall in order to attribute a greater role to revelation in these matters. See *ST* I-II, 91, 4.

[10] Plato, *The Republic* IV, 427e-435.

[11] "Et quidem scimus virtutes esse quatuor cardinales, temperantiam, justitiam, prudentiam, fortitudinem." (Ambrose, *In Lucam*, V, 62, PL XV, 1653c).

the act of hope, and the act of love. But, some may suddenly recall, was there not a fourth act—the act of contrition—which is the one remembered best because it had to be recited in the confessional? Yes, and this demonstrates once again just how much the practice of confession has inundated the formation of theory with regard to morality. Contrition is not a divine virtue and thus does not really belong to the series of the acts of belief, hope, and love.

Now we come to these three divine virtues and the term 'act', which indicates the prayer formula that refers to them, also in respect to very essential matters as far as Christianity as a religion is concerned. The phrase 'as a *religion*' in the previous sentence is not used arbitrarily, because the formula 'Christianity as a *faith*' simply flows out of one's mouth. It seems so obvious, but it is still unique that Christianity is a *faith*. There are religions that do not require faith. They have a number of rituals and one's behaviour is brought into line with particular religious prescriptions, and it is these rituals and prescriptions that parents pass on to their children, but people do not inquire about this specific internal *act* called faith. In contrast, in Christianity one is required to become a believer, which entails appropriating an internal position by holding a number of propositions to be true, accompanying this by the development of a unique relationship to the religious reality. In this a number of specific psychological functions must be activated, such as holding a number of propositions to be true, preparing oneself for something over which one has no control, and the development of feelings of love directed toward an ultimate being. Thus the term 'act' has a pregnant meaning in Christianity.

There has been a great difference of opinion on the relation and interrelationship between these three acts, particularly at the time of the Reformation. Thereafter, after the so-called 'struggle of grace' which was stopped by Pope Paul V in 1607, controversy was suspended on the issue. But a problem that belongs to the core of the issue of faith cannot be resolved by issuing a police order. Now that the polemic context of that time has waned, the problem arises once again, under the probably more familiar distinction between 'believing that' and 'believing in'. Here we find the classic question of whether the Christian attitude begins with 'believing that', believing a number of statements—thus beginning with an act of the intellect—with the more emotionally coloured internal attitudes of 'believing in' (in traditional terminology, the acts of hope and love) following from that, or *vice versa*.

In the latter case, the Christian attitude[12] would begin with being gripped on a deeper level, more totally, and also more emotionally by the absolute, and the rational formulas or at least those which claim to give information are merely attempts to articulate a much deeper and richer experience. The more major theologians have always made room for both views in connection to one of the basic texts on which Christianity rests, Paul's Epistle to the Romans. But the intense debate with the Reformation, which shortly thereafter was forced to cease, has sharpened the positions, with the result that the Catholic stance was 'believing that', the intellectual acceptance of a number of truths, had to primary and that the other psychological acts—hope and love—must flow from this and be led along the right path by faith.

This issue is undoubtedly modern, as becomes apparent as soon as one replaces the old theological terminology with the more modern sounding psychological terms. If one says that faith may not follow from hope, is this not saying that one must beware of projection, that is, that one must be careful not to construct a religious dream world because people need it? If one says that love should not be a source of faith, is that not a warning against the intoxication of a feeling that blinds one to the extent that one no longer has the goal, i.e., that towards which one is directed, in sight? But, on the other hand it seems problematic if one claims that the pure intellectual insight is first in order. This strict and in the long run insupportable stance puts the Catholic position on the same wavelength as scientism, and it is not a coincidence that the debate on the meaning of religion in the nineteenth century (and for some individuals still today) took the form of the struggle between faith and science. It ultimately involves a struggle between hostile brothers. Both parties begin with the same presupposition on the primacy of reason, while it is precisely this that is a current subject of discussion.

The Gifts of the Holy Spirit

However, having uncovered layer after layer, before we come to the present, we once again encounter a sacred group of seven that is to organize and support the Christian life—the seven gifts of the Holy Spirit. The history of these gifts is much more complex than that of the cardinal sins and virtues.

---

[12] Here, for the sake of clarity, we purposely avoid the use of the phrase 'the Christian *faith*', which advocates of the second view would use as a matter of course. The reason is that in their view they use the term faith in a broader way than the meaning than how it is used in the first view with respect to the act of faith.

The text which is referred to is Isaiah 11:1-2,[13] but the symbolism of the number seven has played a role that is at least as important here. The Church fathers linked the gifts with the Christian meaning of the Jewish *menorah*, with the seven spirits, the seven claps of thunder and the seven torches of the Apocalypse, the seven weeks of Easter, the seven planets, etc. It is impossible to recapitulate all the free associations that the meaning produced for symbolism. In this case too it is Thomas Aquinas who left his systematic mark on the teaching, although he was not followed as unanimously here. The theological discussion on the number of the Holy Spirit's gifts and what exactly they consist of waned after the Middle Ages. They are often mentioned in mystical and devotional literature and they continue to be sung about in the Pentecost liturgy, but there is no longer a systematic theological reflection that develops an ethical reflection on Christian life on the basis of these gifts.

The question is whether one can mean something else than the virtues by the gifts of the Holy Spirit, and that was also the opinion of most of the medieval theologians. The list appears to be a series of virtues: wisdom, understanding, counsel, fortitude, knowledge, piety, and fear of the Lord (1831). The fact that the list is different from that of the cardinal and divine virtues is one of the reasons why it proved difficult to fit the gifts of the Spirit into the structure of moral theology. Furthermore, there is the issue of how the term 'gift' must be understood, for it can lead to the suggestion that what is involved here is not something that must be developed in the same way as the virtues. But the discussion on grace which had been discontinued was the reason why a streamlined and generally accepted theory on the gifts of the Spirit was not fitted into the structure of theological ethics. The fate of the gifts in the history of spirituality is all the more interesting, but since Trent spirituality and moral theology have grown further and further apart.

The Practice of Guilt Feeling and the Psychoanalytic Critique

One of the common complaints about the history of the Catholic theology since Trent is that a gap exists between the world of the spiritual authors and that of the moral theologians.[14] There is a growing though often condemned

---

[13] "A shoot will come up from the stump of Jesse; from his roots a branch will bear fruit. The Spirit of the Lord will rest on him—the Spirit of wisdom and understanding, the Spirit of counsel and of power, the Spirit of knowledge and of the fear of the Lord."

[14] See the classic overview in B. Häring, *The Law of Christ: Moral Theology for*

and oppressed world of spirituality and mysticism, in which the theme of the Holy Spirit, as well as a fascination with the figure of the suffering Christ, assumes a large place. Unfortunately, only cliché images of the fascinating Jansenists and quietists remain in the collective memory, while the more dolorous traditions, which left many bleeding hearts behind in iconography, continued until the Second Vatican Council. Yet this fascinating and sometimes bewildering world of spirituality is somewhat isolated. In addition, there is a moral theology that, as is usually said, follows the juridical path. This means that reflection on the moral life is done almost exclusively in the function of the practice of confession. This gap can still be found in the current Catechism. Christian life is divided into a reflection on ethical norms and a relatively small section on prayer (in which one finds relatively little of the moving history of spirituality), but how the two are connected is left rather vague.

We cannot take up the question as to whether confession was so successful because it fit in with developments that affected society as a whole or whether it was confession that also determined that development. There is a general consensus that feeling guilty played an ever growing role in Western civilization. Along with this was the increasingly visible problem of sexuality. This is also encountered in Catholic moral theology. From 1930 on, anti-contraception became elevated to a symbol: this was the year that birth control was accepted by the Anglican Church, whereas they were condemned by the papal encyclical *Humani Generis*. As far as official doctrine is concerned, the struggle rages yet today, and attention is concentrated on the sexual sphere even more by the condemnation of homosexual behaviour (1975) and the discussions on abortion, by which without argumentation with respect to content it is increasingly presented as self-evident that abortion after conception is murder—a position that goes directly against the mainstream of the ecclesiastical tradition.[15]

Priests and Laity (Paramus, NJ, 1961). It is difficult to recommend a more recent overview by S. Pinckaers (*Les sources de la morale chrétienne: Sa méthode, son contenu, son histoire* (Fribourg, 1985)) because it introduces little that is new and ignores current questions. (For our critique, see: P. Vandermeersch, *Ethiek tussen wetenschap en ideologie* (Louvain, 1987), p.23.) On the other hand, much information can be found in J. Mahoney, *The Making of Moral Theology* (Oxford, 1987), which is organized thematically.

[15] See A. Chollet, "Animation," in: *Dictionnaire de Théologie Catholique* I-2 (1923), as well as D. Mercier, *Psychologie, Cours de Philosophie*, Vol. III (Louvain, 1912), pp.323 ff.

In such a situation is it understandable that psychoanalysis should attract the more than ordinary attention of Catholic theologians.[16] But it is likewise understandable that this also caused attention to be paid to what one could learn about guilt feelings and about sexuality from psychoanalysis and not to Freud's view on religion.[17] At the International Congress for mental hygiene, which took place in London in 1948, a number of Catholic participants drew up a plan in the hallways for organizing annual international congresses of Catholic 'psychiatrists, analytical psychotherapists, and child-guidance counsellors'. Pathological guilt feelings in particular seemed a theme that needed to be dealt with urgently. The plan was carried out immediately, and the fifth congress was held in Rome in 1953. Naturally there was a papal audience, and there was suddenly an unexpected turn of events. In his speech Pius XII stated that "no one will deny that there is seldom an irrational, even unhealthy feeling of guilt" but psychotherapy should not tamper with the religious meaning of true guilt feelings.[18]

A. Hesnard's controversial book, *Morale sans Péche*,[19] appeared in 1954. Its thesis was that feeling guilty could induce so much fear in people that they were paralysed with respect to taking any initiative. Their moral reactions began to serve their own psychic self-preservation (do nothing by which you could run the risk of having to endure feelings of guilt) and in no way were they more directed toward a positive pursuit of good. The publication of the book caused quite a stir ecclesiastically. A very intense and complex diplomacy was exercised in order to get Rome to recognize the value of psychotherapy, and, although there were successes, there were also some strange results at times. The newly chosen John XXIII supported the plans to hold a congress on the psychology of guilt feelings in 1960. Milan was chosen as the place to hold it because it was known that archbishop Montini,

---

[16] The pioneer is undoubtedly the Carmelite Br. Bruno of Jesus-Mary (the way of signing one's name at that time allows me to record only his cloister name). Already in 1935 he brought theologians and psychoanalysts together, which resulted in publications in the *Etudes carmélitaines*. The Jesuit Louis Beirnaert and the Dominican Albert Plé are the two other prominent figures in this early period.

[17] The debate of the years 1950-1960 on projection, with which the names of S. Vestdijk, F. Sierksma, and H. Fortmann are linked, is a matter unique to the Dutch, which has not been echoed very much outside of Catholic circles and which, for the rest, was no longer a topical problem of analysis.

[18] Speech by Pius XII to the participants of the fifth international Catholic congress on psychotherapy and clinical psychology on 13 April 1953. AAS, 45, 278-86 (information from the archives of the A.I.E.M.P.R.).

[19] Paris, 1954.

later Paul VI, was sympathetic. But during the preparations for this congress the local synod of the diocese of Rome decided that psychoanalysis was condemned in one breath with magic and witchcraft! With the Second Vatican Council, however, an opening seemed to arise for fundamental discussions. Sexuality remained in the spotlight. A breakthrough was expected in the area of two *hot issues*: birth control and the celibacy of priests. But resistance against rational reflection on these two themes ran deep, for the Council was denied the power to discuss these two (and only these two!) matters. As is well known, ecclesiastical decisions were finally made on these two points that went in a direction opposite to that which was expected. In July 1968 the encyclical *Humanae Vitae* rejected birth control, and in November 1971 the synod on priesthood continued to hold to the obligatory priestly celibacy.

Remaining Questions

Since then the discussion on sexuality operates as a symptom which pulls psychological energy to itself and blocks every in-depth reflection on the core of a Christian ethic and the psychological factors to which it appeals. Because of this, an account has not yet been given of the way in which the course of the history of Catholic ethics has given it the appearance through which it is has become so conspicuous. The discussion still concerns the content of the norms presented—primarily in the area of sexuality. There is still debate on the problematic aspect of what is presented, as if a new content would offer a solution. The real problem, however, lies in the way in which the ethical language in the Church directs itself toward the believer, where completely different motives are at play.[20]

Here lies a possible, more fundamental contribution by the human sciences, particularly psychoanalysis, to moral theology. We will limit ourselves here to briefly mentioning two points: how speaking morally functions and motivates people, whether it does so in a good way or not; the relation between psychological factors that are involved in 'believing' and the way in which people can or cannot develop the inner freedom necessary to arrive at responsible ethical choices.

---

[20] From the perspective of the current language in the Church, one could therefore assume that the problem does not lie in the content but in the form of this way of speaking, were it not that one is thereby led to assume that that form is nevertheless secondary, with the result the problem is once again avoided. Thus, although this formula may sound right, if, in accordance with tradition, one sees the essence in the *forma* or form, I choose not to use this terminology here.

1. The current discussions on the content of what Catholic ethics must present as normative often remain caught in the constriction introduced by the institution of confession and the cultivation of guilt feelings in the structure of ethical language. It is often implicitly assumed that speaking ethically means that one presents a norm. This seems so obvious that even in philosophical reflection on ethics the 'transition from fact to norm' is considered a central problem. There is also an apparent obviousness in this formulation: speaking ethically must induce in the listener the psychology of the feeling of duty or of prohibition. Whoever simply enquires or analyzes will seldom be regarded as speaking 'as an ethicist'. Corresponding to this is the insistence of the sciences, which are so authoritative in our culture, including the human sciences, that they take an ethically neutral stance. In their own way as well, they honour the stance that the uniqueness of ethics consists of presenting specific ethical choices through the knowledge of objective facts which they produced.

The question is whether or not this view on the function of ethics in our society—for we encounter a problem here that is not restricted to the ecclesiastical community—is based on ideology and needs to be reviewed. Apparently, it is still assumed that speaking ethically must awaken the specific psychological motives that support duty and obedience. They are still very much present in our society. However, the question is whether their functioning (and disfunctioning) leads to better ethical insight.

For this reason I have defended the statement that the current problem of speaking ethically does not lie in the transition from fact to norm but in the transition of norm to fact. Before people listen to ethical statements they already have many assumptions surrounding authority, duty, and prohibition in their minds. At the same time they regard a whole set of feelings, expectations, desires, and behaviours as normal and thus as normalizing. Therefore the norm is already present before one begins to speak ethically. This does not support, then, the task of creating the psychology of the normative *ex nihilo*. Today the task of ethics consists much more of appearing analytical and informative and thus coming out with factual material in order to break through the often postulated and irrational *a priori* through which one expects to break through ethical language.[21]

Whatever one may think of my personal view, it is so in every case that the human sciences have more of an eye for the cultural-historical definition of guilt feelings as a psychological factor that is regulated by the ethical interactions between people. That which is raised there could lead to a fundamental reconsideration on both the functioning of moral theology in as far as

---

[21] See the book already mentioned: P. Vandermeersch, *Ethiek tussen wetenschap en ideologie*.

it is a socially recognized way of speaking and the *loci* from which it generates its reflections.

2. The second point that I would like to mention concerns the relation between moral reflection and faith, in which the emphasis lies on the clarification that psychoanalysis can contribute on the function of the second term. What faith is, how it works, how it differs from verifiable knowledge and pure illusion, how it simultaneously entails attachment to a deeper reality but also gives one power to stand at a critical distance: there is still little on the psychological motives that support this complex process that has penetrated theology. Theological circles are still often dominated by the cliché image that a psychoanalytical approach in religion would view it as projection, as if Freud himself had not come to the conclusion that projection is unsatisfactory as an explanation.[22] In order to have genuine faith, it is important to be able to break through that which is literally held to be true in statements of faith and Bible stories. For this reason the discussion on the correct method of employing symbolism has been the subject of debate since earliest Christianity. It is precisely on this point that a closer psychological analysis could have an important contribution, particularly where it exposes the fact that it does not involve a simple alternative in the distinction between illusion and reality, but lies in the truly active and livable relation to reality in a complex mixture of illusionary world and perception.

These insights do not only affect religious faith but all forms of 'theory' or ways of viewing reality. These psychological insights are important not only for dogmatics and spirituality but also for moral theology. There as well one is faced with the question of how the human psyche is able to step back from direct obviousness and to connect old forms of life with possible new ones. It is unfortunate that all of these questions remain hidden. They concern a neglected part of the theological inheritance that is important not only for the way of thinking within the Church but also for secularized reflection on the uniqueness of Western culture.

---

[22] P. Vandermeersch, *Unresolved Questions in the Freud-Jung Debate: On Psychosis, Sexual Identity and Religie* (Louvain, 1991).

SIX

Conscience—A Social-Ethical Reading

Fred van Iersel

Concept Definition

It is extraordinarily difficult to give an exact definition of the concept of 'conscience' (Greek: *Syneidèsis*; Lat.: *conscientia*). Attempts to do so are seldom clear.[1] In view of the complications of arriving at a definition, in this article we will forego this task and make do with indicating important aspects of the concept of conscience, i.e., those aspects that can clarify the specific position of the Magisterium in the cultural dialogue on conscience. The concept of conscience can only be adequately analyzed if one takes into account the following aspects of this concept:
- the relationship between the various sources of the concept of conscience, such as scriptural texts and philosophical systems;
- the relationship between theological views of conscience on the one hand and, on the other, views of this in other disciplines;
- the relation between the various theological perspectives from which conscience can be discussed, such as creation theology, the theology of the Fall (into sin), or covenant theology;
- the distinction between the various levels in discussing conscience: the level of theological anthropology, the discussion of conscience in the context of the dignity of the individual, and the discussion of practical aspects as the realization of the freedom of conscience;
- the relationship between conscience as an 'inner voice representing God' on the one hand, and as a moral judgment brought about by people themselves by means of reason on the other;

---

[1] Cf. G.A. Van der Wal, "Opvattingen over het geweten. Een ideeënhistorische schets," in: *Wijsgerig Perspectief* 27 (1986/87-6): 175-81; H.F.M. Crombach, "Denken en doen. Psychologische theorieën over de ontwikkeling van het geweten," in: *Wijsgerig Perspectief* 27 (1986/87-6): 191-97; B.P. Vermeulen, *De vrijheid van geweten: Een fundamenteel rechtsprobleem* (Arnhem, 1989).

- the relationship between approaching conscience as the ability to judge *versus* approaching conscience *as* moral judgment, a distinction that is closely related to the relationship of conscience to the virtues, particularly the 'cardinal' virtue of prudence;
- the distinction and the connection between conscience as *conscientia antecedens* (prior to an action) and as *conscientia consequens* (a person's conscience after a deed has been performed);
- the connection and the distinction between freedom of conscience as freedom to judge on the one hand and as freedom to act on the other;
- the relationship between the appeal to one's conscience on the one hand and the context in which this takes place on the other.

This article will discuss these aspects of the concept of conscience and their place in the official ecclesiastical discussion of conscience in the Catechism. Since Vatican II, Catholic moral theology has used various means in its search for the ways in which Christian faith and ethics can be connected. The conciliar texts already separate the theology of conscience from a framework dominated by a juridical understanding—a move that has a liberation from legalism in view as well. Its primary theological context became a theology of the human being as the image of God. This article describes how this development is expressed in conciliar documents. It also provides an important aspect of the background of the Catechism: this will, in any case, be a summary of the state of affairs in the Catholic doctrine in the area of faith and morals.

Removing juridical language with respect to conscience from Catholic theology[2] already opened the way in the conciliar documents for placing conscience in a broader context—approaching the human being as an person—and particularly for treating conscience in its relation to moral freedom and moral responsibility. It is all the more interesting to see how the Catechism relates conscience to these other central basic concepts.

In the following section the concept of conscience is analyzed on the basis of a few elements in the Catholic tradition of moral theology (§ 3). In the fourth section the treatment of the theme of conscience in the Catechism is evaluated from various points of view.

---

[2] Cf. A. Moser and B. Leers, *Moral Theology: Dead Ends and Alternatives* (Mayknoll, New York, 1990 (originally published 1987)), p.41; J. Mahoney, *The Making of Moral Theology: A Study of the Roman Catholic Tradition* (Oxford, 1989 (originally published 1987)), pp.33-37.

Vatican II and the Catechism on the Conscience: A Comparison[3]

The Catechism already follows Vatican II in its definition of conscience. For this reason we will now discuss the relation between the relevant documents of Vatican II and the Catechism.

Vatican II on Conscience

The most important discussion on conscience in the documents of Vatican II can be found in the Pastoral Constitution *Gaudium et Spes*, which deals with the task of the Church in the world. In this constitution Vatican II gives conscience primarily an anthropological foundation. The introduction opens with an contextual analysis in the form of an outline of the human situation. The most important theological foundation of the concept conscience is chosen by the Council in chapter one, a reflection on the dignity of the human person. The Council develops this concept on the basis of a theological anthropology of the human being as the image of God (GS 12). This is based on a rereading of its sources: the Scriptures and the Church fathers. Only after sketching the greatness of human beings does the Council outline the tragedy of human existence, in particular sin and death (GS 13). It is against this background that the Council traces its anthropological starting point that human beings are physical and spiritual creatures, and justice must be done to both dimensions (GS 14). The Council subsequently describes human beings as creatures gifted with reason. It does not regard the understanding as accidental; to the contrary, it considers rationality to belong to the nature as such of the human person (GS 15).

Gaudium et Spes deals with three aspects of the concept of the dignity of the human person, which are also recognizable in the concept of conscience as the Council describes and deals with it: the aspect of theological anthropology in speaking about human beings as the image of God, the aspect of the various levels of the dignity of the person, and the aspect of the practical struggle regarding the attack against the dignity of humans.[4]

---

[3] The following abbreviations will be used for conciliar documents, followed by the number of the article quoted (for example, GS 80): DH = *Dignitatis Humanae* (Declaration on Religious Freedom); GS = The Pastoral Constitution *Gaudium et Spes* (on the Church in the Modern World); LG = *Lumen Gentium* (Dogmatic Constitution on the Church); NA = *Nostra Aetate* (Declaration on the Relation of the Church to Non-Christian Religions)

[4] Cf. P. Delahaye, "De waardigheid van de menselijke persoon," in: G. Baraúna (ed.), *De Kerk in de wereld van nu. Commentaren op de pastorale Constitutie Gaudium et Spes* (Bilthoven, 1968), p.215.

In the description of conscience itself the Council maintains its perspective of theological anthropology. Referring to Romans 2:14-16, the Council defines conscience as the location of a law whose voice echoes in its heart. The dignity of conscience consists in listening to this voice, and it is on this basis also that the conscience will be judged. The Council views conscience as the most hidden core and sanctuary of the human being, in which she is alone with God. In agreement with this perspective of theological anthropology, the Council regards loyalty to conscience as the means by which "Christians are joined to other men in the search for truth and for the right solution to so many moral problems which arise both in the life of individuals and from social relationships" (GS 16).

By acknowledging the high theological status of the concept conscience the Council places before itself the task of finding a balance between the maintenance of the objectivity of the norms of morality on the one hand and individual freedom of conscience on the other hand. This freedom of conscience is confronted with a test case in the right to a erring conscience. With respect to this the Council posits on the one hand that the effect of a good conscience is the disappearance of moral caprice and an orientation towards the objective norms of morality. On the other hand, it stresses the fact that, although conscience can err due to an avoidable ignorance, this does not detract from its dignity if the individual is serious in his search for truth (GS 16). The Council goes one step further yet: it links its view of conscience with praise on human freedom. This human freedom also finds a basis in theological anthropology. The dignity of the human being, the Council states, requires a true freedom, an "exceptional sign of the image of God in man." God wished to give people the power to develop themselves so that they would of themselves seek the Creator and would achieve perfection and happiness by adhering to Him in freedom. The Council consistently states that the dignity of the human being requires that she act according to a conscious and free choice and be prompted and moved from within. The Council understands this being moved as a right (GS 17) and that it also applies to children and young people: the Council believes they have the right to be stimulated so that they may assess values according to a right conscience and accept them with personal agreement. With this the Council views freedom of the moral conscience as a right worth pursuing.

The Council also links freedom of the moral conscience with religious freedom based on the recognition of all human beings as the image of God (cf. NA 5). The Council states that the vocation of human beings excludes force (DH 11). Conscience can help people who, through no fault of their own, do not know the Gospel of Christ and the Church to attain beatitude through God's grace (LG 16).

Thus the concept of freedom of conscience that the Council developed does not have primarily a juridical meaning. It reaches deeper and ultimately has to do with theological anthropology. The Council does consider the juridical aspects to be important, although not from the perspective of freedom of conscience but rather from the perspective of the exercise of this fundamental human freedom. This fits in completely with the tendency of the conciliar documents to remove the concept of conscience from its juridical constriction.

By means of the freedom of the human person conscience is linked to the second aspect of the discussion of human dignity: the various levels of the dignity of the person. With respect to this the Council states that the person gains such dignity "when, ridding himself of all slavery to the passions, he presses forward towards his goal by freely choosing what is good, and, by his diligence and skill, effectively secures for himself the means suited to this end" (GS 17). Thus here are formulated the conditions under which people can and must realize freedom of conscience.

The freedom of the human being and his conscience, as affirmed by the Council, does not impede the fact that the people are required to be as informed as possible: only unavoidable ignorance can excuse them (cf. GS 16).

With regard to the third aspect of human dignity, the practical, the Council tends to regard freedom of conscience as an aspect of religious freedom (DH 2 & 3). It is true that religious freedom itself has a basis in theological anthropology based: it applies to every human being and in such a way that no one may be forced to act against his conscience in matters religious nor be prevented, within appropriate limits, from acting in accordance with his conscience either alone or with others (cf. DH 2 & 3). But by placing a strong emphasis on acting according to freedom—and thus not only on freedom of judgement—the Council introduces here, more so than in other documents, the practical aspect of the exercise of religious freedom. This clarifies the first practical aspect of the assertion of the dignity of the human person, i.e., that the human being's freedom of conscience consists not only of freedom of judgement but also of freedom to act. The Council describes 'imbalances' in the contemporary world and their influence on the 'demands of moral conscience' (GS 8). It concerns especially the exercise of freedom of conscience in a concern for 'practicality'.

The second practical aspect of the practice of asserting the dignity of the human being concerns the religious freedom of adherents to other religions and the rights that arise from this (NA 5). The Council argues for the recognition of religious freedom as a civil right (DH 2). In this connection, after a short passage on the social nature of human beings (DH 3), the Council further discusses in particular the religious freedom of communities, which implies a completely different concept of actor.

The third practical aspect concerns the formation of conscience. In connection with its discussion of population growth, the Council states that it considers knowledge of the moral law very important. However, this requires an improvement of the pedagogical methods and social circumstances, and particularly the opportunity for religious education or at least sound moral instruction (GS 87). This insight, that conscience must be supported pedagogically and social circumstances, is connected with the role that the Council attributes to the Church in the formation of conscience. The Council states that Christians must carefully observe the teachings of the Church in the formation of conscience. It also states that: "It is [the Catholic Church's] duty to proclaim and teach with authority the truth which is Christ and, at the same time, to declare and confirm by her authority the principles of the moral order which spring from human nature itself" (DH 14). In my opinion, this view not only refers to the practical tasks of the Church but also has an implication regarding moral theology. It implies namely that conscience—Christian conscience in particular—is not only an individual concern but also has an intrinsic ecclesial dimension because of its formation. The formation of Christian conscience is linked with ecclesial socialization and the pedagogical task of the Church. Is it possible that we are confronted here with an important paradox in the way in which Vatican II speaks about conscience? While freedom of conscience is based in theological anthropology and connected with human freedom, Christians' freedom of conscience, just as that of others, appears to be anthropologically based, while at the same time restricted to some degree ecclesiologically by its ecclesial dimension, that is, Christians' obligation to form conscience with the help of the Church.

The fourth practical aspect is elaborated by Vatican II in its view on war and peace. It is confronted with the question of the extent to which a state may compel civil and military obedience. Here the Council takes an important step by abandoning the principle of '*in dubio pro auctoritate*', which is based on the politics stemming from Augustinianism.[5] Actions that violate the 'natural rights of human beings' and "any order which commands such actions is criminal and blind obedience cannot excuse those who carry them out" (GS 79). This implies that in cases of moral doubt one need not obey the political authority; everyone has the right to obey his conscience. This is the moral theological foundation of the right to refuse to participate in unjust wars, to refuse to participate in morally unjust acts of war in a 'just war', and particularly the right to refuse to serve in the militia. One can observe an ambivalence in the way the Council speaks in this area as well. While the

---

[5] P. Engelhardt, "Die Lehre vom gerechten Krieg in der vooreformatorischen und katholischen Tradition. Herkunft-Wandlungen-Krise," in: R. Steinweg (ed.), *Der gerechte Krieg: Christentum, Islam, Marxismus* (Frankfurt am Main, 1980).

an ambivalence in the way the Council speaks in this area as well. While the Council recognizes the right of the individual to refuse blind obedience, it also recognizes—as long as there is not yet an international authority with its own competence and proper equipment—the right of the state as an institution to self-defense after the possibilities for peaceful negotiations have been exhausted (GS 79). Thus here two actors are placed beside each other: the individual citizen and the militia on the one hand, and that of the state as an institution on the other.

All in all, one must posit that the Council has yielded a perspective on conscience that is characterized by its foundation on an anthropology of the human being as the image of God, by which the conscience is considered not primarily but only secondarily in its juridical aspects.

A Perspective on the Catechism on the Basis of Vatican II

In Article 6 (1776-1802), which deals with conscience, the definition of conscience employed by the Vatican II returns (1776). In the elaboration of the concept substantial differences with the Council's approach appear. The Catechism's treatment is arranged according to the following order: (1) its view on the judgement of conscience, (2) the formation of the conscience, (3) choosing in accord with conscience, (4) erroneous judgement. The concept central to the Vatican II, the dignity of the person, plays a subordinate role, being mentioned only in connection with the requirement of uprightness of moral conscience (1780). The context of theological anthropology, i.e., the view of the person as the image of God, plays no role at all in this text. This has a number of consequences. First of all, the conscience is not regarded as the 'bond' between Christians and non-Christians as it is in Vatican II.

A second, no less important consequence of the omission of the anthropology of the image of God in the article on conscience is that there is no elaboration on the freedom of the human person and the associated freedom of conscience. The former is mentioned only very briefly (1782). In the Catechism all emphasis is placed on the duties that the human person has: the requirement of interiority (1779), the uprightness of moral conscience (1780), the fact that the conscience makes it possible for one to assume responsibility for acts performed (1781). It is illustrative that the interiority of the conscience, which was dealt with as a right in the conciliar documents, has been changed into a requirement (1779). The Catechism devotes the entire second paragraph to the formation of the conscience: the conscience must be informed (1783), the education of the conscience is important (1784); in the formation of the conscience the Word of God is the light by which the Church gives leadership with its authoritative teaching (1785).

roneous Judgement" respectively) come to stand in this perspective, which implies a shift. The documents of Vatican II contain an elaboration of the individual moral freedom on a principial level and on the level of practical aspects of maintaining the dignity of the human person and thus also her conscience as well as its formation an ecclesial dimension. In the Catechism the ecclesial dimension of the formation of conscience receives a more principial significance because of its place in the article and the absence of an elaborated relation with a framework of theological anthropology.

The second aspect of the dignity of the human person—the relation with the functioning of the human person in her context—was only slightly elaborated in the documents of Vatican II, but it was present. That this aspect is absent in the Catechism is a methodical break with the systematics of the Pastoral Constitution *Gaudium et Spes*. Going more deeply into this aspect of the dignity of the human person could have brought conscience into connection with psychological insights and with the critique of religion. Linking up with these approaches to conscience could have made the concept of conscience more accessible, particularly for people in (post)modern societies. Moreover, such an approach could have stimulated a testing of the postmodern relativistic suspicion of conscience. Here perhaps the Catechism's nature as being essentially a compendium of a state of affairs takes its toll. The Catechism appears to close reflection rather than stimulating it. This is also a methodological break with the *aggiornamento* of Vatican II.

More remarkable is that the third aspect of the dignity of the human person is also restricted to a reference to a rejection of any sort of force with respect to conscience in religious matters. Here there is only a reference to *Dignitatis Humanae* and thus no discussion of the freedom of conscience in various actual contexts, such as freedom of conscience in labour disputes or in medical dilemmas. With this the social-ethical dimension of the problem of conscience as an explicit theme disappears from view completely. This is a important change with regard to the Vatican II. After all, the Council had not placed the treatment of the conscience in the Pastoral Constitution concerning the Church in the contemporary world for nothing: reflection on conscience deserves a place in thinking on the organization of society and politics and on the Church's contribution to this.

But not only does Article 6 in the Catechism's section on ethics not broach any new themes, the practical aspects of the exercise of freedom of conscience mentioned earlier are also not actualized. Here the systematics of the Catechism takes its toll. While the text of *Gaudium et Spes* with reference to the Encyclical *Pacem in Terris* gives an important place to the analysis of the human situation, the Catechism's reflection on conscience is presented as a truth without a context. In this area as well, i.e., the analysis of context in which the conscience functions and exercises its authority, more could have been said, in close connection with the social and political praxis of the Church of the last decades. One might think of an elaboration of the role of the conscience in the effective resistance of the Church against totalitarian communism as a source of inspiration for the future—a dimension that is present in the encyclical *Centesimus Annus* and in the encyclical *Veritatis Splendor*.

Aspects of the History of the Theological Concept of Conscience

From the perspective of the history of theology, conscience has received a conspicuous place in the Catechism. It is not remarkable that the Catechism established a relation between *synderesis* (traditionally regarded as a reservoir of fundamental moral knowledge) on the one hand and conscience on the other (1780). That is, the conscience orients itself toward the general knowledge of good and evil which every person possesses. It is good to unite this starting point with the approach in theological anthropology that the person is made in the image of God.

It is remarkable that the Catechism posits that the judgement of conscience must be prudent (1780). In doing so, the Catechism makes a statement on the relation between the 'cardinal virtue' of prudence and (the judgement of) conscience on the other hand. To choose in accord with moral conscience requires that a person interpret the signs of the times with the help of prudence (1788). As the 'first cardinal virtue', prudence thus acquires a function within the concept of conscience. With this formulation the Catechism appears to choose sides in a controversy within the Catholic moral theology with regard to the relation between conscience and prudence—at first glance an understandably technical but nevertheless fundamental discussion.

The background of this debate was Neo-Thomism, but its application extended far beyond this. It concerned primarily the nature and range of moral freedom: Did this apply to the virtuous and therefore prudent individual, who by means of prudence associated with synderesis could choose goals and means for his actions in freedom? Or was this freedom limited to the 'conscience' of the individual, which, analogous to juridical judgements, applies fixed principles to individual cases,[6] through which moral freedom is viewed on a less fundamental level, one where it is applied in practice?

A second aspect of the debate concerned the place of social and political ethics in ecclesiastical ethics. It was not for nothing that in this ethics of an

---

[6] Cf. T. Beemer, "Het voorstel tot kernontwapening: de ethische argumentatie," in: *Tijdschrift voor Theologie* 21 (1981): 245-64.

A second aspect of the debate concerned the place of social and political ethics in ecclesiastical ethics. It was not for nothing that in this ethics of an Aristotelian hue prudence obtained as the political and administrative virtue *par excellence*. For this reason social philosophy from Cicero to Burke was defined as prudence.[7] The science of social administration is also replete with prudence.[8] It implies a pre-juridical freedom from judgement and actions that make prudence into a typically political and administrative virtue. In both social and political philosophy[9] as well as in moral theology[10] one can see a certain loss of prudence that accompanied a ethics of conscience in which the actions of the individual from the perspective of her moral integrity were central.

The twentieth century has witnessed a certain revival of prudence in Catholic moral theology. Deman,[11] in a rereading and reworking of Thomas Aquinas' concept of prudence, has argued for a powerful reevaluation of prudence, also in opposition to conscience (*conscientia*). He strips moral freedom of the framework of the ethics of conscience and, by implication, of its juridical understanding. Thus prudence is placed on a more fundamental and at the same time potentially on a social-ethical level. At the same time, however, in Deman's way of thinking this social-ethical dimension of prudence is not thematized, let alone related to the functioning of state citizens in a democracy.[12]

Another school argues, within the framework of the revival of prudence, for an integration of prudence into the ethics of conscience rather than viewing them as opposed to each other. Thus Furger argues for a 'prudent con-

---

[7] J. Habermas, *Theorie und Praxis* (Frankfurt, 1971), p.49.

[8] H. van de Graaf and R. Hoppe, *Beleid en Politiek: Een inleiding tot de beleidswetenschap en de beleidskunde* (Muiderberg, 1989).

[9] J. Habermas, *Theorie und Praxis*.

[10] J. Schellekens, "Over het 'lot' van de prudentie in de moraaltheologie," in: *Jubileumbundel voor professor magister dr. Kreling OP, aangeboden ter gelegenheid van zijn 25-jarig professoraat in zijn 65ste levenjaar* (Nijmegen/Utrecht, 1953), pp.252-67.

[11] T. Deman, "Probalisme," in: *Dictionnarie de Théologie Catholique*, Vol. XIII-1, Col. 417-619 (Paris, 1936), and the edition of Thomas Aquinas' *Summa Theologica IIa-IIae*, La Prudence (Rome/Paris/Koornik, 1949).

[12] F. Furger, "Prudence and Moral Change," *Concilium* 4 (1968) 5: 66-67.

science'.[13] According to Furger prudence must be able to be corrected by striving for the final goal. He believes that weighing obligation and freedom and the comparison of the concrete situation with precedents can bring about clarity with regard to end and means.[14] In other words, Furger leaves room for a correction of prudence, along the lines of probability, on the basis of casuistry. According to Furger, since Deman moral theology has given conscience the role of leader in assessing the moral life, whereas prudence would be responsible for realizing the potential in the matter at hand.[15] Furger's approach thus implies an instrumentalization of prudence on behalf of the conscience. This is less obvious and more important than first appears. Implied are both the underestimation of the fundamental differences between *prudentia* and *conscientia* and an over-valuing of conscience. Nevertheless Furger specifically indicates the political- ethical dimension of prudence.[16]

The Catechism appears to appropriate Furger's position in the debate surrounding the relation of conscience and prudence in the passages mentioned. Objections can be raised against this. From the perspective of the tradition of Catholic moral theology, particularly in high scholasticism, conscience must be taken seriously: moral freedom extends to the freedom, indeed the obligation, to obey one's conscience, even in the ultimate test case—when conscience errs. At the same time, with the same tradition there is no reason to absolutize conscience, for moral freedom is more fundamental than the freedom, analogous to jurisprudence, to apply fixed principles to individual cases, namely, those cases in which the personal integrity of the agent is at risk. Moreover, fitting prudence into a ethics of conscience can be an indication that the dimension of social ethics in moral freedom can lose importance and have a place only in reflection on the question of how the individual as an individual can maintain his personal integrity in social actions that are coloured by individual intentionality instead of an orientation toward public happiness that is implied in prudence as a political virtue. Such an orientation requires a debate on the claim of the objectivity of Catholic ethics[17]

---

[13] F. Furger, *Klugheit und Gewissen in der katholischen Moraltheologie der letzten Jahrzehnte* (Luzern/Stuttgart, 1968), pp. 75-76.

[14] F. Furger, *Klugheit und Gewissen*, p. 64.

[15] F. Furger, *Klugheit und Gewissen*, p. 25.

[16] F. Furger, "Prudence," p. 66.

[17] Cf. A.H.M. van Iersel, *Op zoek naar een 'gewetenloze' politiek: De tegenstelling tussen gezindheidsethiek en verantwoordelijkheidsethiek in het denken van Max Weber in het licht van de tegenstelling tussen conscientia en prudentia*, Doctoral diss. Catholic University of Nijmegen (Nijmegen, 1982).

and the significance that prudence can have in a democratic and rapidly changing society.[18]

Toward a Theology of Conscience

In this closing section I wish to view conscience from a perspective external to theology, which I believe can contribute to what I think is still a necessary *aggiornamento* of the concept of conscience in theology and Church.

The Relation to Psychological Approaches to Conscience

I stated earlier that the psychology of conscience is not to be found in the text of the Catechism. The Catechism would have been well served if it had taken psychology of conscience into account. The explicit orientation toward the psychology of conscience would, for example, have clarified a tension present in the Catechism—the tension between, on the one hand, a concept of conscience that is grafted onto a model of individual growth and, on the other hand, a concept that sees conscience as a product of socialization. Vatican II sought a solution to this tension by elaborating on the two poles of the ambivalence from another perspective on the dignity of the human individual. The principial aspect of the freedom of conscience was linked with the image of the individual person as the image of God; the practical aspect of this was linked with the need to form the conscience, including the ecclesial dimension. The Catechism deals with the tension in a different way: it changes the hierarchy of the aspects. The formation of conscience under the direction of the Church has increased in importance: it has become principial. The Catechism's change from Vatican II's *right to* interiority to *requirement of* interiority, in combination with the stress on the formation of conscience through the Church, can very well be interpreted as a shift from an approach to conscience that is analogous to developmental psychology to an approach in line with socialization theory.

Certain Aspects of the Theme 'Conscience' in Philosophy

The Greek philosopher Socrates already thematized the conscience as a *daimonion*, an internal voice that influenced his choices at crucial moments.[19] In this article I would like to discuss three philosophical approaches, particu-

---

[18] F. Furger, "Prudence."

[19] Cf. G. Vlastos, *Socrates: Ironist and Moral Philosopher* (Cambridge, 1992 (originally published 1991)), pp. 280 f.

larly with respect to their significance for contemporary reflection on conscience from the viewpoint of moral theology. I will attempt to demonstrate the relevance of this for moral theology.

First of all, the view of E. Levinas, whose approach is that of philosophical anthropology, is important. He speaks of the genesis of conscience. In Levinas' view, conscience does not exist before encountering the other but comes into existence when the other looks at me: a way of overcoming and criticizing autarkic individualist variants.[20]

The second approach is one from social philosophy. Here we join in with the idea thematized in the Vatican II, but not in the Catechism, of conscience as a bond between Christians and non-Christians. In theory, this bond offers points of contact for dialogue with the various forms of ethics of communication that have developed since Vatican II. So, for example, in Apel's philosophy dialogue occupies a central place as an instrument in the finding of truth. In this approach a transcendental intersubjectivity is sought in which the conditions of possibilities for intersubjectively valid knowledge are founded in the framework of a communicative community.[21] For this purpose, in a democratic constitutional state adequate procedures for moral communication should be developed.[22]

Both of these philosophical approaches to conscience are relevant for moral theology. I have already discussed that for Vatican II conscience is the bond between Christians and non-Christians. Levinas' approach from philosophical anthropology deepens one's insight into the genesis of conscience. Conscience appears to have been not individual but social in origin. Because of this this orientation can strengthen the social ethical dimension of an ecclesial ethics of conscience. Levinas' philosophy is, after all, a processing of the dehumanizing violence of the Shoah, which went hand in hand with the attempt at dehumanizing the Jews. Levinas stresses the opposite: recognition of the other as a person implies the acceptance of the commandment in the face of the other: you shall not kill. The implications and consequences of Levinas' concept of conscience deserve further examination if moral theology wishes to surmount the theoretical controversy between extreme individualist interpretations of conscience on the one hand and views of the conscience as a product of socialization on the other.

---

[20] Cf. E. Levinas, "La substitution," *Revue Philosophique de Louvain* 66 (1968): 490.

[21] Cf. C.F. Gethmann, "Realität," in: *Handbuch Philosophischer Grundbegriffe* (Studienausgabe), Vol. IV (Munich, 1973), p.1186; F. Böckle, *Fundamentalmoral* (Munich, 1985 (originally published 1977)), p.22.

[22] Cf. J. Habermas, *Recht en moraal*, (Kampen, 1988).

The various forms of the ethics of communication can, in their turn, draw the attention of moral theology to the process of finding truth and the importance of valid procedures within this process. However, the implications of these forms of the ethics of communication, particularly the presupposition of intersubjectivity as an access to valid moral statements, contrast with the objective orientation of Catholic ethics. For this reason as well, with respect to content, the Catechism cannot be easily linked with this approach because it, like the encyclical *Veritatis Splendor*, maintains a concept of the objectivity of ethics in which there is room for an intersubjective process of finding truth only in the form of obtaining advice in the formation of the judgement of conscience, but not for an intersubjective establishment of the validity of values. Nevertheless, an intersubjectively oriented ethics is important on the methodological level and on the level of its communicative strategy.

A third philosophical approach to conscience is that of philosophy of law, which concerns reflection on governments' recognition of conscientious objections. As Vermeulen has indicated, it is not easy for states to work with the concept of conscience because of the multiplicity of meanings that are ascribed to the concept and by the pluriformity of applications of the concept. Vermeulen describes the secularization of the recognition of conscientious objections on the basis of the development of the refusal to serve in the militia: via a recognition of (secular) conscientious objections it has moved from the recognition of strictly religious objections to the recognition of political objections and even selective objections. The conscientious objection can thereby no longer be identified. The consequences of this become visible in the difficulties that a legislator discovers while testing conscientious objections in the framework of a process for juridical (and political) recognition of them.[23] Therefore, moral theology will have to discuss the issue of the public relevance of the conscientious objection.

The Critique of Religion and Conscience

The Catechism discusses the concept of conscience without an explicit relation being made with the critique of religion. Keeping Nietzsche's critique of religion in mind could have sharpened its eye for a potential effect of conscience's obedience to the law of God: the social subjection of the human being who is called to freedom. Nietzsche's critique of the Christian slave morality forces a clarification of the nature and range of moral freedom in its relation to the standardization of conscience with respect to content.

---

[23] B.P. Vermeulen, *De vrijheid van geweten*.

By means of Freud the requirement of interiority could have been elucidated as the superego. Conscience is then seen as the legacy of the Oedipus complex—the internalizing of the strange authority of parental requirements and prohibitions. In this approach it is the view of conscience as voice that is critically analyzed.[24] A critical theological reception of this could have contributed to the formulation of conditions for a healthy handling of conscience's requirement of interiority.

The religious critique of Marx could have sharpened its eye for the social ethical dimension of the freedom of conscience: does the appeal to conscience not usually arise where the abuse of power in economics, politics, culture, or religion threatens the integrity of the one who has less power? A view to Marx's critique of religion could have clarified the social contextuality of the appeal to conscience.

The Conscience Caught Between Internalized Alienation and Hyper-Individual Autonomy

The concept of conscience as it emerges in the Catechism leads to a dilemma for the Magisterium. The first horn of this dilemma is the idea that conscience is the internal expression of an external (derived from God) wrath. This view makes conscience vulnerable to the classical critique of religion regarding conscience as internalized alienation, the critique of contemporary psychology, and the critique arising from analyses of the context of the appeal to conscience, and moreover restricts the influence of the Church on conscience theologically. The advantage of such a concept of conscience is an explicit relation with revelation theology. But it is precisely because of this that the theological concept of conscience in a secularized culture appears to lose public relevance. In this a concept of conscience characterized as Christian becomes viewed as primarily or exclusively relevant for Churches.

The other horn of the dilemma is a theological foundation of the moral autonomy of the ethical subject. Vatican II's theological anthropology, i.e., human beings as being the image of God, can be employed in this way. Such a foundation can lead to the strengthening of the secularization of conscience as it has already been thematized in various scholarly disciplines and is expressed in Western culture. This secularization can be expressed in, among others, the fact that conscience is viewed merely as a judgement or the capacity of the morally autonomous individual to judge. The theological anthropology of the human being as the image of God who can establish a certain

---

[24] Cf. S. Freud, *Das Ich und das Es*, Gesammelte Werke, Vol. III (1923), p. 282.

degree of autonomy has no place in this. The acceptance of this autonomy in science and culture does not accompany the acceptance of its theological foundation. The concept of conscience, based on the theological optimism of the human being as the image of God, appears to gain relevance, but it loses—not in theology but on the part of its dialogue partners—its theological foundation and thereby its identity. This is all the more dramatic, from the perspective of the Magisterium, in the context of a culture that precisely through its appreciation of the autonomy of the subject becomes vulnerable to totalitarianism: the morally autonomous subject closes himself to a critique from the sources of his autonomy, which intend to preserve proper autonomy in the long run. Symptomatic of this is the liberal philosophical view of the conscience as the non-standardized end of moral development and thereby as *norma normans* of ethics.[25]

Thus in its concept of conscience the Magisterium is confronted with the dilemma between confrontation with the surrounding culture because of a specifically Christian concept of conscience on the one hand and assimilation via a universally human concept of conscience on the other. Both options involve risks. Moreover, both options appear to confront the question of how the theological foundation of the concept of conscience in a modern culture can be communicated, or, even more fundamentally, what its content is and even how it can be developed. It is the question of whether Christian ethics of conscience not only methodologically but also with respect to content, can profit by accepting the intersubjectivity of the validity of ethics. The latter is also rejected by the Magisterium for contextual reasons, which is why this reflection leads to the theme of the contextuality of conscience ethics.

The Contextuality of Conscience Ethics

The Polish philosopher and theologian Jòsef Tischner writes that totalitarianism in the form of communism formed a social context in which an essential and not accidental cohesion between faith and ethics was discovered. Religion and ethics combined in a radical ethical link with a type of society other than the state. Against this totalitarianism only a principial and radical resistance was adequate, given that this totalitarianism attempted to commit people to the evil that it represented according to the principle of revenge: the agent of tomorrow is now made a victim who accepts the norms of the regime and appropriates them. The good was more than a principle: it became visible in its bearers. On the basis of these experiences and insights Tischner posits that the Western Thomistic theology is too much directed toward a

---

[25] J.S. Fishkin, *Beyond Subjective Morality: Ethical Reasoning and Political Philosophy* (New Haven/London, 1984).

synthesis with culture. Tischner's analysis clarifies a question that, as appears from the encyclical *Veritatis Splendor*, the current pontificate submits to every moral system, namely, whether it can resist totalitarianism (*Veritatis Splendor* 99). Thus the idea of moral autonomy, as that can also be expressed in a freedom of conscience based on a fundamental anthropology, is experienced from this perspective not as emancipative, anti-authoritarian, and anti-totalitarian, but rather as a symptom of vulnerability: the 'open-ended character' of an 'autonomous ethics' makes it vulnerable to becoming synthesized with totalitarian systems. Subjects who judge autonomously can, after all, come to different conclusions with regard to the answer offered to the moral challenges of totalitarianism. Moreover, the idea of an 'autonomous ethics' conflicts in its content with the intrinsic relation postulated by Tischner between belief and ethics in the opposition against totalitarianism. Nor is the individualism that can be expressed in a perfect freedom of conscience compatible with the insight that "Totalitarianism arises out of a denial of truth in the objective sense" (*Veritatis Splendor* 99).

If the insight is correct that the ethics of conscience that is recapitulated in the Catechism is contextual in the sense that it is rooted in the struggle against totalitarianism, then it is all the more necessary to assume, as does the Encyclical *Pacem in Terris* and the Pastoral Constitution *Gaudium et Spes*, an explicit analysis of the context in discussing the conscience, so that the application of the ecclesial doctrine is made more accessible for a hermeneutical translation. Here an important question will be: under which conditions can subjectivistic, objectivistic, and intersubjective moral systems stand up to the risks that totalitarianism contains? Because in answering this question *qualitate qua* the social ethical aspects of the conscience will be involved, it is not impossible that by means of the concept of prudence new connections must be sought between politics and ethics and that the relation between concepts of conscience informed by moral theology and the juridical concepts of conscience must be reevaluated as well. But this reevaluation assumes not only a prioritizing of virtue ethics above the ethics of conscience but also a reworking of Aristotelian ethics with its concern for the nature of the human being as a political animal right from the beginning.[26]

---

[26] Cf. M. Nussbaum, *Politieke dieren: Aristoteles over de natuur en het menselijk bedrijf*, Pierre Bayle lecture (1991).

SEVEN

Sin as the Disruptor of Relationships

Annelies van Heijst

Introduction

In 1946 Pope Pius XII expressed the conviction that people of his time were no longer in a position to experience sin. He stated, "The greatest evil of today is that people have begun to lose the concept of sin."[1] What is remarkable about his formulation is that reproach and exoneration go hand in hand. On the one hand Pius XII accuses people of a fading moral consciousness, yet on the other hand it appears that they can do little about it because their knowledge of what sin is is becoming increasingly deficient. Just as remarkable is the fact that this statement does not attest to self-reflection on ecclesiastical proclamations concerning sin. In other words, there is no connection whatsoever between the manner in which the Church proclaims the concept of sin in doctrine and pastoral practice, on the one hand, and the concept of sin that is being lost by believers on the other. Pius XII was not alone when he made this statement. Bernard Häring, author of the standard work in moral theology *The Law of Christ*,[2] remarked that for many of his contemporaries the awareness of sin was no more than a psychological category, a sort of unhealthy guilt feeling, that must be put aside. According to Häring, what was wanted was a morality without sin.

The similarity between Pius XII and Häring consists of both pointing to the hermeneutical hollowing-out of the theological concept as such: apparently it has become difficult to explain in a way that addressed and was comprehensible to people in the second half of the twentieth century the precise existential, believing and experiential reality to which the theological concept of sin appealed. Generally speaking, contemporary theologians demonstrate two types of solutions to this problem. Either they look for the cause in the

---

[1] Quoted by K.-W. Merks, "Omgaan met het kwaad. Een moraaltheologische beschouwing," in: *Contactblad voor het justitiepastoraat* 45 (1994) 3: 2-16, 7.

[2] B. Häring, *The Law of Christ: Moral Theology for Priests and Laity* (Paramus, NJ, 1961).

believers and point out their deficient understanding or else they basically bury their head in their own theological sand and ask whether there is something wrong with the way in which Church and theology today has explained and applied the category of sin. In the first case, the deficient concept of sin is viewed as evidence of a deterioration of moral consciousness or as being itself an illustration of the sinful condition of the modern world. In the second case, the theologian does not point accusingly at the believer(s) but engages primarily theological, ecclesiastical, and pastoral self-criticism.

The Inflation of the Concept of Sin

Whoever says 'sin' says 'guilt'. These two concepts can be distinguished but not separated, and they often appear together in everyday speech as well as in ecclesiastical and theological expostulations. In speaking about sin, the theological dimension of moral guilt is emphatically included. Sin is the recognized and familiar moral guilt 'before God' (*coram Deo*).[3] This distinction does not constitute a problem conceptually, but it is problematic with respect to experience, since contemporary theologians all seem to agree on the notion that the concepts of sin and guilt are subject to strong inflation in the everyday linguistic use.

The Enlightenment critique of Christianity was followed by the sharp condemnation of Christianity in the nineteenth century by Friedrich Nietzsche, who criticized Christian morality in particular. He accused Judaism and Christianity of a "slave morality,"[4] and his criticism turned the Christian scale of values upside down. In his opinion classical antiquity had a morality which "owed its origin to noble, *male* instincts,"[5] sustained by people with a strong will, vigour, power, and beauty. Life is supposed to struggle instinctively toward growth and the accumulation of power: where the will to power is lacking, there is, in Nietzsche's eyes, decline.[6] In his eyes, "Everything that heightens the feeling of power in man, the will to power, power itself" is good; "Everything that is born of weakness" is bad and,

---

[3] D. Mieth, "Wieweit kann man 'Schuld' and 'Sünde' trennen?" in: *Theologisch Quartalschrift* 160 (1980): 184-91.

[4] F. Nietzsche, *On the Genealogy of Morals* in: *Basic Writings of Nietzsche*, tr. and ed. Walter Kaufmann (New York, 1966), p.470.

[5] F. Nietzsche, *The Antichrist* in: *The Portable Nietzsche*, tr. and ed. Walter Kaufmann (Harmondsworth, 1954), p.652.

[6] F. Nietzsche, *The Antichrist*, p.572.

most damaging of all is the "active pity for all the failures and all the weak: Christianity."[7] For Nietzsche, this perversion has caused humanity a great deal of misery, because it is contrary to the process of natural selection: it is not the strong and vigourous who are elevated, but the weak and needy. Nietzsche's implicit anthropological presupposition is that of an independent, fit, adult and strong man: all others, including the people who are in phases of life that require care, are kept outside of consideration. As a concept of people this is too restricted and too vitalistic, but his critique is relevant to those schools of Christianity that have encouraged self-deception, self-humiliation, and suffering as if they were spiritual virtues.[8] Nietzsche felt that sin and guilt were nothing other than discoveries by a priestly caste that wishes to continue exercising their power. By pressing the believers into an awareness of sin and a feeling of guilt, they denied them freedom and autonomy.

Nietzsche's hermeneutics of suspicion with regard to the concept of sin received support in the twentieth century from various social scientific insights. These further complicated the classical concept of sin, particularly with respect to the dimension of deliberate consent and free choice which necessarily accompany the theological concept of sin. Depth psychology, psychiatry, and pedagogy made the definition of guilt even more difficult because the determinations and restrictions due to birth, upbringing, environment, and hereditary defects were increasingly viewed as factors that to a large degree directed human actions. It is very difficult then to determine what room is left for free choice. Because the view of social sciences on human actions is different from that of the traditional religious view, the social sciences generated new views on guilt and led to a different way of dealing with it. It is characteristic that under the influence of the social sciences guilt is no longer seen as something that one can take upon oneself (confession and doing penance) or as something from which one can be freed (based on a model of a transcendental reality of salvation). On the contrary, feelings of guilt are nowadays seen as something from which one can and must free oneself through therapy (based on a model of self-liberation).

In addition to this psychological approach to guilt there is another tendency that has become evident, namely, turing the concept of guilt into a juridical matter. Jurisprudence appears increasingly to be the only remaining public domain in which one can speak of 'guilt' and in which guilt can be connected with (judicial) sanctions. From a theological point of view, there

---

[7] F. Nietzsche, *The Antichrist*, p.570.

[8] H. Fortmann, psychologist and priest, has combatted this type of 'spirituality' specifically and promoted a more integral view on psychological and religious health. See his *Heel de mens: Reflecties over de menselijke mogelijkheden* (Baarn, 1972).

are five restrictions to a judicial view of the concept of guilt. First, guilt can be seen in a juridical sense only insofar as it involves guilt that has been *proven* legally. However, there are many circumstances possible in which a person who has not been judged is nevertheless guilty, or is more guilty than can be expressed in the judgement. In other words, there can be a guilt greater than that which is apparent from the sentence. Secondly, the factor of remorse or repentance cannot be taken into account in the judgement that is rendered. Perpetrators who spend time in jail can emerge with an unchanged (in theological terms) 'sinful' attitude. Thirdly (and the converse of the factor just mentioned), the equality principle of the law leaves no room for the (theological) category of mercy, in which the possibility exists of allowing mercy to take the place of justice. Fourthly, in Western law the victim has structurally marginal place, which means that the offended party, the one who is the victim of the perpetrator and with whom relations are broken, is not involved in the entire process of the law—which also means that the broken relation cannot be restored. (At the very most, a victim can receive reimbursement for damages through a civil suit and feel satisfaction when the perpetrator is sentenced.)[9] Fifthly, there is a discrepancy between the juridical understanding of 'doing justice' and the biblical concept of justice. In the biblical sense of the word, justice implies a restoration of proper relations, with regard to both the offended party and the guilty one, who finds a new relationship toward others, toward him/herself, and toward God. In themselves the restrictions that adhere to the judicial concept of guilt are not bad; the regulations of the law call for certain restrictions. They become bad when, because of the omission of religion as a public domain that obtains for all and from which a moral claim originates, the law is seen as the only and also the most adequate place in which social guilt can be made visible.

As far as 'sin' still functions in everyday language it is used in a morally and religiously neutral sense, as in expressions such as: "It is a sin that the glass is broken," or, "I have sinned against my diet." From the examples that given in Van Dale's dictionary of the Dutch language it is evident that the word sin in the religious sense is loaded primarily with sexual connotations. It is said of an attractive woman that she "is well worth the sin," an unlawfully born child is called "a child of sin," and prostitutes are said to live a life "of sin".[10] Furthermore, the concept 'guilt' is no longer a central category in

---

[9] For a critical discussion on this, see H. Bianchi, *Gerechtigheid als vrijplaats: De terugkeer van het slachtoffer in ons recht* (Baarn, 1985).

[10] Also see H. Wiersinga, *Doem of daad: Een boek over zonde* (Baarn, 1982), pp. 7-8.

the manner in which most Christians view themselves and the world. Christians are much more inclined to see 'neighbourly love', 'justice', and 'liberation/emancipation' as key words for their faith. At the end of the twentieth century the concepts of sin and guilt have been levelled and hollowed out. With regard to overwhelming evil on a large scale in the form of war, violence, and hunger—news and images of which are presented daily by the media—two reactions are dominant: either a resigned pessimism (the absurdity and tragedy of existence) or an optimistic belief in progress (evolution or revolution will make everything turn out right in time). 'Guilt' no longer seems to be an adequate concept for understanding gruesome realities. In the examples above, sin and guilt in the personal as well as the collective sense are hardly relevant categories any more for the understanding of reality.

It is evident, from this sketch of the view of sin and guilt currently dominant in the West European context, that the connection is anything but seamless between contemporary understanding and ecclesiastical language. Liturgical language and sermons show a nearly unbroken and continuous tradition in speaking about sin. Here sin is viewed as an offence against God and the divine law, and Christ who has come to redeem us from our sins. But nowhere is it indicated what experiential reality corresponds to that. That battle of interpretation is left to the believer. But that interpretation becomes increasingly difficult, and so the ecclesiastical vocabulary in liturgy and sermons grows more and more remote from everyday life and experience.

'Sin' in the Catechism of the Catholic Church

Two tracks becomes visible in the late twentieth-century Catholic theological way of speaking about sin. I refer to them as the ecclesiastical way of speaking on the one hand and the theological way of speaking on the other (which is not to say that the ecclesiastical way of speaking could not be theological but it depends on who is speaking). On the ecclesiastical side it is attempted, in line with tradition, to continue to promote that which should be believed about sin: sin as a disruption of the good relations between God and people and as an attack on 'the eternal law' which rational human beings are able to know. The passage on sin in the *Catechism of the Catholic Church* (1846-1876) is an example of this. In this passage the type of concept of God and the scriptural orientation are striking. The concept of God that the reader of this passage encounters already in the first sentence is not that of the patriarchal punishing and wrathful God who will teach the sinner, the trespasser of divine law. Rather, it is the merciful and loving God, who graciously waits for the sinners and has sent his own Son to redeem them.

The first sentence sets a certain tone: "The gospel is the revelation in Jesus Christ of God's mercy to sinners" (1846). This passage actually implies a relationship to the historical ecclesiastical practice because a critical attitude is taken with respect to the legalistic and casuistic interpretation of the concept of sin that has arisen since the seventeenth century and with respect to the rigorous practice of penance that was connected to it (a practice that was legitimized by the image of God as the vengeful and stern Father-God). However, this critical attitude is very implicit. There is no talk of a 'confession' of one's own pastoral deficiency here. Subsequently the classical distinction between 'mortal sin' and 'venial sin' is once again pushed forward as the central structural principle for determining the weight of the sin. A biblical foundation is ascribed to this structural principle, but in the same sentence it is acknowledged that it is particularly a matter of theological tradition: "The distinction between mortal and venial sin, already evident in Scripture, became part of the tradition of the Church" (1854). The description of mortal sin reads as follows: "*Mortal sin* destroys charity in the heart of man by a grave violation of God's law; it turns man away from God, who is his ultimate end and his beatitude, by preferring an inferior good to Him" (1855). To be able to speak of a mortal sin three conditions must be fulled simultaneously: the sin must have grave matter as its object, be committed with full knowledge, and with deliberate consent (1857). A venial sin is committed when, in a less serious matter, a standard prescribed by the moral law is transgressed, or 'when he disobeys the moral law in a grave matter, but without full knowledge or without complete consent' (1862).

For the rest the scriptural interpretation is striking in that it revolves primarily around Paul's texts, the Ten Commandments insofar as they are echoed in the New Testament (Mark 10:19), and the concept of hubris in the story of the Fall. There is an explicit reference to Genesis 3:5, which contains the description of 'the first sin', and the ordinal indication of 'first' seems here to indicate a paradigm or prototype of sin, or original sin in general. This 'first sin' is "disobedience, a revolt against God through the will to become like gods"—a classification that is supplemented with "love of oneself even to contempt of God" (1850).

After, and in addition to this biblical foundation of the concept of sin, there are also many non-biblical distinctions with regard to sin that have arisen in tradition. These distinctions are summed up one after another, through which they collectively yet at the same time fragmentarily evoke an image of many forms of wrong behaviour. They mention, for example, blasphemy against the Holy Spirit, the "capital sins" (St. John Cassian and St. Gregory the Great), and the "sins that cry to heaven" (Peter Canisius). The (also non-biblical) distinction between "venial sin" and "mortal sin" is also heavily stressed once again, which evokes reminiscences of the old style of catechisms. The *Catechism* conforms to tradition by requiring that for sins to be classified as mortal three conditions must be simultaneously met: the sin must have a grave matter as its object, be committed with full knowledge, and with deliberate consent. All explanations of sin involve individual sinners primarily. Only at the end of the treatment, just before the summary "In Brief," is there a discussion of a concept of sin that is suprapersonal. There, in a short paragraph and without further specification, it is remarked that sins give rise to social situations and institutions that are contrary to divine goodness and for this reason are "structures of sin" or "social sin" (1869). The fact that there is no mention of this in the summary demonstrates that this paragraph is regarded as only marginally important.

Given the concept of God, the scriptural orientation, the fact that it does not single out sexual sins, and its mention of the social and structural dimensions of sin, this discussion on sin attempts theologically to initiate an *aggiornamento*, or adapted renewal. But the question is whether this attempt is pursued consistently enough to realize a new interpretation. Between the ordinary concept of sin and the ecclesiastical/theological interpretation such as the one that is sounded once again in the *Catechism* there is a gap that cannot be bridged very easily. This gap has a historical dimension, because a certain type of moral theology has classified negative effects. For this reason the concept of sin should be theologically expressed in a new way so that the one-sidedness and restrictions that for centuries have been characteristic of the Christian way of speaking about sin and guilt can be overcome: a legalistic concept of sin that is geared to the individual and preoccupied with sex (a concept of sin in which the sixth and ninth commandments are regarded as particularly relevant).

Only if the theological concept of sin and guilt is explored once again from the point of view of the experiential categories of contemporary humans living in various situations and contexts can it once again acquire theological relevance. This does not simply ask for an interpretation but demands a *re*interpretation, that is, the discovery (and rediscovery) of expressions, images, symbols, and rituals in the area of sin and guilt that are comprehensible to Christians on the threshold of the third millennium. Given my own horizon of understanding, I will concentrate on the West European context in particular, which is not to say that it must (still) be theologically normative for the entire world. Theoretically, theologians from various continents would, each in their own way, and speaking from within their own situations and in their own stylistic form, make a similar outline. Together, these theologians could give form to a 'Catechism' which, when combined, could speak to people all over the world.

In the above something has already been said about a second track that becomes visible, namely, the track present in the discussions of contemporary theologians. In the last few decades there have been attempts from various theological viewpoints to re-think the concepts of sin and guilt in their topicality and relevance.

New Theological Orientations

In the last few decades various theologians have attempted to contextualize the concept of sin and to make it of current interest. All these approaches, from Piet Schoonenberg to political theology, liberation theology, and women's studies theology, have in common that they define the relation between personal and collective guilt, between individual and communal sin in a new way. Whereas traditional Catholic moral theology placed the emphasis particularly on the individual failures of a person before the face of God, now more attention is paid to the communal and structural dimension of evil and sin. Within the presence of this structural dimension individual persons are both victim and offender: they become involved in a situation that was already characterized by sin and guilt, and they are at the same time jointly responsible (and therefore jointly guilty) for the continuation of this situation.

In this way the dogmatician and exegete Piet Schoonenberg made an explicit connection between 'sin' and 'original sin'. He was concerned with overcoming the division that had developed in Catholic theology in which original sin was treated in the doctrine of creation, while personal sin was treated in moral theology. To convey the cohesion between individual sin and human solidarity in sin, Schoonenberg did not refer to Genesis 3 but to the Johannine concept of "the sin of the world" (John 1:29). In his description sin is the revolt against God in God's salvific actions and creation, and is therefore implicitly a corruption of people and the world. In this sense both creation and redemption are polarities that are held together as God and human beings. Theological drafts, such as that of Piet Schoonenberg (and Edward Schillebeeckx and Karl Rahner, who must be mentioned here) have prepared the way for a new conceptualization of sin and guilt—a way of which grateful use would be made by political theologians, liberation theologians, and feminist theologians.

In political theology, liberation theology, and women's studies theology attention has shifted even more from the individual to the structural component and the individual person is sometimes even left somewhat in the background. In their respective political theologies Johann Baptist Metz and Dorothee Sölle wanted to articulate the ancient theological theme of sin and guilt in the context of contemporary social relationships in the modern period. These relationships were characterized as relationships of injustice. With their social and political critique Metz and Sölle affected the emancipative and progressive beliefs both in the West and in the so-called 'Third' World. This situation which developed historically was classified as 'sinful' and human history was thereby a 'history of guilt'. Although the critique of the political theologians pertained to social structures, it had specific implications on the subject. The sinful situation consisted precisely of large groups of people who were in reality denied the chance of becoming subjects: they could not become that which they potentially were because of social and political repression. This becoming a subject is described by Metz as the realization of God's actual intention for people, and he calls it "downwards transcendence (*Transzendenz nach unten*)".[11] However, becoming a subject requires a radical turnabout. People from the rich Western countries in particular should embark on a process of liberation in which they discard that which structurally marks their sinful situation. They must liberate themselves from riches, consumerism, apathy, the delusion of innocence, political and economic dominance and domination.

Liberation theologians such as Gustavo Gutiérrez[12] and Leonardo Boff, having been taught by Western political theologians, gave their own interpretation of the concept of sin from their 'Third' World context. Linking up with the sorrow and fear of contemporary humans mentioned in *Gaudium et Spes*, particularly among the poor and oppressed, liberation theologians placed the poor at the centre of theological interest. Poverty, underdevelopment, marginality, and oppression of the greater part of the population in these continents were theologically interpreted as institutionalized injustice and a sinful situation. Liberation theologians believed that this situation called Christians to devote themselves to liberation and humanizing commitment. Also within the various types of liberation theology, theology is viewed as the critical reflection on a praxis that has developed historically. This includes not only social praxis but also includes, emphatically, ecclesiastical praxis. For this reason liberation theology is also a self-critical reflection to the degree to which ecclesiastical institutions and ecclesiastical representatives are jointly responsible for the situation of the repression of the poor. This self-critical reflection will not founder in despair but is characterized by the call for *metanoia*: a turnabout that leads to a praxis of liberation.

Furthermore, liberation theology places the poor at the centre as those who embody the hope for change and liberation. In this sense subjects that are practically invisible in theology—the poor and their history—are brought to the attention of theology. Liberation theology is rooted in the experiences

---

[11] J.B. Metz, *Unsere Hoffnung* 1, 5 (94), cited in M. Sievernich, *Schuld und Sünde in der Theologie der Gegenwart* (Frankfurt am Main, 1982), p. 221.

[12] G. Gutiérrez, *A Theology of Liberation* (New York, 1973).

of the anguish of people who suffer injustice. For theology this means that intellectual academic interest must give way to interest in a liberating praxis for and with the poor. This turnabout assumes a conversion of the theologian herself, in the sense of Matthew 20:26-28, where serving is specifically mentioned for the emulation of and in analogy with the Good Samaritan, who revealed himself to be a true neighbour in his caring attitude.

Just as in political theology, in liberation theology sin is not primarily conceptualized as a personal act but as a reality that manifests itself in society and historical reality. This does not detract from the fact that individual people sin and must repent, but the chief emphasis lies on sin as it becomes visible in institutions and structures. These institutions and structures are themselves 'the work of humans' and the (joint) responsibility for them cannot be brushed aside. These structures also need to convert, but they do not convert of themselves unless people are actively involved in such conversion. Thus the liberation from sin, which is both a promise in Christ and at the same time a task for Christians, cannot occur on the level of internal conversion alone but has to take shape in the community.

In women's studies theology 'sin' is thematized in a gender-specific manner. Analogous to political and liberation theology, sin is primarily defined structurally and historically. The domination of the female sex by the male sex—a domination that has acquired its form historically—is sinful.[13] Sexism manifests itself both on the level of social structures and within micro relationships in the private domain. Not only social and political relationships are marked by sexism but personal relationships (even love relationships) are marked in this way as well. Because problems experienced as individual have a social component and a structural root, a division between 'public' and 'private' is a false dichotomy. The sin of sexism pervades the whole societal world on all levels.

It is characteristic of women's studies theology that Church and theology itself are referred to as institutional joint causes of the evil of sexism. Thus Mary Daly, one of the founders of women's studies theology, sees the Genesis story of the Fall as a paradigm for the patriarchal structure of the Christian religion as a whole.[14] There Eve, although the second one to be created (and, on the basis of that 'fact', traditionally depicted as a second-class person), is the first to be deceived, and is thereby the instigator of sin.

---

[13] See, for example, R.R. Radford Ruether, *Sexism and God-Talk: Toward a Feminist Theology* (Boston, 1983), pp. 173-83.

[14] M. Daly, *Beyond God the Father* (Boston, 1973), pp. 47ff.

In the Christian tradition the figure of the guilty and sexually deceived Eve has come to stand in a binary opposition to the figure of the innocent (immaculately conceived) mother-virgin Mary. This bipolar image of women has greatly influenced the Christian image of women, both in the way in which men expressed their desires, longings, and projections concerning women and in the way in which women experienced themselves as women. Women were either thoroughly good or thoroughly bad, with few options between saint and whore. There was no room in this restrictive image for the much less simple way in which most women concretely experienced themselves. It must be established that in the continuation of the formation of the image around Eve 'the woman' in Christianity could obtain as a symbol for 'evil' in general. Tertullian's well-known saying about women being 'the gate to the devil'[15] can be seen as a *pars pro toto* for this sexist tradition.

Beginning with the position that the classical theological concept of sin has concentrated on the revolt against and disobedience toward God and the associated desire—by way of ultimate overestimation of one's powers—to become like God (*hubris* or *superbia*), the following feminist critique on the concept of sin has been developed by theologians such as Valerie Saiving,[16] Judith Plaskow, Christine Schaumberger, and Luise Schottroff. They view the notion of sin as *hubris* as an androcentric conceptualization that completely ignores the experiences of most women. The question is who in fact the people who actually strive to be equal to God are. And what facts are revealed when the life situation of women is investigated? For the answers to these questions Judith Plaskow consulted Simone de Beauvoir, psychology, and literary sources (particularly Doris Lessing's cycle of novels *Children of Violence*, whose main character is a person named Martha Quest).[17] Plaskow—and many feminist theologians with her—established that experiential world of women is sooner characterized by endurance and apathy, by the feeling of having no grip on the situation and a deficiency of initiative rather than by an excessive self-conceit and rebelliousness. Building on Saiving and Plaskow, Marjorie Hewitt Suchocki recently developed a feminist theological

---

[15] Tertullian, *De Cultu Feminarum*, I, 1, in: Migne, *Patrologia Latina* (Paris, 1844), Vol. II, col. 304-05.

[16] Already in 1960 V. Saiving (then V. Saiving-Goldstein) published an article now regarded as foundational for women's studies theology: "The Human Situation: A Feminine View," in: *Journal of Religion* 40 (April 1960): 100-12. Here she elaborates on the differences in how women and men interpret the concepts 'sin' and 'guilt'. With this article she laid a foundation for later feminist critique of sin.

[17] J. Plaskow, *Sex, Sin and Grace: Women's Experiences and the Theologies of Reinhold Niebuhr and Paul Tillich* (Lanham/New York/London, 1980).

interpretation of 'original sin' as "the violence of rebellion against creation."[18] According to her the original sin was not revolt against God but a violent tearing of creation with all that lives in it. In a sexist society it is often women and nature that become the victims of that violence.

Also typical of the experiences of many women is an excess of feelings of guilt, often connected with individual corporality and sexuality. It is precisely because women—not in the least in and through the Christian tradition—are so strongly identified with the physical, sexual, and natural that they have so many undeserved feelings of guilt. The feminine feelings of guilt often exist without an actually demonstrable object, that is to say, that they are not the result of an actual deficiency or mistake committed by the woman in question. The feminist writer Renate Dorrestein indicates this vague feminine feeling of guilt with the phrase, "Sorry for the rain"—an apology by which the woman involved exhibits evidence of feeling guilty for almost everything that goes wrong in the world.

The question posed by feminist theology thus asks: how would a woman in such an experiential context would be guilty of *hubris*, disobedience, rebellion, and too much self-conceit? And, following from this, is it not much more of a sin that women demonstrate too much obedience and too little independence? Does their behaviour not sooner attest to a lack of self-love rather than too much of it? On the basis of this feminist theologians have criticized the universalist claim that is implied by the classical theological conceptualization of sin as *hubris*. After all, *hubris* is 'the' universal human sin. In fact, however, this mirrors the concept of sin chiefly as experiences of men—in particular men who are in positions in which they can exercise power and influence. (Something similar obtains for the subjects of liberation theology, the poor, as for women because they are also in a situation that permits too little self-initiative rather than too much.) In summary, the acknowledgement that the classical theological conceptualization of sin is limited and associated with a certain group necessitates a breaking open of this conceptualization so that experiences of 'sin' other than those mentioned thus far can also be taken into account.[19]

Against the background of the juridical language mentioned earlier in connection with the concepts of sin and guilt, it must be noted that from the point of view of women's studies theology this juridical language has had a

---

[18] M. H. Suchocki, *The Fall to Violence: Original Sin in Relational Theology* (New York, 1994), p.16.

[19] See L. Scherzberg, *Sünde und Gnade in der Feministischen Theologie* (Mainz, 1990); C. Schaumberger and L. Schottroff, *Schuld und Macht: Studien zu einer femistischen Befreiungstheologie* (Munich, 1988).

positive side-effect. In the last two decades a number of abuses with regard to the violation of the physical integrity of women (in particular, the abuse of women by their partners, through incest, rape, and sexual intimidation) have been taken out of the privacy of the private sector and made public as a social problem that is connected with the patriarchal structuring of the relationship of the sexes. It is jurisprudence that has functioned here as the platform and public podium from which violations of the dignity of women could be expressed and, subsequently, charged.[20] The effect of this has been that public opinion concerning this has changed. Whereas the accusing finger used to be pointed quickly at the woman herself and the problem was individualized, now a way of thinking has arisen that places the responsibility where it belongs, namely, with the offender who grew up within sexist social structures. Thus, in the realm of justice it has apparently been possible—to a certain degree—to identify as 'evil', to press charges against, and punish that which previously remained hidden from the eyes of the world. This has led to an increase in moral sensitivity on an international level, as is apparent from the campaign *Human Rights are Women's Rights* that was launched by Amnesty International in 1995.[21]

Central Features

Which central features have emerged in the multiplicity of new theological notions on sin and guilt of the last decades? The first thing that one notices is that there are clear differences of emphasis within schools (this holds, for example, for liberation theology as well as women's studies theology), by which it becomes difficult to outline one all-encompassing framework into which all initiatives fit. These differences are in themselves an expression of the strong historical awareness that has arisen. Theology as reflection on the understanding of faith cannot do anything but indicate this understanding of faith in and from within the historical situation, that is to say, in the context in which questioning and searching people believe, with the result that this

---

[20] See A. van Heijst, "De rechter als God de vader: Over grenzen tussen goed en kwaad als voorwaarde tot vergeving," in: *Tijdschrift voor Geestelijk Leven* 43 (1987) 4: 357-69.

[21] The campaign was launched in the framework of preparation for the World Conference of Women in Beijing (September 1995): the abuse of women within the family is the most common form of violence against women worldwide. Furthermore, the campaign is directed against the murder of female babies, the burning alive of brides in India, and the mutilation of female genitals in Africa, the Middle East, and Asia.

historical contextuality is echoed in theology itself. In spite of the differences, we can distinguish a number of central features that are worth mentioning, since they set the Church's discussion of sin in relief.[22]

The first such feature is the search for an experiential access to the theme of sin and guilt with the purpose of transcending the gap between the spheres of faith and life. The result is that quite a few theologians do not begin with the classical doctrine of sin but with the understanding of sin and guilt as it presents itself in the actual experiences of (groups of) people. A second feature is that theologians rarely begin with individual transgressions in human history but much more often begin with the universal experience of contemporary people who feel they have been handed over to anonymous powers and social structures that control them and in which evil is crystallized. A third feature is that individual guilt against God is scarcely thematized. Much more attention is paid to evil in human history and evil mediated through institutions, through which people have come to find themselves in a situation that is constrained and alienated. This is not to say that theologians completely disconnect sin and guilt from the individual, rendering it anonymous. Rather, they indicate a change in the experience of guilt and of the consciousness of guilt by emphatically placing the individual in his/her concrete social and historically situated background. The personal responsibility for bearing guilt, also before God, is thematized more indirectly than directly.[23] It follows from this that it is apparently no longer obvious that the relationship between people and God be classified as a direct and personal relationship.

A fourth feature is that the moralistic concept of sin that is grafted onto legal categories, has been superseded by a more theological concept of sin that is grafted onto the freedom of the creature before God. At the same time much attention is paid to the way in which this free room given by the Creator to people is restricted by the social and historical reality in which the power of sin is a reality. People are caught up in this constraining reality and contribute to it by being inadequate or sinning. The gift and task of being a co-creator therefore implies responsibility and a chance to achieve, as well as a chance of being inadequate and failing. Thus sin is basically seen as the

---

[22] See F. Böckle, *Fundamentalmoral* (Munich, 1977), particularly the explanation on "Schuld und Sünde in theologischer Reflexion," pp. 121-67.

[23] See, for example, M.H. Suchocki, *The Fall to Violence* (1994), p. 16: "Sin is the violation of creation, and therefore a rebellion against creation's well-being. Insofar as creation involves God as creator, sin also entails a violation against God. But sin is defined primarily from the perspective of its relation to creation, whether self or other, and only secondarily defined in terms of its relation to God."

refusal of (good) relationships, in particular with regard to others, but also with regard to nature (recently given elaboration in drafts on environmental ethics). A fifth feature is that the problem of moral evil is not treated separately from the issue of evil in general—as if this was an issue falling under another category—but to place it within this framework.

A last feature concerns the way in which the new theological outlines on salvation are discussed. On the one hand, it is striking that the theologians mentioned above do not wish to separate sin and redemption. On the contrary, it is precisely from the eschatological, expectant, and hopeful perspectives of salvation that sin and guilt are discussed. On the other hand, it is striking that an awareness of redemption geared purely toward the individual's interiority is dismissed. The salvation that has already been realized through Christ as well as salvation yet to be proclaimed do not occur only or even primarily, in the individual human heart. The reality of redemption is more concerned with objective social structures which need to be liberated from their repressive features and effects. In this connection, salvation through Christ means that the anathema of the objective lack of freedom in which the subject finds herself is broken and a new beginning is made possible. Subjects are addressed with respect to their abilities to be jointly responsible for the rise of new 'just' structures and relations. The eschatological tension between 'already' and 'not yet', also in a situation that is marked by sin, makes it difficult to foster hope and expectation. Redemption that has already been experienced lies hidden in the human freedom to perform 'just' actions and in the ability to aid in the building up of a creation that will ultimately be redeemed. It must be noted (and this certainly obtains for women's studies theology at least) that most theologians give more weight to human responsibility and the nature of reality as a task than to the divine salvific initiative or the nature of reality as a gift.

Furthermore, it can be noted in political theology, liberation theology, and women's studies theology that the imitation motif apparently drowns out the soteriological motif. In other words, proportionally more attention is paid to Jesus than to the Christ. Doing as Jesus did (bringing salvation, restoring good relations among people in the name of God and in this way making the Kingdom of God present) obtains as an important inspiration and evocation in all these types of theology. 'Imitation' is then chiefly following an example, and witnessing to a spiritual/moral attitude of faith from which—in a personal way—Christians can determine what attitude they should have toward fellow human beings, themselves, and God. Ethics and spirituality are interwoven here: a non-legalistic ethic and a spirituality orientated toward Jesus intertwine. From the point of view of imitation, doing good is considerably more important, and considerably more, than simply abandoning evil. Which standards obtain as 'good' can be seen from the example of Jesus.

Re-interpretation

How does the classification of recent theological insights concerning sin and guilt mentioned above relate to the manner in which the *Catechism* speaks about this theme? If we take these insights seriously then a number of 'interpretation problems' arise, which do not make the text more accessible. To begin with, there are various expressions that exclude female readers: a person who considers his/her actions carefully is called 'the father of his acts' (1749); and when a similarity is established between the unity of the divine persons and the harmony among people, the latter is indicated as 'the fraternity that men are to establish among themselves in truth and love' (1878).

Furthermore, there is a strong concentration on the problem of personal guilt and relatively little attention paid to the *Umwelt* component of sin and its collective structural nature which has become so prominent in recent theological approaches. The *Catechism* would have been more persuasive if these insights had been integrated and received more attention. Nor should one neglect to mention, as I have established on the basis of numerous reactions of my students on the passage on sin in the *Catechism*, that for the generation of Catholics who grew up with the old Catechism this new edition gives rise to some resentment because the way in which it is composed causes one to think of the past. What pains this group of readers is the somewhat uninviting atmosphere of 'god and commandment' which they encounter. It must be noted that readers with an ecclesiastical background other than Catholic or readers of a younger generation are conspicuously more positive in their reaction to the text. This is because it involves readers who, given their biography, are much more neutral toward this text and do not have undesirable memories triggered by this text. They bring a different horizon of understanding to the text and apparently read with a different attitude. They said they were particularly touched by various passages and sentences which they called 'concise' and 'beautiful'. A young man said: "'In the heart also resides charity, the source of the good and pure works, which sin wounds.' That is pure poetry!" (See no. 1853).

It may be that contemporary theologians raise issues relevant to the *Catechism*, but, conversely, the *Catechism* also poses a question to the different theological schools mentioned above. It seems to me that the main question is whether something will be lost to view in the exploration of the experiential categories of contemporary people, because it can hardly be mentioned any more in Western culture on the threshold of the third millennium. When it involves sin as a disruptor of relations theologians speak primarily of the relations people have with one another, with nature, and with themselves. The *coram Deo* aspect retreats to the background; if they do speak of the relation to God, they do so by, as it were, embedding it in and making it an aspect of the other relations mentioned. (By this I do not mean to suggest that the relation between people and God could be experienced and theologically conceptualized as separate from the relational connectedness of fellow human beings and the creation; I simply wish to focus attention on the fact that the experience of a personal relation to God has apparently become inaccessible.) In other words, the contemporary theological ways of speaking mirror the existing embarrassment of speaking about the relation between people and God as a personal and relational reality that exists of itself.

It is difficult, apparently, to find images, stories, and symbols that appeal to contemporary believers (and I refer to 'believers' in the broad sense: those who, from an ecclesiastical point of view, are to be found within, on the edge of, or even outside of the Church). Which images, stories, and symbols are still able to express the personal relation of human beings to God, including the social relational dimension and the relation to creation? Viewed in this light one can understand the strong emphasis placed on the personal relation between people and God in the *Catechism* and the *Catechism* can be seen to contain a critique of an opaque modern faith. I read the emphasis on the personal relation between human beings and God as the expression of a particular concern. The concern does not involve primarily a failing knowledge of sin but, if possible, the more fundamental problem of the loss of an awareness of the personal involvement between human beings and God. This (spiritual and moral) reality is no longer a part of everyday experience for most people, and is hardly cultivated any more in the public sphere. From a theological point of view, therefore, there is more going on than a crisis in the understanding of sin and guilt; what is manifest is a crisis of the understanding of faith as such. The appearance of the *Catechism* and the very different reactions that various groups of readers have had to the text brings this crisis to light.

EIGHT

The Theology of Grace as the Hermeneutics of Salvation and Liberation

A.J.M. van den Hoogen

Introduction

The third part of the *Catechism of the Catholic Church* is devoted to "Life in Christ." Chapter three of this part is entitled "God's Salvation: Law and Grace." In this chapter a central aspect of the Christian way of speaking about human existence is discussed, namely, speaking about the reality of grace. This contribution will examine this theme. We will discuss such questions as: the theological connection between speaking about human acts with respect to morality and speaking about grace (1); the experiential reality to which speaking about grace refers (2); the connection between the contemporary experience of reality, the experience of grace, and the moral nature of human acts (3).

Moral Acts and the Experience of Grace

In order to give the fundamental moral character of human acts a foundation, the starting point of the text of the Catechism is a theological reflection with respect to human destiny. We will first determine the course of this reflection and then examine how the moral nature of human acts is described theologically.

Human Acts from the Perspective of Human Destiny

In the structure of the Catechism the moral character of human acts is discussed within a framework that is described as "Life in Christ," and, more specifically, from the viewpoint of "Life in the Spirit." Life in the Spirit describes the vocation of human beings, as the text clearly states.

Now the text makes it clear that human destiny is viewed from the perspective of the human vocation, and that this vocation should be discussed from two viewpoints (cf. 1699-1700). On the one hand, this vocation consists in human dignity, a dignity that is intrinsically related to the creation of humankind. On the other hand, this vocation exists in the growth toward perfection, which is realized in acts directed toward what is good. Thus, in this approach human acts have an intrinsic purposiveness (teleology). The text describes this as follows: "In man, true freedom is an 'outstanding manifestation of the divine image'" (1712). This already demonstrates a certain choice in the Catechism's train of thought, namely, to view human acts less as conditioned by circumstances and more as arising from an initial freedom. It is unfortunate that this choice is not itself defended, as this would have connected the Catechism much more directly with important moral debates that are now taking place in Western culture.

The text of the Catechism does give a theological justification for this choice of a teleological approach to acts. The first dimension of this theological teleology reads: "Christ ... makes man fully manifest to man himself and brings to light his exalted vocation" (1710); the second dimension of this theological teleology states that the human being is able to know this vocation actively, for he is "from his very conception ordered to God and destined for eternal beatitude" (1711). And the third dimension is encountered in the following text: "Man is [consequently, one might say] obliged to follow the moral law, which urges him 'to do what is good and avoid what is evil.' This law makes itself heard in his conscience" (1713).

Law and Grace: The Theological Interpretation of Human Acts

The almost logical (in this case, syllogistic) reasoning that forms the content of the Catechism's theological teleology should not lose sight of the fact that the Catechism's text wishes to place human acts explicitly within a salvific historic framework (cf. also 1739-1742). That salvific historical framework is drawn by means of the Pauline concepts 'law' and 'grace'. I will analyze more closely the way in which the Catechism elaborates on this framework in this subsection. It is an important issue because the Catechism's text wants to place human acts within a theological teleology.

An Example from Paul

That there is a connection between moral acts and 'life in Christ' is probably better worked out by Paul than anyone else when he, for example, in the first letter to the Corinthians traces back the confession that Jesus is the Lord to the working of the Spirit of God and emphasizes that this confession can be understood as a word of true wisdom under the influence of the Spirit of God. This wisdom has its roots in love and its test is suffering. The rule by which people are called to live is a dynamic that is kept under tension by the contrasts between love and suffering. For him, the outstanding reason for speaking of love and suffering is his experience with and insight into the meaning of life and the destiny of Jesus Christ. This specific framework of reference leads him to ask again and again the question of how the Torah developed and was enriched in the history and new life of Jesus of Nazareth. This is Paul's framework of reference when he speaks of love and suffering. Speaking of law and grace, and asking himself the question of what true wisdom includes, Paul asks how the true rule of life is descried in the history, suffering, and new life of Jesus Christ, and how the Jewish Torah ('a lamp for your feet', as the rabbinic metaphor has it) develops and is enriched. It is especially the experiences with the contrasts between love and suffering, also and particularly applied in the history of Jesus of Nazareth, that bring him to the weighty question of the relationship between law and grace.

For Paul there are no general anthropological issues at stake in this, although his Jewish and Hellenistic religious language has constituted the occasion for the outlines and concepts of theological anthropology. It is the fate of Paul's deep searching observations on the history of the Torah that they are not as well received in the rabbinic oral traditions as they are in Stoic, Romance, and scholastic Christian schemes of thought. This still occurs in the Catechism's text, in which, for example, the Pauline way of speaking concerning the law is directly linked to the philosophical category of moral law and Christian Stoic thinking on 'wisdom' (cf. 1950-1951). The Pauline terminology with regard to the old law and the New Law has been linked to various 'worldviews' that have endeavoured to understand the 'law', the '*ordo*', and the '*ratio*' of all reality 'as history (*Geschichte*).'

One of the results of using Paul's theology in this way is that his specific point of reference is sometimes scarcely recognizable in the several theological elaborations on salvation history. The thematic, historical, and, in Paul's eyes, irreplaceable death and resurrection of Jesus of Nazareth was often hidden behind the use of general terminology. These terms no longer make clear that one cannot speak of a theology of grace without speaking of the experience of a rupture. They no longer disclose that one cannot speak of a theology of grace without reference to that irretrievable moment of God's revelatory acts in the tension between love and suffering that has become the historical fate and destiny of the praxis of life and the authentic faith in the God of Jesus of Nazareth. It should also be added immediately that this rupture is also a part of the experience of all who follow in the footsteps of Jesus of Nazareth. The '*metanoia*', conversion, is the 'story' *par excellence* that attempt to give words to the descrying of God's surprising, revelatory acts. Faith implies a discovery that—however described as processual or literary—is immediately joined with a commitment that affects and renews one's life. This commitment discovers 'life' in experiences with 'death' and declares to be 'death' what looked like 'life'. It is a commitment that does not leave a single fragment of someone's life unaffected and knows no way 'back'.

Justification: Rupture and Reformation

Within the theological traditions that appeared after Paul, the schemas of salvation history have often left little room for the 'interruptions' (J.-B. Metz) that are non-negotiable aspects of thinking about God's revelatory acts and of the conversion that occurs among people when they receive a glimpse of these acts of God. That is why it is important to deal explicitly with the framework of salvation history for human acts. The framework and the subject interpret each other mutually.

In the train of thought of the Catechism's authors, emphasis is placed not so much on the experiences of the rupture which lie within "the grace of the Holy Spirit" (1987) as on the renewing connection of the conversion, of the "New Law or the Law of the Gospel" (1965) with the Old Law (1961-1964). The Catechism seems to want to place much emphasis on the fact that the 'New Law', although it is perfecting and renewing, is linked to the 'Old Law'. This terminology entails a problem completely different from that of Paul's presentation of the question. Paul's question was how the Torah's rule for living relates to Jesus' rule for living. As a theological interpretation, the Torah's rule for living held that it was the way of the covenant of Yahweh with his (Jewish) people. Jesus' rule for living, as a theological interpretation, held that it was the way of the new covenant 'through his blood'. Also connected with these theological questions were the questions of theological meaning and of the scope of Paul's mission and the first Christian communities. Already here one can see that orthopraxis precedes orthodoxy. The Catechism's question is a different one, i.e., the question of whether the moral views of the Roman Catholic Church and their foundations can claim universal validity (cf. 1956). The term 'old law' refers primarily to a foundation, viewed as immutable, of the moral acts that endure in the midst of all historical variations (cf. 1958), and which human beings can know through their reason and should follow in conscience. In addition, the term 'old law' refers to the Torah, now summarized in the Ten Commandments. In a Stoicist model of thought, which goes back to the patriarchal theology of Irenaeus and Augustine, as well as others, this 'old law' is described in its two meanings as a "preparation for the Gospel" (1964). Here too one finds reference to an orthopraxis that appears to precede this explanation of the 'orthodoxy'. Now it concerns "the moral catechesis of the apostolic teachings" (1971) and the sacramental praxis of the Roman Catholic Church (1972).

By placing so much emphasis on the renewing connection of the 'New Law' to the 'old law', the emphasis is also placed more strongly on a theology that confirms that faith in Jesus Christ has a significance that can be universalized, and that consequently the moral language of the Roman Catholic Church also has this significance. Because of this, faith assumes the character of endorsing the cooperation between the grace of God and the freedom of human beings (1993) much more than that of a rupturing experience that uproots human beings and confronts them with contextually determined choices. And the renewal that is attributed to the experience of the Holy Spirit is depicted much more as a renewal of humankind in society and culture (cf. 1995). Completely within the tradition of the Council fathers of Trent and their opposition to Martin Luther's theological basis of the 'freedom of a Christian person', the Catechism directs one's attention not so much to the personal relation of the person with his or her God, a relation that is also contextually determined in its experience of rupturing. Rather, the Catechism calls one's attention to the meaning that the sacramental praxis has for the realization and renewal that the faith relation of people with God has for moral actions. Through these accents the Catechism's authors (still) appear to see Kantian moral philosophy as the greatest challenge in our (Western) culture puts to the church and its discussion, which seeks for universality, of the human vocation.

The Experience of Grace

"Since it belongs to the supernatural order, grace *escapes our experience* and cannot be known except by faith. We cannot therefore rely on our feelings or our works to conclude that we are justified and saved" (2005). This quote demands thorough reflection. It is immediately recognizable as fitting into the classic theology of grace, which in its Neo-Thomistic form is characterized by a dualism between the reality of grace and the reality of experience and by a dualism between faith and knowledge. We will first ask whether biblical statements inevitably cause such a dualism, and then we work out what people in the past attempted to achieve with such a dualism.

The Salvific, Conciliatory Concern of God for Human Beings

The word 'grace' is a specifically Christian term insofar as it indicates the totality of God's salvific and conciliatory concern for human beings that has been revealed in Jesus Christ. This salvific and conciliatory concern on the part of God for human beings is indicated in Scripture through several different terms and characterizations, and these terms often stem from the Tanakh, the Jewish tradition of faith.

O.H. Pesch distinguishes five central concepts in reference to this. First he refers to the word *ḥānan*.[1] This term refers to a favour granted to someone upon which that someone cannot make any claim. One experiences it spontaneously and one may pray for it, but it is always given freely to human beings by divine will (cf. Genesis 6:8, Exodus 33:12-16). God's activity of *ḥānan* is expressed through a number of gifts, which are recognized in 'saving from distress', in 'communion with God', and everything the lies between them. In the Septuagint (the Greek translation of the Old Testament, abbreviated as LXX) the word is translated as *charis*, the later 'technical', that is to say, 'summarizing' word for grace in the New Testament. There is, however, also a great difference between *ḥānan* and *charis*. The former concerns one's *turning toward* one's fellow human being, while the initial meaning of *charis* is that which causes happiness, appears to be pleasant, and thus it refers to sweetness, charm, 'grace'. The Hebrew *ḥānan* does not have the dualism of an internal disposition that is externalized in or caused by external deeds of kindness. The 'turning toward' is seen as an answer to a flaw in another, a flaw that is expressed in begging or pleading. Originally, *ḥānan* did not have a religious meaning. Where it did acquire a religious meaning in the Jewish tradition of faith, Yahweh's activity of *ḥānan* has to do with human *life*: healing (for example, Psalm 6:2), salvation from distress (for example, Psalm 9:13-14), release from fear (for example, Genesis 42:21), salvation or redemption (for example, Psalm 26:11), 'restoration' (Psalm 41:4), forgiveness of sins (Psalm 41:3), and strength (Psalm 86:16).

Subsequently, Pesch refers to the words *ḥesed* and *'ĕmet*, usually translated in the Septuagint as *eleos* and *pistis*. *Ḥesed* is often linked to *'ĕmet*. *Ḥesed wa'ĕmet* (grace and faithfulness) is *the* outstanding example of covenantal terminology. Actually, *ḥesed* refers to the attitude and behaviour of the people, that which keeps the nation together. *Ḥesed* means reciprocity and faithfulness; *ḥesed* needs to answered by *ḥesed*. It transcends the scheme of performance and exchange. It has to do with commitment to someone's *life*. The religious and theological meaning of this word has its roots in this view of interhuman relationships. With reference to people and God to use *'ĕmet* in reference to either human beings of God means that one can cast oneself on their actions, words, and love. They can be trusted. It means trustworthiness with the nuance of dignity (from the root *'āman*, which accounts for the meaning of security, endurance, giving certainty). "In determining the relationship between God and his people, the central meaning of

---

[1] Cf. O.H. Pesch, *Frei sein aus Gnade: Theologische Anthropologie* (Freiburg, 1983), pp.115-23; also cf. E. Schillebeeckx, *Gerechtigheid en liefde: Genade en bevrijding* (Bloemendaal, 1977), esp. pp.74-98.

ḥesed becomes apparent from the fact that ḥesed is included in the great hymnic, liturgical proclaimers of God, in which the Tanakh praises the *nature* of God as 'a God of people' (Exodus 34:6-7). God is a 'compassionate and gracious God', patient and rich in ḥesed wa'ĕmet."[2]

A fourth concept that is important is the term ṣĕdâqâh (justice), translated in the Septuagint as *dikaiosunē*. This concept also had a secular meaning originally and received a religious meaning in a time of theocratic, nationalist view of the people of Israel.[3] In Israel all authority was exercised in the name of Yahweh, Israel's only true king, in both secular and religious matters. Human justice had to do with God's justice. Later, in Jesus' time as well, the Jews no longer possessed political independence. Authority and community, authority and religion became separated. The concept 'justice' became desecrated. But it was linked with the meaning that an actual community practises justice. When conflicts are present, there is no 'justice' anymore, neither with the one party or the other. 'Justice' indicates the internal cohesion between human good deeds and the situation with respect to the well-being, salvation, and happiness of the entire community.

The fifth concept Pesch mentions is *raḥămîm*, which is translated in the Septuagint as *oiktirmos*. The word is very affective. *Rāḥam* means womb (cf. Jeremiah 20:17), the soft part of the person (Genesis 43:30). *Raḥămîm* is the plural form of this, referring to the tender, natural, emotional love of a mother for her child, and thus also compassion (cf. Hosea 11:8, Genesis 43:30, I Kings 3:26). Ḥesed is linked to *raḥămîm*, through which God's ḥesed acquires the meaning of tender, vulnerable, motherly love. This is present in Hosea in particular. But this connection within a double linkage becomes more frequent (Jeremiah 16:5, Zechariah 7:9, Psalm 25:6). This is why Yahweh also expects ḥesed from Israel in return, and in his reasoning the prophet says to the people: "'There is no faithfulness ['ĕmet], no love [ḥesed], no acknowledgment of God in the land'" (Hosea 4:1-2). There is then no longer any 'grace'.

In the New Testament *charis* becomes the predominant central concept for 'grace'. This becomes, as it were, the 'technical', summarizing word for God's salvific and reconciling concern for people, creating faith and love and evoking hope. It is through Paul in particular that the term *charis* has received this 'technical', summarizing meaning. The direct background for this lies in the wish for grace that is expressed at the beginning and/or end of Chris-

---

[2] E. Schillebeeckx, *Gerechtigheid en liefde*, p. 82.

[3] Cf. E. Schillebeeckx, *Gerechtigheid en liefde*, pp. 117-18.

tian epistolary literature.[4] Greeks and Greek-speaking Jews began their letters with *chaire* (hail!). Analogous to this, we can find a greeting in the beginning and/or end of each work included in the 'Pauline corpus', the oldest form of which is found in Paul's letter to the Thessalonians: "The grace [*hē charis*] of our Lord Jesus Christ be with you" (1 Thessalonians 1:1, 5:28). For the rest, the reality indicated by the word grace in the New Testament is, again, expressed in many various ways—for example, adoption (Roman 9:4), children of God (Matthew 5:9), the gift of the Holy Spirit (Galations 3:5), being snatched from the dominion of darkness (Colossians 1:13), liberation through purchase or ransom (I Corinthians 1:18, 30), salvation and redemption (Luke 1:69), reconciliation after an argument (2 Colossians 5:18), justification and sanctification (Romans 6:16), the renewal of people and the world (John 13:34), and living in perfection (Ephesians 2:5).

Through Paul in particular, the concept of *charis* has become a summarizing term (a *terminus technicus*) for that which is meant by the 'riches of God's grace' (Ephesians 1:7b, 2:4-7, 3:8) in the New Testament. In 1 Thessalonians, though, it does not appear. Here Paul speaks of the "gospel of God" (for example, 1 Thessalonians 2:2) which is at the same time the "gospel of Christ" (1 Thessalonians 3:2). This gospel entails the confession of "faith in God" and "faith in the coming Jesus Christ." They, the Thessalonian Christians, "turned to God from idols to serve the living and true God," and "to wait for his Son from heaven, whom he raised from the dead—Jesus, who rescues us from the coming wrath" (1 Thessalonians 1:9-10). Here a summary, as it were, is of the original Christian kerygma is given to *pagans*, and there is no trace yet of *charis* and justification, the later key concepts in Paul. A key concept here is Jesus' coming *parousia* (for example, 1 Thessalonians 2:19, 3:13). Not until 1 Corinthians, the letter to the Galations, and 2 Corinthians does the term *charis* become a *terminus technicus*. In 1 Corinthians *charis* appears to mean giving thanks (10:30, 15:57), especially for the giving of alms by the Corinthian Christians for the benefit of the community in Jerusalem (16:3) (also see 2 Corinthians 8:1-9). But *charis* also here means God's salvific revelation in Christ and by this is actually linked to God's election of them to be Christians: "[God's] grace given you in Christ Jesus" (1 Corinthians 1:4). Here the Greek meaning of *charis* still plays a role: God's grace endows Christians with rich gifts (1:5, 6). In the letter to the Galations there is talk of the *charis Theou* (the grace of God) (2:19-21). The 'gospel' is now identified with justification: "... [we] know that a man is not justified by observing the law, but by faith in Jesus Christ. So we, too, have put our faith in Christ Jesus so that we may be justified by

---

[4] Cf. O.H. Pesch, *Frei sein aus Gnade*, pp. 101 ff.

faith in Christ" (2:16a). Paul sees himself as the apostle who is sent to proclaim this message of justification. In contrast to the usual usage of *charis* in the greetings, *charis* receives a very pointed meaning here: Paul was called by *charis* (1:15). "I want you to know, brothers, that the gospel I preached is not *something that man made up*. I did not receive it from any man, nor was I taught it; rather, I received it by revelation from Jesus Christ" (1:11). *Charis* is a revelation, of which Paul is the apostle, and the content of this revelation is justification through faith in Christ, by which people are freed from slavery (5:1).

The biblical statements do not compel one to speak of grace dualistically. Rather, one can establish that the word 'grace' encompasses a variety of human experiences—experiences that for the rest are not traced back to a human subject of actions.

Natural and Supernatural

If the reality of grace is a revelatory reality, does 'grace' then belong to an accessible reality beyond our experience? Does 'revelation' mean that 'grace' falls outside of our experience? Does 'revelation' mean that only the proclamation and *kerygma* make access to 'grace' possible? These questions belong first and foremost in an introduction with respect to fundamental theology. For at issue here are the complicated issues of the relationship between history and revelation, the relationship between faith and knowledge, the relationship between the authority of proclamation and the authority of experience. One issue deserves to be mentioned and discussed here briefly: the conceptual pair 'natural/supernatural.'

The conceptual pair 'natural/supernatural' has long dominated theology in general in the modern period (in fact, since the seventeenth century) and certainly the treatment of grace as well. Although the term 'supernatural' already appears as a *technical term* in Thomas Aquinas in the "Quaestiones Disputatae de Veritate" (1256-1259), the conceptual pair 'natural/supernatural' acquires a specific meaning in the modern period. Thomas refers to God as the 'supernatural principle (*principium supernaturale*)'.[5] But with respect to Thomas one should understand this from a theological view of 'natural' reality. Our concrete reality is, in this view, assimilated into a process. It comes out of (*exitus*) and returns to (*reditus*) God. Creation, people, sin, and grace are given a place in a system of thought that views everything as emanating from God, who creates, preserves, and, when they

---

[5] Cf. "Übernatürlich," in: *LThK*, vol. 10, pp. 437-40.

return to God, glorifies and sanctifies.[6] This schema of emanating and returning does not share our modern concept of historicity, but it is nevertheless a schema in which reflection on concrete reality occurs in the light of God's concern for people and the world, and which has *no* reference to another supernatural 'order'. The state of grace is, in Thomas' view, that the eternal love of God is concerned and related in a creative way with that which is the centre of being human—'freedom', we would say today. Through this concern and relatedness people are, as it were, 'lifted up' out of their finitude, 'pulled up high' to share in the communion with God, to share in the life of God. And from that sharing in the communion with God also flows the involvement of people with God as it acquires shape in faith, hope, and love.[7]

Thus in Thomas' view there is *no* such thing as an *antithesis* between grace and human reality. There is talk of a distinction between grace and human reality, but that distinction arises from the conviction that God's involvement with people is relational in nature and that the concern of God is directed toward the salvation of all people. In the modern period (that is, since the seventeenth century) that distinction becomes an 'antithesis', and the relationship between the reality of grace (supernatural) and human (natural) reality is viewed as a *competition* (Schoonenberg), an idea that has become characteristic of Neo-Scholastic theology.[8] In a well-known Neo-Scho-

---

[6] Cf. M.-D. Chenu, "Le plan de las Somme Théologique de saint Thomas," in: *Rev. Thom.* 45 (1939): 93-107.

[7] Cf. O.H. Pesch and A. Peters, *Einführung in die Lehre von Gnade und Rechtfertigung* (Darmstadt, 1981), p. 89.

[8] Neo-scholastic theology is that theology whose framework is the so-called 'contemporary scholasticism', which began at the end of the eighteenth century and, particularly since the middle of the nineteenth century, continued as a form of Christian philosophy, which is based chiefly on the rediscovery of the work of Thomas Aquinas (cf. "Contemporary Scholasticism," in: *New Catholic Encyclopedia*, Vol. XII (New York, 1967), pp. 1165ff.; "Le renouveau de la scholastique," in *D.Th.C*, Vol. XV/1 (Paris, 1946), pp. 426ff.) Thus initially Neo-scholasticism was a form of philosophy, but very much influenced by theology, particularly by its ideal of knowledge, i.e., the ability to form concepts that give a logical, exhaustive definition of reality and are therefore logically necessary. Since the so-called *'nouvelle théologie'* that arose in the thirties in Europe, in France and Germany as well, it was this ideal of knowledge against which people strove. This ideal denies in particular that theology and faith concern God's mystery and the secret of life of people and moreover denies that faith has reference to salvific *history*. Also cf. A.G.M. Van Melsen, "Wat maakte het neothomisme zo attractief?" in: B. Delfgaauw, *et al.*, *De wijsgerige Thomas: Terugblik op het neothomisme* (Baarn, 1984), pp. 28-48.

lastic textbook for dogmatics by F. Diekamp, *Katholische Dogmatik nach den Grundsätzen des hl. Thomas* (1912-1914), on the relationship between grace and reality one reads: "a nature perfect in itself, equipped with everything that is necessary, appropriates the supernatural like a *superadditum.*"[9] In this quotation two points are immediately striking. First of all, reality is thought of as 'closed'. This does not exclude the fact that this reality is attributed with its own dynamics. "Naturally this is what belongs to nature, that which is constitutive for it, or belongs to its results, or belongs to her requirements," states Diekamp. (For example, it is the nature of the eye that it can see, that it actually does see and that there is light that makes things visible.) The second striking point is that grace is viewed as an 'added reality'. What then is 'supernatural'? The answer is: that which does not belong to nature. Formulated in a positive way, "the supernatural (*supernatura*) is a gift that owes nothing to nature, a gift that is added to nature (*donum indebitum et superadditum*)."

Thus in this Neo-Scholastic view grace and human reality are viewed as 'two levels' (L. Boff) which are stacked upon each other yet have no internal connection. And it is particularly the view of 'nature' that in this view hinders one from being able to conceive of an internal reference between grace and reality. Already years ago the Dutch theologian P. Schoonenberg pointed out the implications this has for anthropology. It is then impossible to reconcile God's real involvement in human reality with the freedom of human beings. In this view God's actions are always at the cost of that of people, and human activity is at the cost of God's involvement. In particular, as long as this involvement of people in the world and of God in human reality is seen as a form of causality, in this view of natural and supernatural one cannot resolve the conflict between these two 'causalities.'[10]

Boff then also correctly concludes that in the Neo-Scholastic view it is impossible to experience grace. Grace belongs to another supernatural order that is inaccessible to human experience. It was not the intention of such a theology to discuss grace as a reality that can be experienced. After all, it was a theology that attempted to formulate "universally valid insights" (Van Melsen). When it is asked today whether people can experience grace, there is a completely different intention in the question, an intention that is fundamentally different from that of Neo-Scholasticism on several points. Two points of difference in particular are important. First, much of contemporary

---

[9] Cited by L. Boff, *Erfahrung von Gnade: Entwurf einer Gnadenlehre* (Düsseldorf, 1978), p.66.

[10] Cf. P. Schoonenberg, *Hij is een God van mensen* ('s-Hertogenbosch, 1969), pp.9-14 especially.

theology has once again discovered that while Scripture and theologians such as Thomas Aquinas do distinguish between grace and human reality, they do not make them antithetical to each other. *Charis* or *gratia* refers to God in his concern for concrete people in their concrete reality. Secondly, much of contemporary theology has once again discovered that we should not think of this concrete reality as a 'closed', albeit 'dynamic', reality. Neither from a metaphysical nor historical quest into reality does our experience of multiplicity and mutability appear to be adequately explained and understood if one takes this as one's starting point. It would be better, Boff suggests, if we stopped speaking in terms of natural/supernatural.[11]

The Experience of Grace as Interpreted Experience

Is one able to experience 'grace'? Even if one has consciously departed from the neo-scholastic schema of nature/supernature and replaced it with the schema of grace and freedom (freedom being understood in the concrete context in which freedom must be liberated), this question cannot simply be answered with 'yes' or 'no'. Whoever answers 'no' thereby probably admits to not having been able to discover anything 'revelatory' in the biblical images and metaphors by which the experience of grace of believers in the Jewish and Christian traditions was expressed. Whoever answers 'yes' does recognize in one's own reality something of those promises of the experience of God's concern which is expressed in the biblical metaphors. Theological reflection can contribute to clearing up misunderstandings that hinder this recognition, and it can also contribute new models of understanding that are justifiable; but it cannot bring it about that a person in his or her own life or a group in its own community come to this recognition.

In the theology of grace, therefore, when it is said that people can experience 'grace', it is an attempt, following the footsteps of those who answer 'yes', to clarify an experience in the presence of those who say 'yes' but also in the presence of those who answer 'no'. It is thus an attempt to clarify an experience that arises in the witness of believing people, where it concerns the experience that *in* our human existence can illuminate a moment of gratuity that can give meaning to our existence, offer a perspective, can become a power for the renewal of people and the world. In the Jewish and Christian traditions of faith there is the trust that 'models of understanding' can also be borrowed from our experience, models that cause one 'to do' and 'to think', in which this "mystery of compassion" (Schillebeeckx) can be expressed in a trustworthy manner, although it is always and by definition partial. For, one can say with Schillebeeckx,

---

[11] Cf. L. Boff, *Erfahrung von Gnade*, p.72.

revelation possesses a structure of experience. The good that certain people experienced in Jesus was experienced and identified as divine salvation. That which was actually experienced in Jesus by Christians was therefore *neither pure 'conclusion' nor pure 'immediate' experience, but interpretive experience—the experience of faith*. Because of the surprising newness of their experience of salvation in Jesus they also wish to place it emphatically in line with their Jewish-religious tradition of experience, which caused them to experience Jesus interpreted in such a way as if they actually experienced him. ... At the same time this led to a reinterpretation of this history from the experience of a renewed history. From this there finally grew a religious view on total history: unity of a divine plan, decree or divine ordainment, that is unfolded *in and through* the history of people. In continually changing situations, in continually new words, the Christian community of faith will ultimately continue to say nothing but that they experience divine salvation in Jesus Christ, even in philosophical concepts that are sometimes very complex. If the old concepts or interpretive moments no longer apply in new situations and if the needs and requirements change, the interpretive concepts also change. But the source experience remains the same in this change: in their own individual situations people continue to experience divine salvation in Jesus.[12]

The Experience of Grace and the Moral Nature of Human Actions

At the end of the first section the question was asked as to whether in the text of the Catechism (still) sees Kantian moral philosophy as the greatest challenge that our (Western) culture puts to the church and its discussion, which seeks for universality, of the human vocation. The second section has indicated a way along which, according to many contemporary theologians, the dilemma between grace and the experience (of freedom) can be transcended and the tension between the two can be made productive. This third section will specifically deal with the moral aspect of the experience of freedom. The question is now whether the tension between the reality of grace as endorsed in faith and the moral aspect of the experience of faith can be made productive.

Morality and the Experience of Grace

In the Catechism much attention is paid to the idea that—first—an inalienable moral dimension should be attributed to human actions and that this moral

---

[12] E. Schillebeeckx, *Gerechtigheid en liefde*, p.55, italics mine.

dimension is, theologically speaking, a free response on the part of human beings to the free intiative of God (see numbers 1996-2005 in particular). The Catechism's text joins in forcefully with the thought of the great theologian Augustine. With this the text also joins in with that which, since Augustine, has become the core issue of the *tractatus de gratia* that originated through his work: the relationship between human freedom and experience of grace. This was a very complicated issue already in the time of Augustine, not in the least because Augustine himself also changed his views during the course of his life and finally came to endorse a view in which there was hardly room to speak of true human freedom. Fortunately, the text of this Catechism does not follow Augustine this far. The view that is present in the Catechism is close to the position to which the Council fathers of Trent subscribed.

A key problem in Augustine was his insight that a fundamental brokenness continued to dominate his moral actions. "What I do not want to do I do, and what I want to do I do not do," he says in his *Confessions*. It is a way of consideration that arises from a glance 'within', a way of consideration that searches for an answer to the (for Augustine) pressing question of why human actions are not thoroughly transparent, why the rationality of the will is apparently insufficient to penetrate the motives of our actions. Apparently, his insight says, the human will to live according to God's law is not enough to deal with God from within one's life.

Augustine then comes to the faithful conviction that life with God has an aspect which he calls *gratia preveniens*. God's grace (cf. 2001) already surrounds people, even before there is talk of exercising human will. For Augustine, especially in his Confessions, this was an insight that created room within the acknowledgement of God's turning toward us to be able to continue to acknowledge that the human will is in our experience so often thwarted by human desires. For the Council fathers of Trent the insight into the *gratia preveniens*—which had in the meantime already expanded into an established element of the treatment of grace—was an important aspect of their resistance to Martin Luther's Reformation. They wanted to hold onto the theological meaning of the sacraments of the church, and according to their insight this meaning lay in the necessary mediation and confirmation of life with God. In the Catechism it almost sounds like a pietistic alternative for the emphasis that since Kant has been placed on the autonomous rationality of the human will: the *gratia preveniens* "is needed to arouse and sustain our collaboration in justification through faith and sanctification through charity" (2001).

Morality, the Experience of Grace, and Historical Awareness

Since Kant, the insight has grown in our Western culture that the autonomous rationality of the human will itself has a public character. The subject is a public subject. The public character and the moral character go hand in hand.

Earlier in this article I pointed out that the text in the Catechism sought another position, a position that cannot be called the 'enlightenment of the Enlightenment' but rather a contra-Enlightenment position. It is typical of the Catechism's position that, among other things, an alternative for the public dimension of morality also fits within this. The public dimension of moral actions is, in the view of the Catechism, fulfilled by the sacramental and judicial aspects of the church.

This view on the church in its function of public dimension of moral actions is candidly discussed in a text that is taken directly from the ecclesiastical codex: "To the Church belongs the right always and everywhere to announce moral principles, including those pertaining to the social order, and to make judgments on any human affairs to the extent that they are required by the fundamental rights of the human person or the salvation of souls" (2032). But the view on the Church as a public dimension of moral actions also appears, albeit indirectly, in the texts on the doctrine of the 'merit' and that of 'sanctification'. The first category as the Catechism gives it is a category that has reference to the public character of moral actions. "Merit," says the text, "refers in general to the *recompense owed* by a community or a society for the action of one of its members" (2006). This recompense rests on the principles of justification and equality. After this definition the text of the Catechism applies this fact to the relationship between God and human being, again in the light of that which is said on *gratia preveniens*. "God has freely chosen to associate man with the work of his grace." God initiates, and human deeds are secondary (2008). The Catechism classifies the 'goods' (*bona*) that arise from these actions as aspects of the "spiritual progress [that] tends toward ever more intimate union with Christ. This union is called 'mystical' because it participates in the mystery of Christ through the sacraments" (2014). In this one can see the crowning of a position that can be described as 'Catholic pietism'. In it is placed the core of the alternative that the Catechism formulates for the moral subject of the Enlightenment.

In order to define clearly the import of this Catholic pietism, I will compare this position with a 'theology of the signs of the times'. This position refers to salvation history when one interprets one's own history from within and bases it in the framework of the promises and fulfilments of divine providence. Such an interpretation of one's own history implies a historical analysis of the developments of the history that we are both witnessing and experiencing now. In *Gaudium et Spes* (GS) this is expressed as follows. It is said of the church that its goal is "to carry on the work of Christ under the guidance of the Holy Spirit, for he came into the world to bear witness to the truth, to save and not to judge, to serve and not to be served" (no. 3). This text concludes the foreword of *Gaudium et Spes*. Following immediately is the statement, "At all times the Church carries the responsibility of *reading the signs of the times and of interpreting them in the light of the Gospel*, if it is to carry out its task. In language intelligible to every generation, she should be able to answer the ever recurring questions which men ask about the meaning of this present life and of the life to come, and how one is related to the other."[13]

The French theologian and historian M.-D. Chenu has given an interesting interpretation of the passage on the "understanding of the signs of the times in the light of the Gospel." A number of aspects of this will be discussed here.[14] In the past acquaintance with the phrase 'the signs of the times' stemmed primarily from exegesis—there was no place for it in contemporary theology. Given its origin (Matthew 16:3), it was linked primarily with the idea of the 'end of time' and not with actual history. The text of *Vatican Council II*, however, links the phrase emphatically with actual and continuing history. With the introduction of the phrase in *Gaudium et Spes* it acquires a new and renewed meaning for theology.[15] There has also been opposition to it. Some have indicated that the phrase has a christological and eschatological meaning in Scripture, while this is not as clearly the case in the conciliar text. Others stress that with the use of this term GS did not give enough attention to the transcendence of the Kingdom of God over against history and not enough attention to the negative aspects of history, evil, and sin. Chenu acknowledges these objections. But more important in his eyes is the fact that the phrase formulates an epistemological principle of a "concrete, historical theology." The phrase 'signs of the times' is therefore the same as understanding which paradigmatic change or renaissance appears in our time. Observation of the signs of the times is therefore also a 'practical' opportunity. It is linked intrinsically to actions that are directed toward the realization

---

[13] Cf. The Pastoral Constitution on the Church in the Modern World: Vatican II, *Gaudium et Spes* (Dublin, 1975).

[14] Cf. T. Van den Hoogen, *Pastorale Theologie: Ontwikkeling en structuur in de theologie van M.-D. Chenu* (Alblasserdam, 1982), pp. 218-23.

[15] The primarily sources in which the phrase has this new meaning are: the summons to the Council by John XXIII, dated 25 December 1961; *Pacem in Terris* (encyclical by John XXIII, dated 11 April 1963); *Ecclesiam suam* (encyclical by Paul VI, dated 6 August 1964); *Gaudium et Spes*, no. 4 (7 December 1965).

of the destiny that a people descries in its history and with being and becoming aware of the roots of that history.

This concrete historical theology also has a moral dimension, as Jon Sobrino, a theologian working in El Salvador, stresses. From the perspective of such a theology the moral issue is characterized not by the question "What should I do?" but by the question "What needs to be done urgently here and now for the sake of justice?" In this framework the words of Jesus—"If anyone would come after me, he must deny himself and take up his cross and follow me" (Matthew 16:24)—do not constitute the final piece of a Catholic pietism with an anti-Enlightenment sentiment (2029) but the starting point of the fundamentally moral dimension that is present in the choice for a faith described as following Jesus. The goal of this moral attitude is universal reconciliation, and this reconciliation is viewed as the fruit of justice.

NINE

The Human Community

Ronald Jeurissen

Introduction

The second chapter on general morality in the catechism, entitled "The Human Community" and consisting of numbers 1877-1948, is devoted to social ethics. In this chapter the most important starting points of Catholic social thought, as that had developed since the time of Leo XIII's encyclical *Rerum novarum*, are brought into the open in a very concise way. In the sixties the Second Vatican Council introduced a radical change in Catholic social ethics. The Council abandoned its earlier pretention of being able to present a well-rounded social doctrine based on the principles of the eternal natural law. Rather than teach humanity, the Council sought dialogue with all people on the actual problems of the world "in the light offered by the Gospel." At the Council the role of natural law as the basis of social ethics was taken over by a theological interpretation of history as *salvation history*. It was not the notion of eternally unchanging nature that functioned as the normative framework of reference but the struggle of humanity toward a better future, in the context of God's kingdom.[1]

If we look at the current Catechism from the perspective of Vatican II, we can ascertain that the farewell to a closed Catholic social 'doctrine' is confirmed. At no point in the Catechism is there the pretence of offering a social ethical doctrine. The Catechism gives primarily the principles and basic criteria of a Catholic social ethic (no. 2423). The text shows directions and also closes others off, but does not fall into pedantic, detailed prescriptions. Vatican II's theology of salvation history, later brought to full flower by theologians like Gutiérrez, Metz, and Schillebeeckx, is not taken over by the Catechism. It is primarily the idea of the human calling to the 'divine glory' (no. 1700) that functions as a theological framework. This vertical metaphysical scheme with its metaphor of 'under and above' 'earthly and divine' is at odds with the eschatology of the theology of salvation history with

---

[1] Vatican Council II, *Gaudium et Spes* 3, 34, 39.

its metaphor of 'past, present, and future'. A dynamic, transformative, and hopeful orientation to the future, which is so unique to the theology of salvation history, is missing in the Catechism. Thus at times the social ethics of the Catechism is somewhat static and non-historical. The texts primarily reveal the conceptual framework of Catholic social thought, but the Church's dynamic view on 'the contemporary world' and her own role in it, as it can be found in *Gaudium et Spes*, is absent from the Catechism. This does not detract from the fact that the Catechism offers a number of basic insights for all who wish to consider issues concerning social ethics, economics, and politics from within the Catholic tradition.

The Structure of the Chapter

The chapter on "The Human Community" gives a very concise rendering of the most important basic assumptions of Catholic social ethics. Concretizations of this are saved for Section Two of the part on morality concerning "The Ten Commandments." The most important paragraphs with respect to social ethics in this latter section are paragraphs 4.V ("The Authorities in Civil Community"), 5.III ("Safeguarding Peace"), and particularly the whole of Article 7, which discusses, among other things, property, the "social doctrine of the Church," economic justice, and love for the poor. Given that this contribution is limited to Section I of the part on morality, these more concrete articles will be referred to only indirectly.

The second chapter forms the middle part of the section on fundamental morality. It is preceded by a chapter on the human person and followed by a chapter on law and grace. This order is important for two reasons. In the first place this division of chapters places the person *before* the community—a structure that is not coincidental. In Catholic social ethics the primacy of the person within the community is in the foreground. Already in the main structure of the Catechism we see this primacy of the person emphasized. In the second place the chapter on social ethics precedes the chapter in which moral (natural) law is treated. Moral natural laws are of an eternal and unchanging nature. Within an ethic that is based on eternal moral laws it is possible to arrive at rigid, absolute, and unchanging moral judgements. That which is morally right is a fixed, clear, and obvious truth. The Magisterium of the Catholic Church makes use of this rigid ethic of natural law, particularly with regard to issues of sexual ethics and medical ethics. The social ethic in the Catechism, however, precedes the discussion of natural law. This order emphasizes a Vatican policy, which is generally clearly recognizable, to take into account thoroughly the contingency of social, political, and economic issues. In social ethics moral good has a certain range—for example, if it concerns the question of the right political order (cf. 1901).

The Second Vatican Council's abandonment of a social ethic based on natural law can be seen in the structure of the Catechism, but the chapter on social ethics nevertheless employs the vocabulary of natural law as well. The argumentation here, however, is not rigid and deductive but evocative and appeals to such self-evident truths as: "Every human community needs an authority to govern it. The foundation of such authority lies in human nature" (no. 1898).

The chapter on "The Human Community" consists of three articles. The first is entitled "The Person and Society" and is completely devoted to the concept of humanity behind Catholic social ethics. Its most important assumptions are that persons are by nature oriented toward living together with others and that the dignity of the human person is the most important criterion for the goodness of the social order. The other two articles give a few basic indications for the correct establishment of society: the primary considerations here are that a society must allow for participation by its citizens (article 2) and be just (article 3). We will discuss the three articles below, focusing on their interconnectedness.

The Central Problem: Person and Society

The title "The Person and Society" evokes three questions:
- what does 'person' mean?
- what does 'society' mean?
- what does the conjunction 'and' between person and society mean?

These questions will bring us to the heart of the social ethics of the Catechism.

The Human Being as a Person

The basis of Catholic social ethics is constituted by the concept of the human being as a *person*. In connection with this, the concept of person entails the following:
- The human being is created in God's image. Being a person consists above all of the fact that human existence is fundamentally characterized by the relation to God. In life, and ultimately through death, this relation must come to completion. The Catholic Church's portrayal of humankind is teleological, that is to say, human existence is oriented toward an ultimate good, an ultimate self-realization, within which it finds its completion (nos. 1699-1709). This teleological portrayal of humankind unites the ideas of biblical eschatology and Aristotelian philosophy.

- As participating in the divine reality people are rational and free (no. 1730), which entails that they also have moral responsibility and are called to the moral completion of their existence.[2]
- The human person is essentially oriented toward living together with others. The Catechism bases the social nature of the human being in the doctrine of the Trinity. There is a certain similarity between the unity of the divine persons (Father, Son, and Holy Spirit) and the fraternity that people are to establish among themselves (1878). Sociality is constitutive for the human person. Without a life in community it is not possible to be a person: "The human person needs to live in society" (1879).
- As the image of God people possess an inalienable dignity and equality. The Catechism states that the human being, gifted with a spiritual and immortal soul, is the only creature on earth that God willed for its own sake (1703; but see also 2415-2418 on respect for animals). On the basis of her dignity as a person, the human being enjoys a number of inalienable moral rights, which she can claim over against society, in this case, the government (1907, 1908, 1911).

Society

'Society' in the catechism refers primarily to 'community'. A community is "a group of persons bound together organically by a principle of unity that goes beyond each one of them" (1880). The meaning of this can be clarified by means of the sociological distinction between *Gemeinschaft* and *Gesellschaft*.[3]

A society according the model of the *Gemeinschaft* is marked by diffuse and unlimited social duties on the part of the members. Social relations within a *Gemeinschaft* are sustained by an attitude of altruistic devotion to others. Characteristic examples are the relations between the members of a family, blood relatives, or a clan. Moral values and norms that sustain the attitudes of benevolence and devotion are important social binding agents.

A *Gesellschaft* is marked in the first place by specific and restricted social duties. A characteristic example is that of a contract. A contract binds the parties involved only to that which is agreed upon in it. Market relations, on the basis of mutual profit, are a typical example of how people deal with one another in a *Gesellschaft*. Altruistic devotion to the other—'doing more than others' as the New Testament puts it—is not expected in a *Gesellschaft*.

---

[2] *Gaudium et Spes* 16.

[3] F. Tönnies, *Gemeinschaft und Gesellschaft* (Leipzig, 1887). T. Parsons, *The Structure of Social Action* (New York: Free Press, 1937), pp. 686-94.

One's own interests and cooperation on the basis of shared interests form the basis of social relations. The *Gesellschaft* has no need of an extended set of social values for its continuity. The 'narrow' ethic of the market (not to lie, to keep one's promises, not to coerce others), and rules established in formal law are sufficient.

Although the Catholic Church has no principial objections to contracts, market relations, and judicial formulations as ways of regulating how people live together, it does object to the increasing dominance of the model of the *Gesellschaft* in society. The predominant orientation toward self-interest in a *Gesellschaft* does not measure up to the vocation of people to become persons. The Church views society as a *Gemeinschaft*. This is evident from the fact that the Catechism views the family as corresponding "more directly to the nature of man" (1882). It is also evident from the description of society as 'organic' and as based on a 'principle of unity' that goes beyond the individual persons (1880). The Catechism argues along the lines of theological ethics that people should live with one another in the manner of a *Gemeinschaft*. Human beings have a religious vocation to become one with the divine. But the love for God is inseparable from the love of one's neighbour, as taught by the Bible (1878). "Charity is the greatest social commandment. It respects others and their rights. It requires the practice of justice, and it alone makes us capable of it" (1889). The love of neighbour must also be manifest in the order of society. This must have a 'spiritual' character (1880, 1886, 1888); it should not be based on material calculations for one's own profit but on a freely assumed conscious solidarity with others. In the Church's view, society is a community of persons oriented toward one another's rights and well-being, not an arrangement of calculating citizens.

There are large and small communities. To begin with, a society of people can exist as a family or as a city. These societal forms "correspond more directly to the nature of man; they are necessary to him" (1882). In addition there are more encompassing societies "on both national and international levels, which relate to economic and social goals, to cultural and recreational activities, to sport, to various professions, and to political affairs." These societies offer people the opportunity to develop their personal qualities, "especially the sense of initiative and responsibility." Moreover, these societies help to guarantee the rights of the person (1882).

Within the various forms of society the Catechism acknowledges a special place to the political society which is guided by a public authority: "Every human community needs an authority to govern it. The foundation for such authority lies in human nature. It is necessary for the unity of the state. Its role is to ensure as far as possible the common good of the society" (1898). The state should be a "state of law," which is to say, a political organization within which the power "be balanced by other powers and by other spheres of responsibility which keep it within proper bounds" and in which "the law is sovereign and not the arbitrary will of men" (1904). The state is the highest form of human society: "Each human community possesses a common good ... it is in the *political community* that its most complete realization is found. It is the role of the state to defend and promote the common good of the civil society, its citizens, and intermediate bodies" (1910).

In order to understand why the state is called the "most complete" form of society, one must turn to political philosophy. According to Aristotle, rational human nature can only become completely developed through participation in the political life of the (city)state. Only the state organizes people's actions in their orientation toward the ultimate good. To begin with, the organizing capacity of the state makes the development of sciences possible. In addition, citizens learn political skills in the state, in particular how to keep the common good of the citizens in mind. Finally, the state is the place where citizens can live as free and equal citizens, determining good and evil in mutual deliberation. The ability of people to live as rational beings develops optimally in the state.[4]

In his *Rechtsphilosophie* Hegel outlines the transition from civil society (*die bürgerliche Gesellschaft*) to state. A civil society is primarily a market community of free citizens. They are primarily oriented toward their own interests and maintain social relations only by means of the principle *quid pro quo*. According to Hegel human freedom and rationality cannot be realized in its full potential on the level of the civil society. This is apparent from, among other things, the fact that the capital concentration in the civil society leads to a structurally impoverished lower class, which undermines the stability of society.[5] Marx would elaborate further on this idea later. Living together in reason and freedom is only possible when all citizens, each from their own particular interests and preferences, orient themselves toward the common good and when an organization of the citizens exists to govern the harmony between particular interests and the common interest. This organization is the state. In the state human society attains the shape of a truly moral community.[6] The view held by Aristotle and Hegel, that the political community of the state realizes the ultimate development of human possibilities of existence, forms the historical background for the Catechism's state-

---

[4] Aristotle, *Ethica Nicomacheia*, 1094. *Politeia*, 1253a.

[5] G.W.F. Hegel, *Grundlinien der Philosophie des Rechts* (Berlin, 1821), §§ 241-45.

[6] G.W.F. Hegel, *Grundlinien der Philosophie des Rechts*, § 257.

ment that the state is the "most complete" realization of the common good of the people.

The Individual and Society

Catholic social ethics places the dignity of the human person first while also attaching great importance to human society. But how must one view the person and the society in relation to each other and how must this relation be organized in real terms? According to the Church, society is not simply an instrument to serve individual interests as is taught in liberalism, nor is the individual subordinate to the interests of the collective as in totalitarian ideologies. What then is the positive meaning of the 'and' between person and society? This is implied in the social nature of the human person himself. The sociality of the human person is the *fait primitif* of Catholic social ethics. It is also its most important problem. The assertion that the community with others is constitutive for the person does imply after all that the interests of society are also those of the person. However, the collective interests of society can sometimes conflict with the dignity of individual persons. How can the profound bond between person and society be stressed without society swallowing up the person in his or her unique dignity? The Catechism attempts to answer this question right from the start by viewing the concepts of 'person' and 'community' not as opposing but as implicating each other, as specifications of each other's meaning. The Catechism's social ethics is based on the two interconnected basic values of human *personality* and *sociality*. In connection with this, one should view sociality as a characteristic of the person, so that the personality of the person is in fact the coordinating concept of the social ethic. The basic values of personality and sociality are inseparably linked together in the fact that on the one hand the community with others is constitutive for being a person, whereas on the other hand the dignity of the person is the criterion for the quality of the community. The two basic values thus continually refer to each other, evoke each other, and each acquires its meaning only in relation to the other. Catholic social thought entails a *dialectic* of person and society. Within this dialectic, however, the one does not merge into the other, nor do both merge into a higher *tertium quid*. The person is and remains something other than society, but a relation of mutual definition does exist.

The two basic values of the person and the community yield two perspectives from which the Catechism develops a number of more concrete *basic norms* of social ethics. From the *perspective of the person* basic norms come to light which the societal organization must meet if it wishes to do justice to the requirements of human dignity. From the *perspective of the community* basic norms come to light for the social actions of individual persons if it is desired that justice be done to the requirements of human sociality. These basic norms are to be found primarily in articles 2 and 3 of the chapter on the human community.

Basic Norms from the Perspective of the Individual

In order to promote the dignity of the human person in societal life the Catechism refers to four basic norms: the *fundamental rights of the human person*, the norm of *social justice*, the principle of *subsidiarity*, and the *right to participation*.

The Fundamental Rights of the Individual

"Respect for the human person entails respect for the rights that flow from his dignity as a creature. These rights are prior to society and must be recognized by it" (1930). The words "are prior to" make the primacy of the human individual in Catholic social thought clearly visible. The rights of the person constitute the first and most important basic norm of Catholic social ethics.[7]

Human rights can be defined as a set of justified claims of people, over against others, to the elementary freedoms, goods, and services that are necessary to lead a dignified life—that is to say, a life in freedom and social-economic security. Rights to freedom have to do with the fundamental 'space' of human liberty that must be respected by others if a human being is to be able to develop as a person. Rights to freedom establish a number of negative obligations for others so that the developmental possibilities of people are not infringed upon and their bodily and spiritual integrity is respected. The Catechism speaks here of the "natural freedoms" of people, "indispensable for the development of the human vocation," which are, in fact, "the right to act according to a sound norm of conscience to safeguard privacy, and rightful freedom also in matters of religion," as well as "the right to establish a family" (1907, 1908). In later chapters the Catechism also mentions the right to establish a business and the right to strike (2429, 2435).

Social economic rights have to do with the goods and services that must be supplied by others if the individual is to be able to develop as a human being and attain social security. Rights that are mentioned by the Catechism

---

[7] *Gaudium et Spes* 25-27. For a complete list of the Catholic concept of human rights, see H. Zwiefelhofer, *Neue Weltwirtschaftsordnung und katholische Soziallehre* (Munich, 1980), pp. 33-37.

in this connection are: "food, clothing, health, work, education and culture, suitable information" (1908).

The summary of human rights in the Catechism is exemplary by nature. A more elaborate summary can be found in the encyclical *Pacem in Terris*.[8] As regards the content, the Church's thinking on human rights corresponds to the secular definition as it is formulated in the United Nations' Universal Declaration of Human Rights. A unique characteristic of Catholic thinking on human rights is that the Church not only speaks of the fundamental rights of humans, but also of their fundamental *obligations*. This obtains not only in the tautological sense that the right of the one always entails a corresponding obligation for the other.[9] A person has a number of intrinsic obligations that are inseparably linked with his existence as a social person. As a person the human being is also called to contribute to the social life with others. Insisting on human rights can easily lead to an individualistic attitude in which collective arrangements are reduced to instruments that serve private interests. This results in the loss of the communal character of the society. An explicit linking of human rights and obligations can only be found in passing in the Catechism (for example, 1886); more exhaustive treatments of this can be found in *Pacem in Terris* and *Gaudium et Spes*.[10]

Social Justice

The second basic norm from the perspective of the person is social justice. The Catechism says with respect to this: "Society ensures social justice when it provides the conditions that allow associations or individuals to obtain what is their due, according to their nature and their vocation" (1928). The phrase 'what is their due' harks back to the Thomistic doctrine on justice. In his *Summa Theologica* Thomas Aquinas (1225-1274) defines justice as "a habit whereby a man renders to each one his due by a constant and perpetual will."[11] Thomas distinguishes between *commutative justice (iustitia commutativa)* and *distributive justice (iustitia distributiva)*. Commutative justice regulates the mutual relations between individuals. Actions that take place mutually between two persons (for example, employment and payment) should always be in a proper relation to each other. Distributive justice establishes a norm for the relation of the community, particularly political authority, to

---

[8] John XXIII, *Pacem in Terris* 11-27.

[9] *Pacem in Terris* 30.

[10] *Pacem in Terris* 28-36; *Gaudium et Spes* 30.

[11] Thomas Aquinas, *Summa Theologica* II-II.58.1, 8.

the individual: the community must ensure that the communal goods are divided "in proportion" (cf. 2411).[12]

The concept of 'social justice' was officially introduced into the Catholic Church by Pius XI in his encyclical *Quadragesimo Anno*. This came about as a reaction to excesses of economic liberalism, which had produced a distressing social inequality. Pope Pius writes: "To each, therefore, must be given his own share of goods, and the distribution of created goods, which, as every discerning person knows, is laboring today under the gravest evils due to the huge disparity between the few exceedingly rich and the unnumbered propertyless, must be effectively called back to and brought into conformity with the norms of the common good, that is, social justice."[13] It seems that already here social justice is intrinsically determined by distributive justice. Social justice is the organization of people living together according to the principle of distributive justice, or, distributive justice on the level of society. The emphasis on the aspect of distributive justice within social justice is retained in more recent Vatican texts, and in the Catechism as well. *Gaudium et Spes* views social justice as the removal of social and economic inequality; *Populorum Progressio* urged an improvement in trade relations between rich and poor nations by invoking the notion of social justice.[14] These views return in the Catechism (1939, 1941, 2437-2442).

The Catechism bases the requirement for justice on the principle of the *equal dignity* of all people (1934). Equal dignity, however, does not mean *equality*, since "the 'talents' are not distributed equally" (1936). The inequality of talents is not viewed by the Catechism as an evil but as a given that is, in principle, positive. Because people differ from one another they can complement one another and thus form a society. Inequality makes it possible for the social virtues in the human person to develop (1937). Thus the Catechism approvingly quotes a text from the *Dialogo* by St. Catharine of Siena, which is at first glance surprising: "... And so I have given many gifts and graces, both spiritual and temporal, with such diversity that I have not given everything to one single person, so that you may be constrained to practice charity towards one another" (1937). This quote surely should not be read as if the Church itself would not wish to see something positive in "such diversity," although the wording of the text does suggest this interpretation. In other documents the Church identifies and condemns the 'sinful structures' in soci-

---

[12] Thomas Aquinas, *Summa Theologica* II-II.60.1.

[13] Pius XI, *Quadragesimo Anno* 58.

[14] *Gaudium et Spes* 29; Paul VI, *Populorum Progressio* 44.

ety, by which riches are acquired at the cost of poverty to others.[15] Thus it appears that the quotation must be read hyperbolically, more in the light of Aristotle's statement that someone who does not need others to live is either an animal or a god, but certainly not a human being.[16] In any case, the necessary correction follows immediately: "There exist also *sinful inequalities* that affect millions of men and women. These are in open contradiction of the Gospel" (1938).

Inequality among people may not lead to "discrimination in fundamental personal rights on the grounds of sex, race, colour, social conditions, language, or religion" (1935). Hopefully, the Magisterium will someday find in this definition in its Catechism a reason to give up the unequal treatment of men and women in its own practices, following the ancient principle to 'practice what you preach.'

Subsidiarity

Respect for the person requires that the state's authority not reach too far into the life of society. After all, "Excessive intervention by the state can threaten personal freedom and initiative" (1883). Here one must first think of totalitarian forms of government, but in principle the state can have too much influence in every political order. In addition to the minimum of respect for human rights and the requirements of social justice (2236, 2237), the Church therefore also indicates a maximum of state interference. This is the famous *principle of subsidiarity*, which entails that "a community of a higher order should not interfere in the internal life of a community of a lower order, depriving the latter of its functions, but rather should support it in case of need and help to coordinate its activities with the activities of the rest of society, always with a view to the common good" (1883, cf. 2431).

The term 'subsidiarity' was introduced into the Church's language by Pius XI, who intended to give direction to the state's intervention in socioeconomic life. Generally the principle deals with the help (*subsidium*) that society owes to its members. The best help is the help for self-help. All help must stand ready to serve the personal development of the individual by stimulating his or her own power and initiative.[17] Pius XI expressed the principle of subsidiarity as follows:

---

[15] John Paul II, *Sollicitudo Rei Socialis* 36 f., *Centesimus Annus* 38.

[16] Aristotle, *Politeia*, 1253a.

[17] O. von Nell-Breuning, *Soziallehre der Kirche: Erläuterungen der Lehramtlichen Dokumente* (Vienna, 1983), p.53.

Just as it is gravely wrong to take from individuals what they can accomplish by their own initiative and industry and give it to the community, so also it is an injustice and at the same time a grave evil and disturbance of right order to assign to a greater and higher association what lesser and subordinate organizations can do. For every social activity ought of its very nature to furnish help to the members of the body social, and never destroy and absorb them. The supreme authority of the State ought, therefore, to let subordinate groups handle the matters and concerns of lesser importance...."[18]

The principle of subsidiarity flows directly from the fundamental principle of the dignity of the human person, who as a free and intelligent creature is called to develop his or her human capacities, a process that society may not obstruct. Nor does the principle of subsidiarity imply that the care of the government for its citizens must be restricted as much as possible. Rather, the government must continually endeavour to maintain and increase the chances for its citizens' development. According to the principle of subsidiarity the community at the higher level must offer help when the lower community or the individual is unable to achieve its goal.[19] The principle of subsidiarity is not an argument for dismantling the welfare state, even though the limitations of the welfare state have been pointed out by the Church in the name of the principle of subsidiarity.[20]

The Right to Participate

The Catholic Church continually emphasizes a right that is closely related to the intention of the principle of subsidiarity to preserve the independence of individuals and groups in society—the right of the individual to *participate* in the responsibility and the decision-making process within social institutions, particularly in economic and political areas. When the community with others is constitutive for one's personhood and when human sociality attains its ultimate fulfilment in the political community, then political participation is a condition for being able to live and act as a person.[21] We find this line of force in Catholic social thought in the Catechism as well. In the state "the choice of the political regime and the appointment of rulers are left to the

---

[18] *Quadragesimo Anno* 79-80.

[19] S.H. Pfürtner and W. Heierle, *Einführung in die katholische Soziallehre* (Darmstadt, 1980), p.142.

[20] *Centesimus Annus* 48.

[21] John XXIII, *Mater et Magistra* (1961) 82 f.; *Pacem in Terris* 73-74. Paul VI, Apostolic letter *Octogesima Adveniens* (1971) 47. John Paul II, *Laborem Exercens* (1981) 15.

free decision of the citizens" (1901). This means that the state must follow a democratic pattern. "The Church values the democratic system ...."[22]

Basic Norms from the Perspective of Society

Because of the sociality of people society is also a source of orientations in the social thought of the Church. However, the Church is intent on not placing society as a value *over against* the individual, which could lead to the totalitarian subordination of the individual to the collective (1885). One must respect "the just hierarchy of values," and not allow the inversion of means and ends, which results in "viewing persons as mere means to that end" (1886-1887). On the other hand, the just hierarchy of values also entails that individuals may not view society merely as means for their particular ends. After all, society is comprised of other people who, in their dignity, also may not be reduced to means. It is precisely because living in society is a condition of true personhood that communal life may also dictate certain expectations with regard to the attitude and behaviour of individuals. Society cannot exist without an orientation toward the good of society on the part of its members. Important basic assumptions for the social actions of individuals that ensue from this are: *social love, solidarity, responsibility* and the *obligation to participate*.

Social Love

"Love is more fundamental than justice," Pius XI taught, for by itself justice is not a sufficient basis for the community: "in the assumption as well that everyone will ultimately receive what he deserves there will always be ample scope for love: justice alone, while able to remove the causes of social conflicts, can never create good understanding and a feeling of fellowship, no matter how faithfully it is practised."[23] *Gaudium et spes* links love with unity among people. Because God created people as a unity, with the wish that they form one family and treat one another in a brotherly way, the love for God and for one's neighbour is the first and greatest commandment.[24] In the Church's social thought love appears to relate to the fellowship and unity of the community. Love is the orientation of individuals toward the good of their fellow human beings, which consolidates them into an actual

---

[22] *Centesimus Annus* 46.

[23] *Quadragesimo Anno* 26.

[24] *Gaudium et Spes* 24.

community. Thus the Christian duty to love one's neighbour is indirectly but fundamentally a norm for individual actions from the perspective of society. The catechism links the call to love with the call to conversion. "It is necessary, then, to appeal to the spiritual and moral capacities of the human person and to the permanent need for his *inner conversion*, so as to obtain social changes that will really serve him" (1888). "Charity is the greatest social commandment. It respects others and their rights. ... [It] inspires a life of self-giving: 'Whoever seeks to gain his life will lose it, but whoever loses his life will preserve it'" (1889). An attitude of love and conversion does justice to the "spiritual reality" of human communal life. Life in a community is not simply materially motivated, based on physical needs or material advantage. Life in a community also entails that people "always be readily disposed to pass on to others the best of their own cultural heritage; and eagerly strive to make their own the spiritual achievements of others" (1886).

Solidarity

Closely connected to social love is the *principle of solidarity* (1939-1942). The concept of solidarity refers more clearly to the structure of human society than does love. Loving one's neighbour is first of all a moral attitude. Solidarity is also a moral attitude, but in addition to this it is also a social fact, namely, the showing of a common destiny.

According to the literal Latin meaning, 'solidarity' denotes the connectedness of several persons who together have to perform a duty in such a way that each of them can be called to account for the entire obligation and must vouch for the others in this. Solidarity is the collective responsibility of everyone over against everyone. Consequently, the solidarity principle expresses mutual reliance on one another, the mutual dependence of the members of the community.[25] Solidarity is an ontological principle of human beings that issues directly from their social nature. Actually, solidarity is nothing else than the origin of society in the will and actions of each individual. Only those who show solidarity can form a society.

The catechism stresses that solidarity is necessary in order to allow a good society to exist—that is, a society in which the dignity of the individual is protected by justice: "Solidarity is manifested in the first place by the distribution of goods and remuneration for work. It also presupposes the effort for a more just social order where tensions are better able to be reduced and conflicts more readily settled by negotiation" (1940).

---

[25] A. Rauscher, *Personalität, Solidarität, Subsidiarität* (Cologne, 1975), pp. 22-25.

The Catholic Church's concept of solidarity refers to a solidarity that is universal and not one that is linked to groups. In principle the circle of solidarity is unlimited: it encompasses the entire family of God's children and also reaches out to future generations (2415) and, within certain limits, to animals (2615-2617). When necessary the Church also urges solidarity *within* groups which experience discrimination, especially labourers and the poor, who can only effectively demand their rights through united actions.[26] Group solidarity, however, should not lead to forcing the issue of class distinctions.[27] The Catechism also stresses the importance of solidarity in international situations: "World peace depends in part upon this" (1941), or, in the words of John Paul II, *"opus solidarietatis pax."*[28]

Responsibility and the Obligation to Participate

The Catechism mentions the concepts of responsibility and participation in one breath (article 2, III). Nevertheless, one could distinguish the terms in such a way that participation is first and foremost a way of acting, whereas responsibility is first and foremost a situation: people *are* responsible. The specific nature of every person's responsibilities then determines the manner in which each person participates in society: "'Participation' is the voluntary and generous engagement of a person in social interchange. ... Participation is achieved first of all by taking charge of the areas for which one assumes *personal responsibility"* (1913-1914).

We referred earlier to the *right* to participate as a basic norm of social ethics from the perspective of the individual (4.4). From the perspective of society, participation is also an *obligation* of each individual: "It is necessary that all participate, each according to his position and role, in promoting the common good" (1913). The obligation to participate is closely related to the moral requirement of solidarity. People realize their mutual solidarity when each person in his own way participates in societal life.

'Responsibility' generally refers to (having to) give an answer, explaining one's conduct to a 'forum' that establishes requirements and promotes expectations with regard to individual actions. This can be the *'forum internum'* of one's own conscience, or the external forum of society. One can distinguish between a forward-looking and a backward-looking form of responsibility. Backward-looking responsibility takes the form of liability, guilt, and

---

[26] *Laborem Exercens* 20; *Sollicitudo Rei Socialis* 39.

[27] *Mater et Magistra* 147; *Laborem Exercens* 20.

[28] *Sollicitudo Rei Socialis* 39.

the obligation to restore or compensate for damages. In contrast, forward-looking responsibility refers to that which someone should do in relation to his social tasks and functions. A task is, after all, nothing other than a description of responsibilities. Finally, responsibility can refer to the *virtuousness* of a person whose decisions and actions attest to foresight, wisdom, and concern for the good of all those involved.

The Catechism speaks of responsibility in particular as a task and a virtue. Then responsibility is the orientation of one's actions toward the good of others within each person's specific task and function in society. The Catechism refers in particular to the responsibilities that ensue from tasks of educating the family, from professional tasks, and from each person's task as a citizen (1914-1915).

Responsibility also has the critical function of stimulating one to self-examination with regard to one's own involvement in social problems.[29] Thus the responsibility that one has as a citizen can also be described negatively as the obligation to avoid "fraud and other subterfuges, by which some people evade the constraints of the law and the prescriptions of societal obligation" (1916). In Catholic social thought responsibility is an obligation of the part in relation to the whole. As such it is an important concretization of solidarity, which forms the cement of society. Society comes into being because of solidarity, and solidarity is expressed in participation and the shouldering of responsibility.

The Common Good

The concept 'common good' has occurred above several times. The original Latin term for this concept is bonum commune, which literally means 'the communal good'. Freely translated, one could say that one could speak of *bonum commune* when there is a 'good society'. But then the term could easily be misunderstood if the *bonum commune* only referred to a correct social and political organization, to respect for human rights, the legal state, and social justice. It is true that these are essential elements of the *bonum commune*, but the concept entails more than that. '*Bonum commune*' is in fact the shortest possible summary of Catholic social thought. It is the point from which all its lines of thought arise and to which they return. More concretely, the *bonum commune* is where the perspectives of the individual and the community within Catholic social thought encounter each other and medi-

---

[29] This critical function emerges particularly in the document by the Pontifical Justice and Peace Commission, "An Ethical Approach to the International Debt Problem," in: *Origins*, Vol. 16 (1987), no. 34, pp. 601, 603-11.

ate with each other. It is therefore also the point in which the above mentioned basic norms from the perspectives of the individual and the community encounter each other: on the one hand, respect for human rights, social justice, subsidiarity, and the right to participate; on the other hand, social love, solidarity, responsibility, and the obligation to participate. Where the communal order is first and foremost based on respect for the human individual with his inalienable rights *and* where the individual persons are jointly oriented toward one another's well-being, *that* is where human society exists as a *bonum commune*. The Catechism defines the common good as "the sum total of social conditions which allow people, either as groups or as individuals, to reach their fulfilment more fully and more easily" (1906).[30] This is subsequently specified in three elements, all of which have reference to the responsibilities of public power: respect for the human person's rights to freedom, concern for development and social economic rights, and finally concern for peace, that is to say, the "stability and security of a just order" (1907-1909). The common good appears here primarily as a task of the government, which is the organization responsible for the promotion of the common good within society (1897, 1902, 1903). "Legitimate defense," the practice of legitimate violence against threats from within or without, is a means that the government may employ for this in extreme cases (cf. 2307-2314).

The reference to the public power that is charged with the concern for the common good should not be thought simply to mean the national state. The Catholic Church is generally very reserved with regard to national politics. Ultimately the Vatican itself is a state and, in its political capacity as the Holy See, is bound by the diplomatic taboo of 'meddling in domestic affairs' of other states. This reservation also has to do with the Aristotelian Thomistic concept of a political community, within which the modern distinction of state and society are difficult to place. A "public power," as the Catechism uses the term, can also refer to a local, regional, or international government.

The Church has always mourned the lack of an effective organization for the universal common good on a world-wide scale. In 1963 John XXIII wrote: "Today the universal common good poses problems of world-wide dimensions which cannot be adequately tackled or solved except by the efforts of public authorities endowed with a breadth of powers, structure and means of the same proportions: that is, of public authorities which are in a position to act in an effective manner on a world-wide basis."[31] The Catechism re-

---

[30] Cf. *Gaudium et Spes* 26.

[31] *Pacem in Terris* 137.

peats the plea for an effective "organization of the community of nations" and also states the most important task of this organization, which is, "to provide for the different needs of men; this will involve the sphere of social life to which belong questions of food, hygiene, education, ... and certain situations arising here and there, as for example ... alleviating the miseries of refugees dispersed throughout the world, and assisting migrants and their families" (1911).

Where the Catechism explicitly discusses the common good (1905-1912), it is regarded as a task of political leadership in particular. This does not mean that one may overlook the eminent importance that the Church attaches to the *obligations* on the part of the citizens with regard to the common good. After all, "it is necessary that all participate ... in promoting the common good. This obligation is inherent in the dignity of the human person" (1913). Concern for the common good is not only a task that the citizens may require of the government, but also a task that they may expect from one another and to which all persons should devote themselves.

The Catechism rephrases the social ethic of the Catholic Church as a dialectic of individual *and* society, of rights *and* obligations—above all, as a vision of the 'spiritual' nature of the human community that is led primarily by values and not by interests. Within the actual discussions on the moral foundations of society, on the demand for limits to a liberal ethics, in the discussion between liberalism and communitarianism, the Catholic tradition of social ethics takes a position that is very original and deserves to be heard more.

TEN

The Moral Law

Theo C.J. Beemer

In this article we will look first at the place that the treatment of the moral law occupies within the systematics of the first section of the part on morality in the Catechism, i.e., the section on general morality. How important is the concept of law in this section which bears the title: "Man's Vocation: Life in the Spirit"? Next, in the second section of this paper, we will analyze the article on the law (1949-1986) and provide some commentary on it. Here the following topics will be discussed: law and grace, the origin of the concept of law, and an attempt to understand what the natural law is. In the next section we will look, by way of illustration, at how the concepts of moral law and natural law function in the applied, concrete teaching on morality in the Catechism, which claims that various practices conflict with the moral law or with the natural law. Finally, we will discuss the text on the old law and the New Law or Law of the Gospel: a theme that is rich for believers but which functions little in the concrete ethics of the Catechism (section 2).

Moral life and a Christian View of It

More than ever before Christians are aware that moral knowledge and moral life on the one hand, faith knowledge and living out of one's faith in Christ on the other are by no means identical. We owe this sharpened awareness to the historical and geographical fact that we live in a secularized society, in which, moreover, Christians, i.e., those who confess Jesus as Lord and Christ and are taken up into his community through baptism, no longer constitute a majority of the population. Furthermore, Christians live in a society in which non-Christian religions are more and more clearly present: Judaism, Islam, and Hinduism. The peculiar question, "Are Christians morally better than others?", was previously often posed with people outside the church (sometimes called 'humanists') in mind. At present, however, it is more often asked with respect to those who adhere to a different faith. We understand that moral insight and a morally good or bad life are more general phenomena than faith in Jesus Christ. But this does not detract from the fact that something as general as the humanity of the human being, human actions with respect to good and evil, and a good organization of society are viewed from the perspective of the Christian faith in a *unique* way.

To investigate something as universally human as morality from the perspective of the Christian faith in God-with-us has occurred for centuries in moral preaching since the earliest Christian communities in the Roman Empire, and later in moral theology. Here the Catechism has nothing new to offer—though that was not its intention. Moral theology has never allowed itself to be reduced to a teaching on behaviour that was intended only for baptized Christians or Catholics. This does not happen in the third part of the Catechism either. At least, that is what I will attempt to prove in what follows, for at first glance the systematics of the Catechism do not give a clear answer to this.

I can illustrate the practical implications of this hypothesis for moral discussions in society by means of the following example: whenever the Catholic Church teaches that a specific practice, such as euthanasia, is in conflict with the moral law or the law of God, does it mean that Catholics may not engage in such a practice (or: that the church forbids it to her members)? Or does it mean that people may not do it because it is not good and that it should not become a socially accepted practice? Put more simply: if the Catechism speaks about the moral law, does it then intend a rule that obtains for Catholics or a rule that, according to it, obtains for all people?

Let us return to the hypothesis. Part Three of the Catechism bears the general title: "Life in Christ." And the short introduction that precedes the division into section one and section two (1691-1698) concerns Christians unambiguously, those who wish to follow the way of Christ and are initiated into him through the baptism. But the first section, which, as we already stated, treats general morality and fundamental concepts, has the heading, "Man's Vocation: Life in the Spirit." There are three subheadings under this caption: 1. The Dignity of the Human Person; 2. The Human Community; 3. God's Salvation: Law and Grace. The titles "Life in Christ" and "Life in the Spirit" point in two different directions. Life in Christ is, as it were, intended for baptized Christians. Life in the Spirit is intended for all people on earth. Nevertheless, according to my assessment of the texts, the second train of thought is the dominant one.

The text speaks in a believing way about the vocation and way of life of human beings—thus of all human beings. This is evident from the short description in number 1700: beginning with the dignity of the human person, which is rooted in her being created in the image of God, it indicates how people can come to the perfection of love and find true happiness in God. Numbers 1701-1707 then follow the splendid explanations of the Second Vatican Council in its document concerning the church in the contemporary world (*Gaudium en Spes*) of 1965 on the dignity of the human person. One can follow the references to this in the footnotes to these numbers. And here we already encounter the concept of moral law. Number 1706 reads:

> By his reason, man recognizes the voice of God which urges him "to do what is good and avoid what is evil." Everyone is obliged to follow this law, which makes itself heard in the conscience and is fulfilled in the love of God and of neighbor. Living a moral life bears witness to the dignity of the person.

And by way of summary, number 1713 repeats: "Man is obliged to follow the moral law, which urges him 'to do what is good and avoid what is evil'. This law makes itself heard in his conscience." However, numbers 1708 and 1709 depart from the council in a remarkable way (the references in the footnotes also stop). What is the difference?

The Council concludes the chapter on the dignity of the human person with a reflection on Christ the new Adam (*Gaudium et Spes* 22). This human being has paved the way for us and people are restored in their humanity through association with his suffering, death, and resurrection, indicated briefly as "the paschal mystery."

The Council then states expressly:

> All this holds true not for Christians only but also for all men of good will in whose hearts grace is active invisibly. For since Christ has died for all, and since all men are in fact called to one and the same destiny, which is divine, we must hold that the Holy Spirit offers to all the possibility of being made partners, in a way known to God, in the paschal mystery.

In this text J. Ratzinger, who commented on this part of the conciliar document, praised not only the connection of human salvation with the Easter mystery but also the explicit recognition by the church that the possibility of salvation for people is not dependent on their explicit recognition of God, let alone on the explicit confession of Jesus as Christ.[1]

In contrast, the Catechism closes the section on the human person as the image of God in the following way: "He who believes in Christ has new life in the Holy Spirit." A religious description of the moral life of human beings, guided by moral law and sustained by grace, is concluded in this way with a remark on the Christian believer. In my view, this is a short circuit. One does not have to believe in Christ in order to share in the new life in the Holy Spirit.

---

[1] J. Ratzinger in: *Das Zweite Vatikanische Konzil: Dokumente und Kommentare* (= LThk, 2nd. ed., Supplementary vol. III) (Freiburg, 1968), pp. 350-54.

Precisely whenever one wants to talk about morality—and not about articles of faith or the sacraments—it is of great importance to adhere, with the Second Vatican Council, to the position that every person has the possibility of coming to God through living a good moral life—understood as a life in the Spirit. This possibility is not connected to the condition that the person believes in God or is a Christian or a member of a church community.[2]

This also answers the question of whether the Catechism, whenever it states that a specific practice conflicts with the moral law, intends to address only Catholics. It does not—the church expresses its judgement that this conduct is not good for people. It does not enact an ecclesiastical law, as many Catholics incorrectly think. It places before all an instruction about what, according to its insight, is good for people and what is not. That in a number of cases the hearers, including Catholics themselves, do not simply accept that instruction as moral truth is another question.

Analysis and Commentary on the Article on Moral Law (1949-1986)

Law and Grace

As already stated, the Catechism discusses the moral law already elsewhere (1706 and 1713), namely in connection with the issue of conscience, treated in another article in this book. But we find a somewhat systematic discussion of the concept of moral law only in the third and last chapter of the doctrine on general morality. This chapter's heading reads: "God's Salvation: Law and Grace." Number 1949 states: "Divine help comes to him [the human being] in Christ through the law that guides him and the grace that sustains him." The discussion of these two themes in one chapter causes one to recall the arrangement of moral theology in Thomas Aquinas' *Summa Theologica*. He opens his treatment as follows: "We have now to consider the extrinsic principles of acts. Now the extrinsic principle inclining to evil is the devil, of whose temptations we have spoken of in the First Part (Q. 114). But the extrinsic principle moving to good is God, Who both instructs us by means of His Law, and assists us by His Grace."[3] For a correct understanding I will note that the extrinsic principles of our actions are distinguished here from the intrinsic principles which Thomas treated in the preceding questions, such as our capacity for knowing and striving and the formation of

---

[2] This is the case, however, in numbers 846-848 in a different conceptualization.

[3] *Summa Theologica* I-II.90.Prologue. The translation is taken from Thomas Aquinas, *Summa Theologica*, tr. Fathers of the English Dominican Province (London, 1922).

'habits' that prompt us to good or wrong actions (virtues and vices). 'Extrinsic' of course does not mean that God's Spirit does not work in our hearts but it does mean that God is somebody other than we are, that God's wisdom is not our wisdom, God's will is not our will. The German theologian O.H. Pesch, famous for his studies on both Thomas Aquinas (13th century) and Martin Luther (16th century), corrects the misunderstandings that this prelude on "law and grace" has caused for Protestant Christians.[4] At the same time he praises Thomas' for connecting these two themes, which were divided in the theology of later centuries into two disciplines: the teaching on the law became treated in ethics and that on grace in dogmatics. The Catechism thus returns to a premodern schema, and this has its advantages.

After treating law in article 1 and grace in article 2 this chapter has yet a third article on "The Church, Mother and Teacher." Because a specific task is given here to the Magisterium of the Pastors of the Church in instruction on the moral law, this section will also be involved in my discussion.

The Origin of the Concept of Law

The general remarks on law that the Catechism makes in numbers 1950-1953 are brief as well as incoherent and confusing. The term 'moral law' needs to be delimited over against the concept 'law' as that appears in the (natural) sciences. There a law is an established regularity with respect to the appearance of phenomena and processes. To this belong the laws of nature as well as economic laws (the Catechism opposes the "law of the market" to the moral law once).

Originally, however, the concept of law belonged to the language of morality, in which it concerned the freedom of human actions, which via a binding rule is directed to specific ends. It is clear that the concept of law has its origin in the experience of political life, which in its turn is a part of the moral order. Number 1951 also gives—with a few omissions—the classical definition of law as it appears in every textbook on moral theology. This classical definition is taken over from Thomas Aquinas: a law is a rational ordering for the sake of the common good (this term presupposes a community), enacted by those who are charged with the care of the community ("by competent authority," says the Catechism).

It is confusing, indeed misleading, that in the same number (1951) this definition of law is applied to God *without explanation*: God as a lawgiver, who as a 'competent authority', as a governor, is concerned about a particu-

---

[4] O.H. Pesch, *Thomas von Aquin: Grenze und Grösse mittelalterlicher Theologie* (Mainz, 1988), esp. ch. 12: "Gesetz und Gnade oder: Theologie der Geschichte," pp. 284-317.

lar community. But which community? With this is connected the fact that the classical but alienating concept of 'eternal law', which does not play any further role in the Catechism, is mentioned here but not really explained. Only someone well trained in theology would recognize the concept of eternal law in the second full sentence of 1951 concerning "the rational order, established among creatures." Indeed, 'eternal law', a concept which entered Christian theology via St. Augustine from Stoicism, refers to the administrative plan of divine wisdom for bringing the universe to its ultimate destiny. In that sense, even nonrational creatures 'obey' God's plan, as is stated often in the Psalms. In the concept of eternal law God is conceived of as the Lord of the cosmos and of world history who prepares a policy for bringing the universe to his Kingdom. For humans this policy is unfathomable and hidden: it is 'the mystery of [God's] will', as it is called in the letters of Paul (cf. for example Ephesians 1:9). But God has nevertheless given people some insight, namely by bestowing on them the gift of intellect which can recognize both what is good and appropriate and evil and destructive for human beings and the community. This intellectual knowledge is a reflection of the wisdom of God and is called 'the natural law'. God bestowed more insight into his ordinance, subsequently, through the historical Revelation of his intentions in the people of Israel and in Jesus Christ.

The Catechism states in number 1952 that the moral law has different expressions: the eternal law, the natural law (the term natural law is more correct since it is thus distinguished from physical laws of nature), the revealed law, and finally the civil and ecclesiastical laws. Civil and ecclesiastical laws correspond in that they are enacted by human authorities for their communities; they are always subject to being tested with respect to their justification against the 'higher' law.

I object seriously to the term 'expressions' in this text. In the first place, it is incorrect to call the eternal law, the administrative plan of God's wisdom, the expression of something else. However, more serious is that the text suggests that 'moral law' is a primary concept under which different kinds of laws are said to fall which are all equally compatible with the definition of a law.

It is of essential importance to understand *and* to say, in connection with a Christian and theological use of the concept of law, that it is *not* a general concept that is applied to kinds in a *univocal* way, but that an originally political concept is applied in an *analogous* way (thus with correspondences and considerable differences) to other phenomena. The definition of law is to be used for God as a lawgiver or for human reason as a lawgiver (empowered by God) only by way of comparison and taking account of the differences.

Pesch[5] points to this, but the British moral theologian J. Mahoney does so more extensively and acutely.[6] That God is named a lawgiver in a univocal way has for centuries had the result that 'living in the Spirit', i.e. moral life, was depicted in legal terms in which all legalistic scholarship could be indulged: when is the law proclaimed? what dispensations are possible or impossible? what sanctions has the lawgiver instituted? where is the court of justice? This legalistic language is, according to Mahoney, purely analogous: it attributes to God the words and ideas of our social experience. For centuries moral theology has already considered itself exempt from the rule that obtains everywhere else in theology, when we dare to apply concepts from our human experience to God: we can speak about God as a lawgiver only if we understand that we are speaking analogously, which can be very misleading if we do not take into consideration the differences with what we understand by a law.

All this will immediately become apparent when, in looking at the sections on the natural law (1954-1960) and those on the New Law or Law of the Gospel (1965-1974), we keep in mind the elements of the definition of law in 1951: a law is a code of conduct, enacted by competent authority for the sake of the common good.

The Natural Law: What is It?

The concept of a natural law has been an extremely important, indeed indispensable, part of the Christian reflection on the moral life for a long time, particularly with respect to its cognitive aspect: how do people know what is good? It is primarily the Catholic tradition of thought, much more than the Protestant, that has adhered to the view that human reason is in a position, independent of the biblical revelation, to recognize at least the principles of a good life. Two faith convictions are present here: first, that reason and conscience have been given to human beings by God; secondly, that the spontaneous, premoral urges (in that sense 'nature') of human beings also come from God, such as the urge for self-preservation, aggression, affection, the need for sociality, the urge to examine. This is not to say that these spontaneous urges already contain a rule or law for human action, but one can speak of a natural law in the sense that human reason, taking account of the 'nature of the beast' can devise norms for the good life and for society. Giving to everyone what is his or her due is an example of such a law. The natural law is the rational knowledge of the universal principles of humanity,

---

[5] O.H. Pesch, *Thomas von Aquin*, pp. 287-88.

[6] J. Mahoney, *The Making of Moral Theology: A Study of the Roman Catholic Tradition* (Oxford, 1987), esp. ch. 6, "The Language of Law," pp. 224-58.

both in the form of rights as well as duties. The idea of human rights and the summary of these rights are, historically seen, of much later origin than the idea of the natural law. But one could compare the knowledge of the fundamental rights and their corresponding duties with the knowledge with which the natural law provides us.

The doctrine of the natural (moral) law is important because it defends the idea of a norm that is prior to every positive law enacted by any human government, such as the constitution of a state or a church; an idea of a norm that in addition enables a rational critique of laws and historically developed customs. On the other hand, this doctrine is also unsatisfactory, because and insofar as it still leaves open all kinds of conclusions and concretizations. It does not offer any explanation for the differences among the moral traditions of different peoples. The moral theologian Bernard Häring has written that the norm that human beings must always act in accordance with the demands of the historical situation is also a part of the principles of the natural law:

> Only the knowledge of the immutably valid essential laws of natural right and of the historical situation makes it possible to form a judgment in every individual instance as to what is "historically right" and therefore also, in the full sense, "right according to nature."[7]

The Catechism states that the natural law, enacted by human reason (1955) and at the same time characterized as a very good work of the Creator (1959) offers a *foundation* on which human beings can build *the house* of moral rules for conduct which will determine their choices. This is an apt and striking metaphor, because it delineates the particular, concrete morality as a house built by human beings. (The original meaning of the Greek word *èthos* is 'stable, accustomed place'.) Morals are thus a cultural achievement, brought into existence on the basis of principles of humanity recognizable to everyone: the natural moral law. In the meantime it has become clear how much the analogy has already advanced with respect to the original concept of 'law'. It is almost superfluous to point out that from antiquity the natural law was characterized as a law written on the hearts of human beings by God. It is thus 'written' in an entirely different way than an ordinary law and is not codified.

In the presentation of the doctrine of the natural law by church and theology, doubt is usually expressed (also in the Catechism) about the ability of human reason to know what is truly human. This doubt arises in the consideration of the sinful situation of the human family (1960). Our (moral) un-

---

[7] B. Häring, *The Law of Christ: Moral Theology for Priests and Laity*, vol. 1 (Paramus, NJ, 1961), pp. 246-47.

derstanding is darkened: the power of evil is indeed so great that we not only act in contradiction to our moral insights but can also arrive at wrong insights as to what we are to do. However, I believe that this doubt can be removed if we make the reliability of our moral reasoning and of our conscience dependent on the demand that it be opened up to every unselfish instruction by others, in particular by wise and experienced people. One no longer has to suspect an understanding that is continually open to unselfish instruction; only moral self-conceit need be suspected.

The construction of the house of morals on the foundation of the natural law is, of course, possible only if one can draw conclusions from moral principles, or when one, with an eye for the historical situation, can give further human determination. As far as drawing conclusions is concerned, the following questions arise. Who draws them? And who guarantees that the conclusions are drawn in the right way?[8]

The Catechism states, in imitation, incidentally, of a doctrine that was already developed in the second century after Christ, that the principal precepts of the natural law are expressed in the Decalogue (1955). In the 1939 question and answer catechism of the Dutch bishops, which (or at least the answers) I had to learn by heart in school at that time, Question 191 reads: how has God given the ten commandments? Answer: "God has impressed the ten commandments in the hearts of people right from the outset; he gave them to the Jews through Moses, and Christ confirmed them in the New Testament."

Here we come to a thorny topic, namely how and with what authority specific commandments can be deduced from natural law and from the Decalogue. In the treatment of particular morality in the second section the Catechism follows the arrangement of the biblical Decalogue. At the same time, however, the Decalogue functions as a peg on which to hang the whole of Catholic instruction in morality, including the smallest details. The Catechism states it more splendidly: the Decalogue is the foundation for the whole edifice of the church's instructions on morality, the *depositum* of Christian ethics that was built up through the centuries by way of tradition through the Catholic church (2033; see also 2065, 2199 (in connection with the fourth commandment) and 2336 (in connection with the sixth commandment)). In number 2036 it is said that the Magisterium of the Pastors of the Church also extends to the *specific* commandments of the natural law, thus beyond general principles.

---

[8] According to O.H. Pesch, *Thomas van Aquin*, p. 289.

If one does not at all doubt the competence of the ecclesiastical leadership to give moral instruction by way of deduction and conclusion from the principles of human dignity, one is still obliged to pose a few questions: how do the pastors of the church know for certain that they always make the correct deductions from these principles? What role have historical circumstances played (and do play) in the establishment of their moral teaching? And what authoritative instruction other than themselves do the leaders of the church recognize? With respect to the last question let me point out that number 1783 speaks of authoritative instruction in general in the formation of moral conscience, whereas number 2039 speaks only of the authoritative instruction of the Magisterium of the Roman Catholic Church.

Contemporary society surely has a need for reliable and unselfish moral authorities that present human beings, society, and government with fundamental and critical insights. But it is difficult to understand why the pastors of the Roman Catholic Church should have a monopoly in this. In addition, it should be acknowledged that already within the Catholic community itself the task of finding moral truth requires that the pastors be more in tune with believers, in particular believers with moral experience in particular areas of life. Mahoney, whom we cited earlier, is of the opinion that precisely in the formation of moral opinion and judgement the distinction between an *ecclesia docens* and an *ecclesia discens* is completely inadequate and antiquated.[9]

How do the concepts of moral law and natural law function in applied morals?

Topics and issues from the particular morals of the Catechism do not constitute the theme of this book. By means of the index of key words in the French and English editions of the Catechism we can illustrate how the phrases 'moral law', 'law of God', and 'natural law' appear in the assessment of all kinds of practices. At the same time it becomes clear that legal terminology is not used in a systematic manner but, rather, incidentally.

In connection with the fourth commandment of the Decalogue, regarding the duties of civil government, we read that "No one can command or establish what is contrary to the dignity of persons and the natural law" (2235). In its treatment of the fifth commandment, in the paragraphs dealing with intentional homicide the Catechism states: "The moral law prohibits exposing someone to mortal danger without grave reason, as well as refusing assistance to a person in danger" (2269). "Direct abortion ... is gravely contrary to the moral law" (2271). "[Prenatal diagnosis] is gravely opposed to the

---

[9] J. Mahoney, *The Making of Moral Theology*, ch. 4, "Teaching with Authority," pp. 116-74.

moral law when this is done with the thought of possibly inducing an abortion" (2274). "Voluntary co-operation in suicide is contrary to the moral law" (2282). "The Church and human reason both assert the permanent validity of the moral law during armed conflict" (2312). With respect to the sixth commandment of the Decalogue we read: "[Homosexual acts] are contrary to the natural law" (2357). "Divorce is a grave offense against the natural law" (2384). "However polygamy is not in accord with the moral law" (2387). "[Free unions] are contrary to the moral law" (2390). The treatment of the seventh commandment includes the statement: "Willfully damaging private or public property is contrary to the moral law" (2409).

Honesty compels one to say that the use of legal terms occurs almost haphazardly. A number of practices are also fundamentally rejected without the use of this terminology. In such cases one sees, for example, the phrase "intrinsically evil" as in the judgement on contraception in number 2370. My conclusion therefore is that the Catechism does not attribute any high systematic value to the concept of moral law. Rather, it concerns the belief of the official moral teaching of the church that it can determine all kinds of practices as objectively wrong, conflicting in themselves with the moral order of humanity instituted by God. This was also one of the most important topics of the 1993 papal encyclical *Veritatis Splendor*. The question, "Why are you so certain of it?" refers us then to the argumentation in each case and not so much to the appeal to a law.

The Old Law and the New Law of the Gospel

According to the subdivision of the moral law in its kinds or "expressions" submitted in number 1952, the natural law is followed by the law revealed by God in history, which is also an instruction given in grace. The first form of this historical revelation is the law of Moses. The Catechism discusses this in numbers 1961-1964.

The text scarcely expresses the fact that it concerns a covenant law, in which first the saving and liberating acts of the God of Israel are recounted and only then the rules for living that Israel needs to remain in the Covenant and in the freedom bestowed on the Israelites. The harmonization of the Decalogue with the natural law, which—as already stated—originated in the second century, obscures the insight of faith that moral instruction always follows the gracious gift of liberation.[10] Even the command to love God and our neighbour as ourselves is secondary to faith in the love of God for us.

---

[10] Cf. K.-W. Merks, N. Poulssen, W. Weren, *Weg of Wet? Over de tien woorden* (Boxtel, 1989). The article by the moral theologian Merks takes up the significance of the Decalogue as social legislation and as a law of freedom.

The doctrine of the natural law does not recognize the presupposition of a prior covenant of grace and that is a loss. (Some authors refer to the Noahic covenant as such—a presupposition; theologically, this is a very interesting suggestion.)

Mahoney notes concerning the law of Moses that the analogical character of the concept of law is not pertinent to the faith of Israel. This people saw itself as a theocratic society, established in history by God's saving intervention and dependent for its existence on its faithfulness to the Law that the Lord had given Moses. The God of Israel was indeed really the ruler, the politician, simply and directly and not in an analogous sense. Why did the people need to have a king?

Jesus of Nazareth was a teacher who presented his Jewish hearers with the idea that nothing of "the Law and the prophets" would pass away. But he did radicalize this law "with authority" (Matt. 7:29). Can one now assert that Jesus was a lawgiver in the strict sense of the word? To call his instruction about how we must live a law is still possible in a metaphorical way. But as the Catechism teaches in accordance with Thomas Aquinas: the New Law is not essentially an instruction in words—it is first and foremost the grace of the Holy Spirit who influences and moves the hearts of human beings to participate in the Easter mystery of Jesus Christ, the new Adam.[11] The analogous application of the original concept of law is now stretched to the outer limit of comparability or even beyond it.[12] The Spirit instructs the hearts of people who are receptive with respect to the good that they must do. The Spirit supports their powers for the sake of the common good: the completion of the human race in the kingdom of God. Obedience to the law becomes, in this extremely metaphorical application of the concept of law, a prayer for the enlightenment of our understanding as to what we must do and for obedience to what the Spirit inspires in us.

The language of law in morality is not wrong, although it can have a wrong effect. It has a positive meaning for moral life, in particular whenever one keeps in mind its orientation to the common good. But its importance is limited. Through its haphazard and infrequent use of the term in applied morality but primarily through the title of its section on general morality, "Life in the Spirit," the Catechism actually gives the impression that the language of law is not all that important.

---

[11] Cf. O.H. Pesch, *Thomas von Aquin*, pp. 307-08.

[12] J. Mahoney, *The Making of Moral Theology*, p. 255.

ELEVEN

The Authority of Church Teaching on Matters of Morality

Joseph A. Selling

It is clear that the subject of this essay goes far beyond the new *Catechism of the Catholic Church*. Indeed, if one turns to the *Catechism* itself in search of enlightenment on this question one will probably be somewhat surprised to find that the text offers relatively little on the topic. The entry on "Authority" in the index directs the reader primarily to questions of civil authority. Under "Church: teaching ministry" one finds a fairly long list of topics which ultimately comprise only two treatises: one on the office of bishops (888-892) and the other on moral life and the magisterium (2032-2040). We will return to these texts later, after we have had the opportunity to sketch a broader context within which to interpret what the *Catechism* has to say on the matter.

It also occurs to me that our subject area might convey two, somewhat different topics: the methodological and ecclesiological questions about the sources and exercise of authority within the Catholic Christian community, and the practical and content-oriented question about what constitutes specific moral teaching and what binding force might be attached to an individual pronouncement. I believe that these two questions must be approached in the order that they are presented here, for without a sound basis in the knowledge of the sources, stating whether one or another teaching carries any binding authority will be little more than an expression of personal opinion. We therefore need to look at the "larger picture" if we hope to make any sense out of what has become a high profile issue within the church.

In one sense, we could speculate that contemporary moral theology has been preoccupied with the question of authority since 1968, when Pope Paul VI published his famous encyclical on the regulation of fertility, *Humanae Vitae*. More than a quarter of a century later, the issue of contraception is still capable of stirring heated debate at every level and in almost every corner of the church. While the teaching itself is clear, i.e., "every action which, either in anticipation of the conjugal act, or in its accomplishment, or in the development of its natural consequences, proposes, whether as an end or as a means, to render procreation impossible, is to be excluded" (HV 14), it is something of an understatement to suggest that the teaching has not been unanimously accepted within the body of the faithful.

A certain preoccupation with moral matters has been further brought to a head with the promulgation of Pope John Paul II's encyclical on moral theology, *Veritatis Splendor* (1993). Although I speculate that this text will rather quickly fade into oblivion, if for no other reason than its lack of accessibility to anyone who is not a professional moral theologian, the months following its appearance generated a plethora of commentaries and criticisms.[1] The principle subject matter of the core of this letter is moral methodology. However, the appearance of this treatise under the aegis of a papal encyclical itself raises questions about authority in this field: does hierarchical authority extend to the sanction or proposition of (moral) theological methods and tools?

Veritatis Splendor itself refers the reader back to the *Catechism* "as a sure and authentic reference text for teaching Catholic Doctrine."[2] Thus, one comes full circle with respect to the statement of the hierarchical magis-

---

[1] I will cite here only three books: J. Wilkins (ed.), *Understanding Veritatis Splendor: The Encyclical Letter of Pope John Paul II on the Church's Moral Teaching* (London, 1994); D. Mieth (ed.), *Moraltheologie in Abseits? Antwort auf die Enzyklika Veritatis Splendor* (Freiburg, 1994); J.A. Selling and J. Jans (eds), *The Splendor of Accuracy: An Examination of the Assertions made by Veritatis Splendor* (Kampen/Grand Rapids, 1994).

[2] This statement is actually a quotation taken from the Apostolic Constitution *Fidei Depositum* (11 October 1992), no. 4. I include here the last paragraph of *VS* 5:

If this Encyclical, so long awaited, is being published only now, one of the reasons is that it seemed fitting for it to be preceded by the *Catechism of the Catholic Church*, which contains a complete and systematic exposition of Christian moral teaching. The *Catechism* presents the moral life of believers in its fundamental elements and in its many aspects as the life of the "children of God:" "Recognizing in the faith their new dignity, Christians are called to lead henceforth a life 'worthy of the Gospel of Christ' (Phil 1:27). Through the sacraments and prayer they receive the grace of Christ and the gifts of his Spirit which make them capable of such a life" (*Catechism* 1692). Consequently, while referring back to the *Catechism* "as a sure and authentic reference text for teaching Catholic doctrine" (*FD*, 4), the Encyclical will limit itself to dealing with *certain fundamental questions regarding the Church's moral teaching*, taking the form of a necessary discernment about issues being debated by ethicists and moral theologians. The specific purpose of the present Encyclical is this: to set forth, with regard to the problems being discussed, the principles of a moral teaching based upon Sacred Scripture and the living Apostolic Tradition (*Dei Verbum*, 10), and at the same time to shed light on the presuppositions and consequences of the dissent which that teaching has met.

terium about its own authority in moral matters. It is almost as if the source of this authority is contained within the statement of the claim itself. It is self-referential.

The General Claim to Authority

A preliminary look at the *Catechism* at this point sets the scene for the more specific discussion about morality by first looking at the source for all (teaching) authority, namely Scripture and Tradition. In Part One, Chapter Two, Article Two, on "The Transmission of Divine Revelation," the third section discusses "The Interpretation of the Heritage of Faith" (84-95). The text begins in para. 84 by recounting the role of the apostles as the recipients of the faith: "The apostles entrusted the 'Sacred deposit' of the faith (the *depositum fidei*), contained in Sacred Scripture and Tradition, to the whole of the Church." This is followed with a quotation from *Dei Verbum*, 10 § 1 on the apostolic heritage.[3] The next three paragraphs purport to build on this idea, but the way in which this is done can be appreciated only by examining the text itself.

> 85 'The task of giving an authentic interpretation of the Word of God, whether in its written form or in the form of Tradition, has been entrusted to the living teaching office of the Church alone. Its authority in this matter is exercised in the name of Jesus Christ.' [DV 10 § 2] This means that the task of interpretation has been entrusted to the bishops in communion with the successor of Peter, the Bishop of Rome.
>
> 86 'Yet this Magisterium is not superior to the Word of God, but is its servant. It teaches only what has been handed on to it. At the divine command and with the help of the Holy Spirit, it listens to this devotedly, guards it with dedication and expounds it faithfully. All that it proposes for belief as being divinely revealed is drawn from this single deposit of faith' [DV 10 § 2].
>
> 87 Mindful of Christ's words to his apostles: 'He who hears you, hears me' (Luke 10:16), the faithful receive with docility the teachings and directives that their pastors give them in different forms.

---

[3] DV 10 § 1: "By adhering to [this heritage] the entire holy people, united to its pastors, remains always faithful to the teaching of the apostles, to the brotherhood, to the breaking of bread and the prayers. So, in maintaining, practising and professing the faith that has been handed on, there should be a remarkable harmony between the bishops and the faithful." See note 46 in the text for further references.

Between two quotations (successive in the original) from DV 10 in paras. 85 and 86 there is a strategically placed interpretive sentence that identifies 'the bishops (in communion with the successor of Peter)' as 'the living teaching office of the Church alone'. The 'teaching office' of the first quotation is then translated with the latinized word, 'Magisterium', when it is pointed out that this office is not superior to the Word of God. Finally, para. 86 cements the implication of the episcopal-magisterial identification by using the words of Christ to direct the faithful to be 'docile' toward this 'teaching-office/magisterium' in accepting its "teachings and directives." What begins in *Dei Verbum* as an explanation of the transmission and maintenance of the integrity of Scripture and Tradition as the source of our faith is put forth by the *Catechism* as a justification why the faithful need to adhere to the "directives" of their bishops.

This is what one might call 'creeping authoritarianism', formulated in a language which can defend itself against the charge of being inaccurate on the grounds that a 'catechism' is not a proper place for technical language, and yet simultaneously abusing the technical theological language that was so carefully respected in documents like the very "Dogmatic Constitution on Divine Revelation" that is quoted. The authors of the *Catechism* apparently did not experience a need to remain within the bounds of technical distinctions and consequently attribute the same 'authority' by which the church protects Scripture and Tradition to the issuing of unspecified 'directives ... in different forms'. Does this include *all* different forms? Are the faithful to exercise the same docility toward the decision of a local 'pastor' with respect to which films they should see as they are called upon to demonstrate with respect to the interpretation of Sacred Scripture? Does this expectation of 'docility' extend to the elaboration of moral method, principles, or specific norms?

Furthermore, placing the 'magisterium' virtually on the same plane as Scripture and Tradition[4] is particularly dangerous when this 'magisterium'

---

[4] The last sentence of DV 10 reads: "It is clear, therefore, that sacred tradition, sacred Scripture, and the teaching authority of the Church, in accord with God's most wise design, are so linked and joined together that one cannot stand without the others, and that all together and each in its own way under the action of the one Holy Spirit contribute effectively to the salvation of souls." This statement is not intended to put the 'magisterium' on the same level as Scripture and Tradition, but rather to recognize that it is the community of the church itself, exercising its mandate (office) to teach, that is responsible for the determination, transmission and maintenance of the primary source of our faith. The canon of Scripture itself is determined by the church, and the meaning (interpretation) of scripture is continuously held within the community of the church. The 'third dimension' of the phrase from *Dei Verbum* must

is interpreted not in its broad traditional sense but rather in the "restricted modern sense"[5] of the late nineteenth century, namely as an office exercised by a relatively few number of persons whose principle qualification is membership in the hierarchy rather than theological training. In this relatively recent understanding, the meaning of 'magisterium' as a teaching office "refers not to the function but to the functionaries."[6] The source of interpreting and understanding Scripture and Tradition, then, is attributed not to an office (task, mandate) of the church but merely to certain individuals who happen to occupy a particular place in the hierarchy.

The first attempt to come to terms with the meaning of authority and authoritative teaching according to the *Catechism*, then, does not shed a great deal of light upon the problem of identifying either the agents or the nature of the work of interpreting and teaching what is essential to the faith and authentically (i.e., authoritatively) part of the sources of the faith (Scripture and Tradition). Rather than relying on the *Catechism* itself, then, we need to return to a more historical sense of tradition.

Authority and Tradition

In many ways, the question of authority is very much a question of tradition, not simply because Tradition in the technical sense is recognized as a source of authority, but also because the question of authority has its own tradition (in the non-technical sense of history). In my opinion, one of the more prominent authors who cannot be ignored in any study of authority (and morality) is Yves Congar, O.P., whose extraordinary studies of the magisterium as an expression of (teaching) authority in the church have been an inspiration to a generation of post-Vatican II theologians.[7]

---

be interpreted cautiously, lest one falls to the temptation to place it on a par with the Word of God itself.

[5] R. Murray, "The Human Capacity for God, and God's Initiative," paras. 26-141, in: M.J. Walsh (ed.), *Commentary on the Catechism of the Catholic Church* (London, 1994) pp.6-35, Excursus on "Further Reflections on magisterium, and 'Magisterium'" 34-35, p.35.

[6] M.A. Fahey, "Church," in: F. Schüssler Fiorenza and J.P. Galvin (eds), *Systematic Theology: Roman Catholic Perspectives* (Minneapolis, 1991) pp.1-75, "Magisterium," 49-50, p.49.

[7] See especially two articles in *Revue des sciences philosophiques et théologiques* 60 (1976): "Pour une histoire sémantique du term 'Magisterium'" (pp.85-98) and "Bref historique des formes du 'magistère' et de ses relations avec les docteurs"

Congar's studies revealed the shortsightedness of considering the teaching authority exclusively in terms of the hierarchical magisterium. Such a view would presume that history began, or goes no further back, than the first Vatican Council (1870), a statement that would in its own right be shocking to those who presume that the 'modern' concept of magisterial authority is traceable at least as far back as the Council of Trent.

Up to and including the time of the Council of Trent (1545-1563), although the term itself is not used with any great frequency, 'magisterium' refers to the position and authority of a teacher in matters of the faith, what we would call a theologian. Around the eleventh century, the term began to take on a more juridical overtone, as the one who decides or judges in a dispute. Nevertheless, this power of judgment resided not in a position as such but in a certain level of established learning (competency). Magisterium was considered a ministry and not a quality acquired *ex officio*.

By the twelfth and thirteenth centuries, after the split between the Eastern and Western traditions, in the West we witness the growth first of the cathedral schools and eventually the universities as centres of higher learning. In this context, the 'magister', a term that survives today as the title of the ultimate degree in sacred theology, was a learned teacher, usually the holder of a particular chair. In the Middle Ages, it was the scholars who looked after the integrity of the faith and upheld 'orthodox' theology. Increasingly, however, the resources of the universities were used at the convenience of ecclesiastical powers, which in turn became more conceptual in the expression of dogmas. The fear of heresy, the repeated affirmation that the church of Rome never erred, the progressive insistence that magisterial judgment put a definitive end to theological debate, and the claim (traceable to the time of Gregory VII and the 'false decretals' in the eleventh century) that the pope had the exclusive right to convoke a council, all contributed to the growing centralization of authority, including that of teaching the 'true faith', that eventually became identified as a form of 'magisterium'.

More important for the evolution of the concept of magisterium than the consolidation of power in the modern church, however, is a fundamental change in the notion of theology itself as a form of intellectual knowledge. It is primarily the Enlightenment that gave rise to the rationalistic tendencies

---

(pp.99-112); reprinted in English in C.E. Curran and R.A. McCormick (eds), *Readings in Moral Theology, No. 3: The Magisterium and Morality* (New York, 1982) as "A Semantic History of the Term 'Magisterium'" (pp.297-313) and "A Brief History of the Forms of the 'Magisterium' and Its Relations with Scholars" (pp.314-31). For a wider background to these studies, see also: *Tradition and Traditions: An Historical and Theological Essay* (London, 1966), originally published as *La Tradition et les Traditions: Essai Historique* (1960) *Essai Théologique* (1963).

of eighteenth and nineteenth-century theology that culminated in the pronouncements of the first Vatican Council. If theology becomes merely propositional, it is easy to understand how one might conceive the role of 'authority' to be little more than judging the correctness or incorrectness of a given proposition or deciding between one proposition and another. It is thus as much the responsibility of a theology that presents itself primarily as a matter of conclusions that the authority-theology issue becomes reduced to a question of approval or condemnation, since it is the accountability of those who exercise the hierarchical form of teaching office in a way that does not rise above a legislative notion of the faith and a juridical concept of authority.

Up until the time of the French Revolution, centres of theological learning continued to play an active part in the 'development' of theological insight, insofar as that was possible in the post-Tridentine age.[8] Rome played the part of intervening to solve controversies as well as judging theological orthodoxy in the light of the Tridentine expressions; but for the most part, Rome initiated hardly any theological 'teaching' itself, being content with the competence of trusted experts on theological matters.[9] As the church approached the eve of the Vatican Council in the last century, however, things were again changing. Among other things, a tremendous revival of religious and church life was going on amidst the tumultuous evolution of political life in most of Western Europe.[10] With democracies being built throughout Europe and monarchies either being destroyed or relegated to formalistic positions of power, the 'authority question' was not only on the lips of churchmen but signified a controversy that was typical of the age. When Vatican I

---

[8] On 16 January 1564, Pius IV issued the bull, *Benedictus Deus*, according to which no commentary or interpretation was allowed to be given to any document or decision of the Council of Trent, with the exception of those official explanations provided by the official Vatican sources. In fact, the official "Acts of the Council" of Trent were only published in this century. See P. Fransen, "A Short History of the Meaning of the Formula *fides et mores*," *Louvain Studies* 7 (1978-79): 270-301, p.289.

[9] At both Trent and Vatican I, official commentators on the conciliar texts, as these texts were subject to the processes of drafting and editing, would make continuous references to 'the fathers' and to 'commonly held theological opinions' to substantiate the positions they took with respect to revisions of the texts under their charge. These 'opinions' were considered to be an important *locus theologicus* in determining the mind of the church on particular matters.

[10] See P. Hughes, *The Church in Crisis: The Twenty Great Councils* (London, 1961) pp.294-302.

addressed the question of authority from an ecclesiastical point of view, then, it was not as 'out of step' with actual events as a retrospective view of things might suggest.

'Fides et mores' from Trent to Vatican I

Maurice Bévenot[11] points out that at Trent there is a direct parallel between *fides et mores* and *veritas et disciplina*. His concern is a comparison of the use of these phrases in the Councils of Trent and the Vatican with a view toward clarifying the meaning of *fides*. He argues, successfully I believe, through an analysis of *fides* and of what was considered to constitute 'heresy', that the decrees and canons of the Council of Trent took a much broader approach to this topic than would later be the case at the Vatican Council.

At Trent, the two phrases are used more or less interchangeably. This Council, we must remember, was concerned with the Reformation and was attempting to address a broad range of matters, not all of which are directly traceable to revelation. When Trent issued condemnations, and even when it used the term *anathema sit*, it included a broad range of things that are not only based upon revelation, not only deducible from revelation or necessary to protect the integrity of revelation; it also included disciplinary matters that have little or nothing to do with revelation.

We must also remember that the fathers at Trent were not concerned with such distinctions, and so we should not draw unwarranted conclusions from this observation. The simple point to be made is that, concerned with the integrity of the Catholic faith and attempting to counter the attacks of the reformers, Trent issued decrees and condemnations on a broad range of things, up to and including merely disciplinary matters. When Trent turned to its 'second agenda', as it were, namely the need to reform the church itself from within, its decrees, and its condemnations as well (though these did not include *anathema*'s), even more frequently extended to items that were not connected with revelation at all but with the day to day (e.g., liturgy) and generation to generation (e.g., seminaries, priesthood) running of the church.

All in all, the concern of the fathers at Trent was more disciplinary than propositional. The 'truth' of the 'faith' was taken for granted. The principle

---

[11] "'Faith and Morals' in the Councils of Trent and Vatican I," *The Heythrop Journal* 3 (1962): 15-30. Bévenot is dependent upon the early work of, among others, Piet Fransen on Trent and concludes his contribution with a remark that more work still needs to be done on the precise meaning of the term *mores*, something that may have prompted Fransen's deepening investigation of the issues.

issues concerning the reformers were jurisdictional, so that a number of condemnations were formulated not with respect to whether a particular teaching was 'true' but rather in reference to the competence of the church to proclaim a teaching or make a (practical) judgment based upon that teaching.[12]

Thus, an analysis of the meaning of *mores/disciplina* at Trent, in close parallel with the meaning of *fides/veritas*, was very broad. It was neither as technical nor as restrictive as later pronouncements would be, and the area indicated by *mores/disciplina* encompassed much more than what we would today call "morality."

The atmosphere at the first Vatican Council, however, was very different. The principle concern here was the relationship between reason and faith, and the emphasis of its decisions and teaching concerned an intellectual assent to the truths of faith.[13] Such truths, approached in the climate of a declining but still very much present rationalism of the (post-)enlightenment period, were considered beyond the powers of natural reason and therefore did not demand any logical demonstration. Giving intellectual assent to such truths was a matter of decision, not reflection and conclusion. The definition of papal primacy and infallibility included the right to teach these truths (*doctrina de fide vel moribus*, to be believed and held by all the faithful): those that are contained in the sacred scriptures, those that are 'manifest' in the scriptures, and those "so intimately bound up with revelation, that a man who denied them would, to say the least, be putting his very faith in danger."[14]

At the same time, at Vatican I a sharp distinction is introduced between the *doctrina* (*fides et mores*) and *disciplina*. In the former phrase, used to delineate the scope of papal teaching that might be declared to be infallible, there is a clear reference to revelation; while in the latter, we are confronted with matters of church administration.

> That is why it was laid down that, as we have seen, all have a duty of subordination and obedience to the Pope, not only in matters that concern faith and morals [i.e. when he teaches the *doctrine* about them], but also in those matters that belong to the discipline and government of the world-wide Church [i.e. when he issues some specific regulation]. If this is how the passage should be understood (and so, I think, it should), then *disciplina* means executive meas-

---

[12] See especially some of P. Fransen's later work on this question, "Divorce on the Ground of Adultery—The Council of Trent (1563)," *Concilium* 6 (1970): 89-100.

[13] P. Hughes, *The Church in Crisis*, pp. 302-312. See, also, F.A. Sullivan, *Magisterium: Teaching Authority in the Catholic Church* (Dublin, 1983).

[14] M. Bévenot, "'Faith and Morals,'" p. 18.

ures imposing (or forbidding) action, in contradistinction to decrees laying down what must be believed or held as true (*doctrina* de fide vel moribus).[15]

The conclusions I would draw from this and subsequent studies is that distinctions were introduced at the time of Vatican I that have had an important influence on the further development of theology. In one sense, Vatican I represented an effort to *extend* hierarchical and especially papal authority throughout the church. The difference between Trent and Vatican I was the insistence upon the 'truth value' of various papal pronouncements. In the sixteenth century it was sufficient to declare what was expected of the faithful in regard to what one professed and what one did. In the nineteenth century, there was an overwhelming concern about the validity of ecclesiastical and papal statements themselves. While Trent, therefore, could combine various levels of 'truth', certainty or necessity in its pronouncements, Vatican I had to be extremely careful in how it phrased its statements. The distinction between *mores* and *disciplina* is significant not so much for what it says about conduct or behaviour (*disciplina*) but for the level of restriction that is placed upon the truth of those things considered to be morals (*mores*). The former is placed under papal (and presumably also episcopal) jurisdiction and everyone is called upon to obey ecclesiastical authority, while the latter falls under the rubric of infallibility, so that one is obliged to submit not to the person or office of the Bishop of Rome but rather to the absolute truth value of a statement.

This, of course, immediately begs the question of how one could be (so) certain of the truth of a pronouncement. For the believing Christian, truth is preeminently found in the Word of God, in revelation. *Fides et mores*, then, in some distinction with the understanding at Trent, is strictly tied to revealed truth, especially in its written form as the scriptures. First, whatever is clearly present in scripture and tradition constitutes something known as true because of its origin in the Word of God and thus something that is proclaimed by the church infallibly. Secondly, however, there are other things that, though not necessarily 'contained' in revelation are so closely connected with revelation that they may also be said to be true and thus able to be proclaimed infallibly by the church. These are the so-called 'secondary objects' of infallibility and encompass those things flowing directly from revelation as deduced from the revealed truth itself and those things without which (because they would be necessary) or with which (because they would constitute an obstacle to faith) revelation itself could not be known and maintained.

Rather surprisingly, there is very little theological discussion with respect to what might constitute the 'primary object of infallibility' with re-

---

[15] M. Bévenot, "'Faith and Morals,'" p. 18.

spect to *mores*. Apparently there is a general (theological) consensus about what might constitute 'revealed morality'. I would venture to go even further and speculate that the content of such a category would be exceedingly small. The 'closer' one comes to sacred scripture, that is, the more deeply one studies the scriptures with the aid of all the available tools (that have been approved by the 'magisterium' itself), the more one realizes that there is precious little that can be found in the Bible that would offer a clear, explicit and immediately applicable behavioural norm that one would classify as 'moral'.[16]

It is quite another matter to consider the so-called 'secondary object(s)' of infallibility, which, by definition, are already at least one step removed from revelation. Two questions seem particularly pertinent to us here: whether what one might call 'natural morality' constitutes part of this secondary object, and whether specific moral norms (on their own, or a group of norms related to each other in some manner) might ever be considered part of this secondary object.

F.A. Sullivan appears to provide an adequate rejection of the first proposition, offering, among other things, a comment by Bishop Gasser, official spokesperson for the Theological Commission at Vatican I. The Commission had to deal with a suggestion to substitute the phrase 'principles of morals' for the technical term *res [fidei et] morum*. This suggestion was rejected because, "principles of morals can be other merely philosophical principles of natural morality, which do not in every respect pertain to the deposit of faith."[17] Sullivan concludes, and I agree, that this position is sufficient evidence to demonstrate that, at least at Vatican I, the area of 'natural morality' as such does not constitute material for the (secondary) object of infallibility.

Before moving on, it is perhaps worthy to point out that the rejection of 'natural morality' as something at least indirectly or implicitly related to revelation pertains to the *content* of what one might include in this category

---

[16] Most discussion about scripture and morality centres upon questions of motivation, orientation, and direction rather than upon the elaboration of specific norms. Besides the classic study by R. Schnackenberg, *Die sittliche Botschaft des Neuen Testamentes* (Munich, 1954); *The Moral Teaching of the New Testament* (Freiburg, 1965); for a sampling of contemporary literature on the subject, see C.E. Curran and R.A. McCormick (eds), *Readings in Moral Theology, No. 4: The Use of Scripture in Moral Theology* (New York, 1984).

[17] F.A. Sullivan, *Magisterium*, pp. 131-42, p. 140. The English translation is that provided by Sullivan, who includes the original Latin: "Insuper principia morum possunt esse alia mere philosophica naturalis honestatis, quae non sub omni respectu pertinent ad depositum fidei."

and not necessarily its existence. *That* a 'natural morality' exists would appear to be implied, if not contained, in the famous statement of Romans 2: 14-15b: "Indeed, when Gentiles, who have not the law, do by nature things required by the law, they are a law for themselves, even though they do not have the law, since they show that the requirements of the law are written on their hearts." By the same token, one could propose that any statement that denied the existence of 'natural morality' made it impossible to accept that there is a law written on persons' hearts, or for that matter that refused to accept that persons could come to correct moral conclusions using 'natural morality' would also have to be (authoritatively) rejected as erroneous, perhaps even rejected 'infallibly'.

Exactly *what* a so-called 'natural morality' might contain is an entirely different question, one which brings us to the second proposition mentioned above with respect to individual (or groups of related) specific moral norms. Can specific moral norms ever be considered part of the 'secondary object' of infallible statements? Although it would appear that the restriction mentioned above with regard to the fact that some 'merely philosophical principles' would not necessarily have anything to do with the deposit of faith, there are those who persist in hypothesizing that indeed some specific moral statements may be classified as infallible, at least as far as the 'ordinary magisterium'[18] is concerned. One such example would be the attempt of Ford and Grisez to suggest that the prohibition against the use of contraception constitutes infallible teaching, a position that has sparked a continuing debate in moral theological literature.[19] Most of that debate centres around searching for arguments to establish a candidacy for belonging to that body of material that *might* be considered capable of being proclaimed infallibly. (Too) little attention, in my opinion, is given to the question whether there could possibly be any connection with this specific norm and revelation in general.[20] Most of the argument, from those who claim infallibility for this

---

[18] See J.P. Boyle, "The Ordinary Magisterium: Towards a History of the Concept," *Heythrop Journal* [1] 20 (1979): 380-98, [2] 21 (1980): 14-29.

[19] J.C. Ford and G. Grisez, "Contraception and the Infallibility of the Ordinary Magisterium," *Theological Studies* 39 (1978): 258-312. F.A. Sullivan, *Magisterium*, pp. 119-52, esp. pp. 142-152, made a particular effort to take on the hypothesis of Ford and Grisez. This was followed by G. Grisez, "Infallibility and Specific Moral Norms: A Review Discussion," *The Thomist* 49 (1985): 248-87; Sullivan, "The 'Secondary Object' of Infallibility," *Theological Studies* 54 (1993): 536-50; and Grisez, "Quaestio Disputata: The Ordinary Magisterium's Infallibility," *Theological Studies* 55 (1994): 720-38.

[20] F.A. Sullivan, "The 'Secondary Object' of Infallibility" (1993), p. 545, notes

specific norm, appears to centre around the somewhat reversed argument of constancy (cf. *Humanae Vitae*, 6 on this issue as well): because either the magisterium states or theologians assume that a teaching must be held as definitive, it is presumed to be irreformable. Theologically, the argument actually works the other way around: because a teaching is proposed as irreformable, it is expected to be held definitively. Nonetheless, the lack of evidence for any basis in scripture sometimes leads proponents of the theory that specific moral norms are contained in revelation to the argument of last resort: the norm so stipulated is actually a manifestation of the "will/plan of God".[21] Until someone provides us with a clue of how a mere mortal can definitively know what the will of (this anthropomorphic image of) God might be, we will simply leave such arguments aside.

Dogma, Doctrine and Teaching

When Vatican II took on the question of episcopal and papal authority in *Lumen Gentium*, it did not go very much further than what had been accomplished at Vatican I except, perhaps, to reinstate the importance of *communio*, collegiality and the generally underplayed role of the bishops throughout the world and throughout history in maintaining and teaching the integrity of the faith. At the very least, the question of who forms the 'subject' of authority was very much part of the agenda of the council. The

---

that recent scriptural scholarship has more or less discredited the story of Onan (Genesis 38:4-10), such that while Pius XI alluded to the story in *Casti Connubii* in 1930, Paul VI avoided any mention of it in *Humanae Vitae* in 1968. Grisez, on the other hand, "Quaestio Disputata," p.722, states that, "while it is true that Ford and I prescinded from the question whether the norm excluding contraception is revealed, we argued that the widespread use in the past of the Onan story and other scriptural texts to illustrate the Church's teaching rejecting contraception, together with other facts suggesting that the norm is revealed, tends to show that this teaching is at least connected with divine revelation in such a way as to fall within the secondary object of infallibility." It is incredible how a simple phrase like "tends to show" is presumed by Grisez to demonstrate that his point has been proven. It would be interesting to exegete what Grisez claims are "other scriptural texts to illustrate the Church's teaching rejecting contraception." If these are sound sources, it is not at all clear why Paul VI would have omitted them from his encyclical.

[21] On a parallel issue, namely the question of artificial insemination *in vitro* and the official position of the magisterium on the question, see J. Jans, "God or Man? Normative Theology in the Instruction *Donum Vitae*," *Louvain Studies* 17 (1992): 48-64.

lively discussions that took place during and ever since Vatican II testify not only to the importance of this issue but also to a certain sense that it is not yet resolved.[22]

I would suggest that the question of the 'object' of authoritative statements stands in need of clarification as well. Although it is possible to appreciate the transition that took place between Trent and Vatican I with respect to the distinction between *doctrina* and *disciplina*, it appears that such distinctions have escaped the authors of the *Catechism*, not to mention the speculations of theologians like John Ford and philosophers like Germain Grisez.[23] There is something to be said for the use of technical language in theological discourse, even if this remains difficult to communicate on a popular or pastoral level.

The distinctions that were traditionally (debated and ultimately) accepted with regard to the primary and secondary object of authoritative statements, particularly those that might be pronounced in an irreformable manner, may still be helpful in shedding light on the matter of *mores* and *disciplina*. Thus, we can refer to those things that are directly traceable to revelation, being explicitly stated or implicitly present in scripture and in apostolic tradition, as *dogma*. 'Secondarily', we can refer to those things that are intimately connected with the content of revelation, necessary for the maintenance of its integrity or (negatively) to be avoided as a threat to its integrity as *doctrina*. This would simultaneously explain the extent of irreformable pronouncements being described with the phrase *doctrina de fide vel moribus* (*Pastor aeternus*, *Denz-Schoen*. 3074) and the notation of Vatican II that the object of this teaching "extends as far as extends the deposit of divine revelation" (*Lumen Gentium*, 25).

What we need, I suggest, is a third, more clearly delineated category that indicates an area that has little or nothing to do with revelation, at least in the manner described above. This we can designate by the vernacular word 'teaching' (*leer, Lehre, enseignement*) that must not be confused with being a simple translation of the technical word *doctrina*. If we need to draw parallels with the Latin terminology, 'teaching' would be related to *disciplina*, a general category that describes a way of doing things, a manner or style of behaviour. The word 'discipline' refers not only to formal control (particularly of oneself as well as of a certain type, as in 'military disci-

---

[22] See, for instance, E. Schillebeeckx, "Breuken in christelijke dogma's," in: *Breuklijnen: Grenservaring en zoektochten. 14 essays voor Ted School bij zijn afschied van de theologische faculteit Nijmegen* (Baarn, 1994), pp. 15-49.

[23] See the article mentioned above, J.C. Ford and G. Grisez, "Contraception and the Infallibility of the Ordinary Magisterium."

pline') but also to a body of knowledge, a science or skill. Hence, physics and mathematics are both disciplines but so is physical training and physical education.[24]

This third category would encompass the broadest scope of material, quite unlike the well-defined terms *dogma* and *doctrina*. Exactly what it might encompass, however, is still a matter of speculation. Most Catholic Christians would agree that one who hears and professes to believe in the Gospel of Jesus Christ should exhibit a particular kind of life-style that would not only not contradict but actually reflect such a belief. It is on this basis that even scripture (1 Corinthians 6) testifies to the exclusion of those who lead a certain way of life from the Kingdom of God. The scriptures, however, do not address specific, isolated acts performed by human persons, nor do they call into question what were at the time established practices considered to be 'natural or normal'. Thus, St. Paul questions neither the institution of slavery nor the idea that women should assume a lesser place, even within the Christian community. It goes without saying that these notions are not warmly received in our day.

The farther away one gets from revelation, therefore, the less certainty one can have about the accuracy or lastingness of particular (moral) propositions. In comparison with the highly restricted *doctrina moribus*, what is taught as *disciplina (mores)* constitutes a very wide category indeed. This insight is aptly reflected in the contemporary moral theological distinction between 'fundamental norms' and 'concrete norms', the first of which refer to attitudes or dispositions (virtues) and the second to behaviour. Fundamental norms are basically compatible with and to some extend even contained in scripture, finding their strongest expression in the Sermon on the Mount (Matthew 5-7). We are all called to live our lives in the love of God and of neighbour (Matthew 22:37-40; Mark 12:39-31; Luke 10:27). When we apply this attitude of love to the different dimensions of our lives, we begin to elaborate a list of virtues: love applied to human relations is called justice, applied to communication it is called honesty, or to sexuality is called chastity, and so forth. None of these fundamental norms tells us precisely what to do; they only indicate the attitude that we should bring to human situations.

Concrete norms, on the other hand, address the area of human behaviour and are basically of two types. 'Concrete *material* norms' (CMNs) de-

---

[24] Similarly, another synonym for 'teaching', the word *praecepta*, which also refers to commands or rules (norms), is derived from the verb *praecipio*, which indicates the taking or receiving of something 'in advance'; hence the receiving of instruction so that one is prepared for one's task; as it were, learning the 'rules of the game' before we begin to play.

scribe behavioural actions (or omissions) in a descriptive manner, indicating the real or potential presence of good and/or evil in that activity. Positive and negative examples would be: return borrowed property, do not kill. 'Concrete *synthetic* norms' (CSNs) purport to account for not only what takes place but also the motive for acting and any relevant circumstances. Positive and negative examples would be: keep the Lord's day holy, do not murder.

While the '*synthetic*' variety of concrete norms appears to address specifically moral incidents, the simpler, '*material*', variety is limited to the describable aspects of human behaviour which, in themselves, are inadequate for making a moral judgment. Furthermore, specific moral norms are usually historical (time bound), cultural (emanating from the consensus of a moral community), and ultimately human (fabricated to suit human situations and circumstances). What is more, the very fulfilment or negation of a CMN usually results in a change in the situation that was initially addressed by that norm, altering the circumstances in which its further (repeated) application must be reassessed.

Authority in Moral Teaching According to the Catechism

With this admittedly brief, sketch of the background issues, we can now turn to the *Catechism* itself and ask how it addresses the issue of 'authoritative' moral teaching. As stated above, there are two places in which this topic surfaces. The first has to do with the 'subject(s)' of this teaching and the second with its 'object'.

Paragraphs 888-892 of the *Catechism* form a subdivision of a larger text on "The Hierarchical Constitution of the Church" (874-896). This entire treatise is divided quite logically but is written somewhat inconsistently. It has five sections, the first two on the function and structure of the hierarchy and the last three on the triple episcopal office of teaching (888-892), sanctifying (893) and governing (894-896). The opening section first explains what is meant by "ecclesial ministry" (874-879), quoting liberally from scripture and apparently following the conciliar teaching (*Lumen Gentium*) by emphasizing this ministry as service, exercised in both a collegial and personal way. The second section explains the relations between "the episcopal college and its head, the Pope" (880-887), stressing rather ardently that "the *college or body of bishops* has no authority unless united with the Roman Pontiff, Peter's successor, as its head."

Beginning the section on the threefold office, the 'teaching office' is first described in relation to the bishops.

888 Bishops, with priests as co-workers, have as their first task 'to preach the Gospel of God to all men', in keeping with the Lord's command. They are 'heralds of faith, who draw new disciples to Christ; they are authentic teachers' of the apostolic faith 'endowed with the authority of Christ'.

Neither in this, nor in the two following sections on sanctifying and governing, do we see a return of the ideas of service, collegiality and personal vocation that were indicated in the opening paragraphs. What we do see in the following four paragraphs on the teaching office is an emphasis on the Magisterium, on infallible teaching, and on 'The Roman Pontiff' as the principle bearer of this 'charism'. It is almost as if the only 'teaching' worth talking about is infallible teaching. Or is the implication that virtually all teaching, particularly that which emanates from the Roman Pontiff, somehow shares the mark of infallibility, lies in its shadow or in some way or another is implicated by association?

Here we find no distinction between *dogma*, *doctrina*, and the far more general category of simply 'teaching', *disciplina*. The average member of the church reading this text could very well get the impression that it is a question of 'all or nothing'. There appears to be little room for 'daily teaching', 'general guidance', 'fraternal counsel', or even that (recently) famous phrase 'ordinary magisterium' which, in this text at least, appears to enjoy a kind of 'virtual infallibility', demanding 'religious assent, which though distinct from the assent of faith, is none the less an extension of it'.[25] The 'creeping authoritarianism' mentioned above is here turned into a kind of 'creeping infallibility' that seems to make most episcopal and just about the totality of papal teaching absolute.

To see how this impacts upon the specific area of 'moral teaching' we need to consider another treatise, this one comprising the first part of Article 3, "The Church, Mother and Teacher," of the third Chapter, "God's Salvation: Law and Grace," in the first section of Part Three of the *Catechism*, "Life in Christ." As this article concludes the introduction to the so-called moral teaching of the church as presented in the *Catechism*, it concentrates

---

[25] Cf. E. Schillebeeckx, "Breuken in christelijke dogma's," pp.44-45: "The response to *ex-cathedra* pronouncements is expected to be an 'obedience of faith' (*obedientia fidei*); while the proper response to the fallible statements of the 'authentic teaching office' is only 'religious assent' (*obsequium religiosum*). This is already a substantial and fundamental distinction, recognized by Vatican II. Canon 833 [sic; cf. 752] of the new Code explicitly determines this *obsequium religiosum*. There is, according to these documents, no question of demanding an assent of faith or an irrevocable inner assent to the moral details of this encyclical [*Veritatis Splendor*]; simply religious respect" (translation is my own).

upon the teaching office, under the title, "Moral Life and the Magisterium of the Church" (2032-2040).

The first paragraph of this treatise consists of three quotations which symbolize, with all due respect to Canon Law, a movement from the sublime to the ridiculous.

> 2032 The Church, the 'pillar and bulwark of the truth' (1 Timothy 3:15), 'has received this solemn command of Christ from the apostles to announce the saving truth' (LG, 17). 'To the Church belongs the right always and everywhere to announce moral principles, including those pertaining to the social order, and to make judgements on any human affairs to the extent that they are required by the fundamental rights of the human person or the salvation of souls' (CIC, can. 747 § 2).

My respect for Canon Law was inspired by my teachers and is currently upheld by my colleagues who continuously remind us that the Code of Canon Law is not the place to look for either theology or morality. The Code is, rather, adapted from these other disciplines and so forms only a secondary reference to the primary sources. Nevertheless, the *Catechism* does not hesitate to present three quotations from three sources that contain three different statements.

The words taken out of (the context of) 1 Timothy are directed more to the 'local church', the life of which the author of this epistle is attempting to characterize for its recipient, than it is to the church universal. The demeanour of bishops and deacons is the topic of this third chapter, and the author gives advice on "how one ought to behave in the household of God, which is the church of the living God, the pillar and bulwark ...." This is neither an endorsement of the magisterium nor a confirmation of any specific truths that are taught by that office.

The second quotation, from *Lumen Gentium*, also refers to the 'truth', but when these words are read in context it is clear that 'the truth' spoken of here is 'the gospel', the good news of Jesus Christ. Reading the 'Dogmatic Constitution on the Church' we find parenthetical references to Acts 1:8 and 1 Corinthians 9:16, unquestionably indicating that this statement has nothing to do with pronouncements, rulings, or magisterial teaching.

The third reference, then, places us in the Code, Book III, on the teaching office. The first part of this canon (747 § 1), like the rest of mainstream tradition, places the competence of this teaching office clearly within the 'deposit of faith' and links it inextricably to revelation.[26] The second part,

---

[26] Can. 747 § 1. Ecclesiae, cui Christus Dominus fidei depositum concredidit ut ipsa, Spiritu Sancto assistente, veritatem revelatam sancte custodiret, intimius per-

which is quoted exclusively here, resurrects an idea discarded at Vatican I during the discussion of the object of infallibility. The council refused to admit such a vague term as 'moral principles' to be included in the definition because these could include 'merely philosophical principles' that have nothing to do with revelation. The use of the phrase here in the Catechism appears to be a conscious attempt to link every 'moral teaching' with the same note of authority (authenticity) that is attached to the proclamation of the truth of revelation. Such a usage even appears to go contrary to the few commentaries on the code itself that I have consulted. None of these commentaries even imply that the text constitutes a claim to teach about the most particular of moral matters.[27]

The following paragraph, 2033, while at first appearing to give recognition to 'catechists, preachers, theologians and spiritual authors' manages to slip in a surprising reference to something the *Catechism* calls "the deposit of Christian moral teaching." This obvious echo of the standard, technical phrase 'deposit of faith' is unfortunate, I think, because it appears once again

---

scrutaretur, fideliter annuntiaret atque exponeret, officium est et ius nativum, etiam mediis communicationis socialis sibi propriis adhibitis, a qualibet humana potestate independens, omnibus gentibus Evangelium praedicandi.

§ 2. Ecclesiae competit semper et ubique principia moralia etiam de ordine sociali annuntiare, necnon iudicium ferre de quibuslibet rebus humanis, quatenus personae humanae iura fundamentalia aut animarum salus id exigant.

[27] J.A. Coriden, T.J. Green, and D.E. Heintschel (eds), *The Code of Canon Law: A Text and Commentary* (New York, 1985) pp. 546-547, refer to § 2 of the canon to the *Lex Ecclesiae Fundamentalis* (c. 57) and to *Gaudium et Spes* 36, on the special question of the church in relation to the political order [and which also addresses the issue of "the autonomy of earthly affairs"]. L. de Echeverria, *Code de Droit Canonique Annoté* (tr. from Spanish, Paris, 1989) p. 444, draws attention to and quotes *GS* 42: "Christ did not bequeath to the Church a mission in the political, economic, or social order: the purpose he assigned to it was a religious one. But this religious mission can be the source of commitment, direction, and vigor to establish and consolidate the community of men according to the law of God." E. Caparros, M. Thériault, and J. Thorn (eds), *Code de Droit Canonique: Édition bilingue et annotée* (tr. from 4th Spanish ed., Montreal, 1990) pp. 442-443, even appear to limit the entire meaning of "moral principles" to those of the social order. "Paragraph 2 specifies two areas of competence of the Church: to explain the moral principles of the social order and to pass judgement on human activities in the light of the requirements of the fundamental rights of the human person or the salvation of souls (cf. *GS* 76)". It is curious how each of these three commentaries refer to different paragraphs of "The Pastoral Constitution on the Church in the Modern World." It is at the same time significant that each of the commentaries draws attention to the use of the Pastoral Constitution in order to interpret the canon.

to lump together just about every single form of 'teaching' with the same note of authority. The content of this 'deposit' is said to extend from the Creed to the Lord's Prayer, while "the basis for this catechesis has traditionally been the Decalogue." On this last point, the text is only partly correct, for alongside moral teaching based upon the ten commandments, which was set down in the Catechism of the Council of Trent and which the present *Catechism* emulates, many renowned theologians, not the least of whom St. Thomas Aquinas, choose to build a moral teaching not on the commandments but on the virtues. In fact, Thomas' 'virtue ethics' remains an inspiration today for those who are attempting to revise moral theology according to more scriptural and theological rather than legal lines.[28]

To say that the Decalogue is a source of moral teaching is not so much wrong as narrow-minded. On the one hand, moral teaching goes so far beyond the decalogue that the latter is hardly recognizable in that teaching except in the most obscure manner. The *Catechism* itself bears testimony to this observation, as even a cursory reading of the text will reveal. Things are forced into the individual articles on the commandments in an almost arbitrary way. On the other hand, the commandments themselves constitute a 'mixed' collection of parenetic statements (especially the ninth and tenth commandments) and concrete material as well as synthetic norms. The fifth commandment, for instance, forbids 'killing'. If this is so, simply and literally, one may wonder how Christians came to accept the teaching on just war. Proposing that the fifth commandment implies the 'intentional, unjust taking of the life of an innocent person' or murder, begs the question as to what constitutes murder and what does not. The commandment on its own does not provide answers to such questions.

The next two paragraphs, 2034-2035, reintroduce the high degree of concern on the part of the authors to emphasize the role of the 'magisterium' and especially the "charism of infallibility." The extent of such teaching is

---

[28] J.A. Selling, "You Shall Love Your Neighbor: Commandments 4-10," in: M.J. Walsh, *Commentary on the Catechism of the Catholic Church*, pp.367-394, p.368: "It is simply observed by the official commentators that this third part will be based upon the ten commandments, as if it is a foregone conclusion that the similar structure of the *Roman Catechism* (the catechism of the Council of Trent) is normative or even desirable. One could ask whether this is a sufficient excuse to adapt a system that ultimately led to being one of the pitfalls of counter-reformation theology, giving rise to the debates about probabilism, making itself vulnerable to rationalism, and fostering a legalistic ethics devoid of scriptural, theological or christological insights. Overcoming these biases turned out to be a tremendous task that culminated in the achievement of Vatican II. Is it therefore necessary to repeat the experience all over again?"

explicitly limited to divine Revelation and "all those elements ... without which the saving truths of the faith cannot be preserved, explained, or observed." At first, this text appears to be more respectful of the tradition than the previous treatise we saw on the subject of authoritative moral teaching. However, the next immediate paragraph returns to the tendency of all-encompassing authority. "The authority of the Magisterium extends also to the specific precepts of the *natural law*, because their observance, demanded by the Creator, is necessary for salvation" (2036).

No reference is given for this statement which, as far as I am aware, represents an unprecedented claim to the broadest scope of authoritative competence to date. The text does not attempt to define what are meant by 'specific precepts', thankfully leaving the entire statement open to interpretation: are all 'specific precepts of the natural law' to be observed because they are necessary for salvation? Or are all specific precepts necessary for salvation to be observed? How can one tell the difference between primary, secondary and peripheral precepts of the natural law? Does this authoritative competence extend to the statement by Leo XIII that there is a natural inequality between employer and employee (*Rerum Novarum*, 1891), or to the statement of Pius XI that women should be subject to men (1930)?

The sentence that follows the one quoted here is equally obscure.

> In recalling the prescriptions of the natural law, the Magisterium of the Church exercises an essential part of its prophetic office of proclaiming to men what they truly are and reminding them of what they should be before God.

This statement is inspirational, but remains vague. What does it mean to speak about "what [men, (sic)] truly are and ... should be before God"? All the emphasis is given to form rather than content. In general, this would be understandable; but in the present context, with the claim to the 'specific precepts of the natural law' hanging in the balance, this kind of sweeping statement inspires little more than disappointment. Further, the footnote reference given to this text, *Dignitatis Humanae*, 14, hardly substantiates the claim being made.

> In the formation of their consciences, the Christian faithful ought carefully to attend to the sacred and certain doctrine of the Church (*Ecclesiae doctrinam*). The Church is, by the will of Christ, the teacher of the truth. It is her duty to give utterance to, and authoritatively to teach (*authentice doceat*), that Truth which is Christ Himself, and also to declare and confirm (*declaret atque con-*

firmet) by her authority those principles of the moral order which have their origin in human nature itself.[29]

The authority mentioned here is that of the church, not merely that of the magisterium; the 'truth' mentioned here is that of Jesus Christ, not the natural law; the 'principles of the moral order' are said to be 'declared and confirmed', not taught with the same authority as the Gospel (revelation) itself. Again we find a sloppiness of language in the *Catechism* that implicitly supports sweeping claims to authority in moral teaching without offering comprehensible evidence for those claims.

Following a fleeting recognition of various 'ministries' in the church, we finally come to the notion of conscience that is functionally present in the *Catechism*.[30] I expect that the author(s) did not even realize that the last two sentences of para. 2039, at least from one interpretative perspective, are contradictory.

> As far as possible conscience should take account of the good of all, as expressed in the moral law, natural and revealed, and consequently in the law of the Church and in the authoritative teaching of the Magisterium on moral questions. Personal conscience and reason should not be set in opposition to the moral law or the Magisterium of the Church.

The first sentence implies a certain relation between the person and the sources of understanding and wisdom. Conscience is, in the spirit of the conciliar teaching (*GS* 16), a means of discernment. With the words "as far as possible", the *Catechism* even seems to imply an appreciation of the limitedness of human knowledge and the important distinction between descriptive

---

[29] "Declaration on Religious Freedom", in: A. Flannery O.P. (ed.), *Vatican Council II: The Conciliar and Post Conciliar Documents* (Dublin, 1975), pp. 799-812, p. 811: "However, in forming their consciences the faithful must pay careful attention to the sacred and certain teaching of the Church. For the Catholic Church is by the will of Christ the teacher of truth. It is her duty to proclaim and teach with authority the truth which is Christ and, at the same time, to declare and confirm by her authority the principles of the moral order which spring from human nature itself."

[30] The treatise on conscience is to be found in Article 6 (Chapter I, Part III), paras. 1776-1794. Although clearly more elaborate than what is present here, one finds the same ambiguity in that text as is contained in this single paragraph. It is, however, beyond the scope of this essay to investigate the concept of conscience in the *Catechism* and I will limit myself to these few remarks.

(logical) and evaluative (psycho-logical) knowledge.[31] The following sentence, however, suggests that conscience can be turned on and off, for or against any of the sources upon which it was just recognized to be dependent. While even the conciliar teaching recognizes that one's conscience can slowly go blind, especially "as a result of habitual sin", neither the Pastoral Constitution nor any other serious theological document presents a picture of conscience that can shift so completely, as it were, between discerning faculty and arbitrary judge. One might suspect what the authors of the *Catechism* were concerned about (a misuse of the word 'conscience' to signify a simple rejection of authority), but the text of the *Catechism* contributes nothing to understanding this issue. It therefore fails to teach or even offer guidance. More in the spirit of canon law than theology, it simply makes a ruling.

Method and Content in Moral Teaching

The *Catechism of the Catholic Church* appears to be chiefly concerned with the content of morality and moral teaching. While it makes sweeping claims about the competence of the teaching office (magisterium) to instruct and direct all persons in the care of the Church, it presumes the validity of its own method for making moral judgments and concentrates on the content of those judgments by demanding some things and forbidding others. The *Catechism* gives little attention to the issue of moral methodology.

The encyclical *Veritatis Splendor*, however, represents a quite different picture. In the text we find judgments about methods for analyzing and deciding moral issues that have been a matter of professional theological debate for three decades, since the time after the council and certainly since *Humanae Vitae*. *VS* presumes its own authority for formulating judgments and defers to the *Catechism* for "a complete and systematic exposition of Christian moral teaching" (*VS* 5). It makes a difference which document one reads first. The *Catechism* was published in Italian, French and German before *VS* was promulgated. The opposite was the case in the English-speaking world. If one reads *VS* first, one may still be able to appreciate the complexity of the issues and the tentativeness of positions formulated in the central, second chapter of the encyclical. If one reads first what the *Catechism* proposes about the scope of 'authoritative' teaching in matters of morality, however, one may approach the encyclical with a very different attitude.

---

[31] Cf. K. Rahner, "Zur Enzyklika «Humanae vitae»" *Schriften zur Theologie*, Vol. IX (Einsideln/Zürich/Cologne, 1972): 276-301, 288.

The issue here is whether the teaching office extends into the area of methodological questions in Christian ethics. If the 'extraordinary' authority of this office is bound to (extend as far as) the 'deposit of faith' (revelation) and those things which are directly associated with this faith, it is difficult to envision how methodology might be incorporated into the scope of authoritative pronouncement. It is even more difficult to imagine how specific items would fall within that range, except in the most general of terms.

I propose that we return to some of the more technical distinctions that have been made on the issue of authoritative teaching in general and see whether they can be specifically applied to the area of morality. The terms *dogma* and *doctrina*, then, would refer to those things that are contained in or related to revelation, including those things that are essential to the moral life of Christians. Certainly, the Decalogue belongs to this category, but so too does the double command to love God and neighbour. Also connected with this terminology are those things that may be connected with revelation in an indirect or secondary manner. This is the meaning of the phrase *doctrina de fidei vel moribus* at Vatican I. It incorporates not mere policies or opinions but those things, the necessity of which are crucial to maintaining the integrity of revelation. This might include the affirmations of the basic goodness of human nature/persons, the ability (not the guarantee!) to reach correct moral decisions through the use of reason, or even a general proposition such as the existence of freedom (and the error of the doctrine of predestination).

We then come to specific questions that might fall under the category of *disciplina* and have relatively little to do with the deposit of faith at all. Questions about private property, justifiable warfare or human rights might fall within this broad scope of 'teaching'. This is the area of policy (-making), advice (-giving) and administration. To effectively develop this teaching, it continues to be necessary to gather information from (several) pertinent disciplines, to take account of historical and cultural circumstances, and to exercise great care in the manner of formulation and presentation. Teaching on this level involves many factors, hardly any of which are connected with the faith as such.

Yet, the one thing that does connect even this form of (moral) teaching with the more general mandate of the teaching office is the consideration of whether certain—always situated, circumstantial and complex—(patterns of) behaviour(s) are compatible, appropriate or fitting for one who claims to profess the faith and witness to the truth of the Gospel of Jesus Christ. Clearly, the answer to such questions can and must remain flexible and open to reassessment. To use only one example, the policy on the possession and use of military force may be one thing when (a) civilization feels that its very existence is being threatened, another when the possessor of dominant force is exploiting weaker people for its own gain, and yet a third in the face of the manufacture and possession of weapons of mass destruction.

How, and with what appropriateness, whatever decision one makes reflects a life being led in the light of the faith describes the competent area of the teaching authority of the church as the entire people of God. It is not the content, per se, of this decision that falls immediately within this competence, since that content, as just pointed out, remains humanly contingent. Much less is it the method of observation, analysis or argumentation that falls within this competence since (or, to the extent that) none of these things have a bearing upon the meaning of a life in faith.

Moral reasoning, or to use its more contemporary name, Christian ethics, is a matter of investigation for those who have been adequately trained in the discipline and have developed a proficiency with the appropriate tools taken from philosophy, sociology, communication theory, and so forth. It is therefore perhaps more appropriate to speak of a theology of morality than about a moral theology when we consider this level of argumentation. The teaching office has the duty to protect the integrity of theology insofar as this represents the deposit of faith, revelation. It has the obligation to remind us that whatever is decided as policy or individual decision must reflect a life in faith. It enjoys, however, no special competence for predicting which policies or decisions will necessarily form the most appropriate vehicle for achieving that end, since it has no more insight into the future than anyone else.

"See How the Christians Love One Another"

In order to come to terms with the question of authority and morality, it is not only necessary to analyze the meaning of authority; one must also take a hard, long look at what we mean when we use the word 'morality'. If by morality we refer to the designation of behaviour as right or wrong, we imply a legislative/executive type of authority that acts either to tell us the rules or enforce them, like a policeman.

If, on the other hand, we have a broader notion of morality, one that encompasses a 'way of life',[32] then the function of authority must be conceived quite differently. For Christians, 'the way' signifies a way of life that is compatible with and/or appropriate for those who share a belief in the message of the Gospel, or to put it another way, who consider themselves to

---

[32] Living in 'fellowship' with our fellow Christians ("see how they love one another"), all our fellow human beings, and ultimately all the things of creation. Setting the order or priorities here is very much the work of ethical reflection.

be (the) followers of Jesus Christ. Quite the contrary of the 'Pelagian' notion that we act well so that we can 'earn' our reward, or that we act well as a 'condition' to the (fruitful) reception of God's grace (salvation), this idea presumes that grace is given, salvation is offered and received, and or way of life is a *result*, rather than a cause, of grace.

It remains important what that way of life is: what is the content, the contour or detail of such a life? Individuals, surely, do not invent the moral life, living according to 'the way'. This is something that is both built upon the wisdom of centuries and constructed spontaneously on the solid ground of data that needs to inform every ethical decision that we must make. The epitome of a life that is lived according to 'the way' ultimately resides in the community. In the Catholic Christian tradition, this community is perhaps too easily identified with 'church'. However, Vatican II made its contribution to enriching this image by restoring the idea of the church as the 'people of God'. This ecclesial image is not merely institutional and hierarchical; it is particular (local) as well as universal, inculturated as well as traditional, contemporary as well as apostolic, secular as well as sacred.

It is from a community that one learns 'how to live'. In most cases, this 'community' consists of family, neighbourhood, school, peers, state (nation), union, political party, ethnic heritage, and so forth. Some of these communities may overlap with the specific community of the church (as the people of God who share a belief in the message of the Gospel). In other instances, membership in one's 'church community' may be coextensive with the family, implying that the 'other' fellow believers are drawn from a mixture of groups that do not always coincide. This, I believe, is one of the riches of the Catholic Christian Communities in our times. But that is another story. The point here is that this particular community plays a significant role in the formation of one's notion of how one 'should' live: what is the shape of 'the way'?

In this paradigm, it is the community that functions primarily as the source of moral authority. However, this function is achieved in a very different manner than legislation—even though each community will eventually legislate its daily and yearly activity by building up agreements (e.g., about liturgical celebrations) or rules of decorum (e.g., who is [not] expected to do what at which time). The authority of the community flows through example, or to use a more biblical term, through witness. The community witnesses to (demonstrates) 'the way', the members of the community witness (both demonstrate and observe) 'the way' being lived out. Through this process, one learns—and helps to fashion—what 'the way' might[33] look like.

---

[33] We must say 'might' because one cannot fully predict the specific circumstances of every single human decision.

I would suggest that the principle features of this model of morality demand an authority that is communicative, credible and convincing.

It must be *communicative* because the failure to communicate results in the failure to (bear) witness. This, as any communications specialist will remind us, involves not merely a 'message' being communicated but, just as importantly, the character of the communicator and the person(s) with whom one is communicating.

Authority must be *credible* in the sense that or own tradition speaks of being *reasonable*. Here we signal not a sense of 'adapting' to the times (being merely contemporary) but rather speaking *to*, and occasionally even *at*, the times. Typical faults in this area are characterized, among other ways, as being a-historical or classical. Are we addressing real issues in a real world, or are we living in a dream world of unreached and unreachable ideals? Saying we should all love one another is nice, but hardly credible. Demonstrating how to work through conflict in a creative manner is far more plausible, credible, than pretending that conflict does not exist, or worse, that it comes about merely because someone is at fault.

The *convincing* character of the moral authority of a community is demanded more by the integrity of the community than by the receptivity of the observer. Typical of the problem would be the young adult who observes that certain 'authority figures' do not practice what they preach. Laying down a set of rules that are honoured more in the breach than in being followed raises questions about consistency that undermines (moral) authority.

To be convinced, one must first be attracted. This does not call for accommodation, but rather for letting it be known precisely what has convinced those who already embrace what is being held out for consideration. Justifiably, there is a strong criticism of a kind of 'soft Christianity' that appeals to 'feeling good' or 'being happy', in the superficial meaning of the term. This would extend to the kind of 'Christianity' that is peddled in the media, selling beauty, success and social status for the price of a tithe.

What is attractive in this case is the life of the believing community, in good times and in bad, in face of adversity as well as success. What is attractive is the experience of the believing community as a whole and over time. How the community deals with tragedy, for instance, contributes to its convincing character. How it deals with success is equally important. The point is that one cannot grasp the entire meaning of a community in only one time, one set of circumstances, or from one perspective.

Ultimately, it is the entire story of that community that will provide the background against which one might assess its communicative, credible and convincing character. This does not mean that the story of a community must be spotless or without fault. On the contrary, how the community deals with its own faults, its shortcomings or its mistakes will play an important role in its convincing character.

The church is a community of believers, but it is simultaneously a moral community, one in which the way of life of the community as well as its individual members defines who and what that community is. As a moral community, it is not merely a community of moral persons, for most of us are sinners, knowing that we are still in the process of striving toward (God's) righteousness. More than that, a 'moral community' is one that shines out (Matthew 5:14-16) and sets an example for the entire community of humankind. If it fails in this, if it is not communicative, credible and convincing, no amount of claims to moral authority will make it so.

TWELVE

Scripture and Morality

Karl-Wilhelm Merks

In the publication of the *Catechism of the Catholic Church*, the pope's preface, "Apostolic Constitution *Fidei Depositum*," calls the Holy Scripture the source and frame of reference for the doctrine that is set forth in the Catechism. "The presentation of doctrine must be biblical and liturgical," and, "A catechism should faithfully and systematically present the teaching of Sacred Scripture, the living Tradition in the Church and the authentic Magisterium...."[1] Thus the Catechism is "a statement of the Church's faith and of catholic doctrine, attested to or illumined by Sacred Scripture, the Apostolic Tradition, and the Church's Magisterium."

At the same time the Catechism is an extension of Vatican II, being "the most mature and perfect fruit of the teaching of the Council."[2] In a short passage on the renewal of moral theology, this Council itself had emphatically demanded that moral theology would have to "feed more richly from the doctrine of the Holy Scripture" (*Optatam totius* 16).[3] With this the Council took note of a deeply felt dissatisfaction with regard to the standard type of moral education that existed at the time, on which A.-G. Sertillanges OP (1863-1948) had com-

---

[1] The text continues, "... as well as the spiritual heritage of the Fathers, Doctors, and saints of the Church, to allow for a better knowledge of the Christian mystery and for enlivening the faith of the People of God."

[2] Cited by H. Verweyen, *Der Weltkatechismus: Therapie oder Symptom einer kranken Kirche?* (Düsseldorf, 1993), p.11; cf. Catechism, number 10. Here and in the following the translation of quotes from other languages are mine unless otherwise indicated.

[3] Cf. the commentary by J. Neuner in *LThK*, Erg.-Bd.2, p.345: "Desired above all is a renewal of the teaching in moral theology, which was frequently based too much on principles of the natural law and canonical norms and was not theological enough. The decree speaks of the necessity to construct a moral theology more on Scripture and to derive its moral claims from the grandeur of the Christian vocation and Christian responsibility for the world."

mented, "In all of contemporary Catholicism, morality and the elite who provide moral instruction reveal themselves to be the weakest points."[4]

Preliminary Hermeneutical Considerations

In a critique of the genre in which this doctrine of morality found its expression—handbooks such as had been developed in the last three and a half centuries—the theologian and psychiatrist Marc Oraison points to the fact that, in addition to its static essentialist rationalist nature as a natural law morality, it had become quite meagre primarily with respect to its theological quality, and this was even sometimes completely absent.[5] To demonstrate this he cites a passage from the beginning of the much used handbook by Heribert Jone O.F.M., called *Katholieke moraaltheologie*: "A person must attain his end through *personal acts* that correspond with the remote (objective) and the immediate (subjective) norm of moral actions, that is, with the *law* and *conscience*. People deviate from these norms in *sins* while the virtues help us to act in agreement with them. This indicates the arrangement of the doctrine of principles [thus, fundamental moral theology]."[6] In Oraison's opinion Jone's moral theology—and he is no exception in this—lacks almost all of that which should be central to a *theological* ethics: there is no reference to an active God, no connection to Christ. The meaning of belief, the gift of salvation, which we do not make ourselves, all play a minimal role.

A few other examples point in the same direction. Thus one can read in the introduction of a moral handbook by the English theologian T. Slater (d. 1928): "... manuals of moral theology are technical works ... as the text-books of the lawyer and the doctor. ... They deal with what is of obligation under pain of sin; they are books of moral pathology."[7]

The conciliar requirement of more use of the Scripture in morality seems surprising on the one hand, at least in its generality. Were not a number of the

---

[4] Cited by J. Leclercq, *L'Enseignement de la Morale Chrétienne* (Paris, 1950), p.9. Our own view is that "morality" can mean the moral qualification of human behaviour as well as systematic reflection on it (moral doctrine, ethics). Because this article concerns ecclesiastical statements, it is usually the second meaning that will be used, without excluding the connection with the first meaning.

[5] M. Oraison, *Une morale pour notre temps* (Paris, 1964), pp.60 f.

[6] H. Jone, *Katholieke Moraaltheologie* (Roermond-Maaseik, 1953), 7th ed., no. 4.

[7] T. Slater, S.J., *A Manual of Moral Theology for English-Speaking Countries*, vol. 1 (New York, 1918), pp.6 f.

handbooks set up biblically, following the Decalogue, as does the Catechism (2052-2557)? Certainly the critique of these manuals did not have reference to the section on special morality in the first instance but to the section that deals with *De principiis*, the principles, and is called "Fundamental Morality" (and thereby the section that corresponds to the numbers of the Catechism that are the subject of this volume: 1691-2051). Naturally, it also makes one think that special morality (with which, according to Thomas Aquinas, all moral reflection is ultimately concerned[8]) did not have a retroactive effect on the shape of the previous general section. For the section on general morality was not articulated in biblical categories, but according to a systematic conceptual framework (human act, law, conscience, sin, etc.). In addition, however, as a separate study could demonstrate, it is also the question with regard to concrete moral theology based on the Decalogue as to how biblical these handbooks actually were. There are justifiable suspicions that other influences were also at work here.

The latter can lead us to initial conclusions with regard to our theme: a *biblical framework* as such does not guarantee the *biblical character* of a moral statement. Neither is a biblical character guaranteed by quoting and weaving biblical citations as such into the doctrine of morality. Non-biblical formulations can breathe the spirit of Scripture just as scriptural texts can be used in an non-biblical spirit. Thus not only the fact *that* the Bible is used but *how* it is used determines whether a theological discourse can be considered biblical. The same obtains for dealing with texts of the Second Vatican Council. Here as well the text, even where it is correctly quoted (which is not always the case), does not yet guarantee a theology in the 'spirit' of the Council. However, I cannot go into this any further here.[9]

The question of the relationship between Scripture and morality is therefore not a matter of the actual use of Scripture as such, and the question of the biblical character of a moral statement is not answered by counting the number of quotations. How can (the doctrine of) morality then be given a biblical character? Before one can speak of the biblical character of morality or a biblically-oriented morality[10] in a meaningful way, a series of preceding questions must be clarified.

---

[8] *ST* I-II.6 prol.; II-II.Prol.

[9] For a few examples (revelation, tradition, Scriptures; ecclesiology) of a restorative re-reading of Vatican II (*Dei verbum; Lumen gentium*) by the Catechism, see H. Verweyen, *Der Weltkatechismus*, pp. 26 ff, 74 ff.

[10] I am speaking intentionally of a biblically-oriented morality and not directly of a biblical morality. I understand the latter to be a morality as it arises (historically) from the Scriptural texts; the question of whether or not this morality is directly applicable to our time is already the first step from a biblical to a biblically-oriented morality.

These questions are partially inherent to a good analysis of the biblical text itself. For example, what is biblical morality? Where can it be found in the texts (in legal documents, norms, stories, events, actions)? How does Scripture view the relation between that which we understand to be morality (the question of good and evil in acts) and other dimensions of faith (the concepts of God, humankind, the world, etc.)? What role does morality play in the whole of the experience of faith? Is it so self-evident to speak of *one* biblical morality? In addition, other questions which need to be clarified beforehand concern the problem of how the gap between the moral views and practices of two thousand or more years ago and the moral views and practices of today can be bridged. For example, is a literal appropriation (sometimes?) possible? How can/must we interpret and transpose views of that time to our time? What, for believers, is antiquated in Scripture and what continues to obtain for today?

Even though we cannot deal with all these questions here, they nevertheless form the background for a sound assessment of the use of Scripture in the Catechism and the biblical character of the doctrine of morality which is explained in it. In any case, we must be well aware of the fact that the question of the relation between the Bible and moral theology is anything but simple. More generally, it has been established that in the Catechism "(almost) unrelated ... are two ways of approach (*Denkansätze*) at work: that of biblical salvation history and that of the natural law/Neo-Scholasticism."[11] The latter appears to have a very negative connotation, which is the result of an old dissatisfaction with the neo-scholastic abstract way of thinking. Insofar as the Catechism links up with this way of thinking—and there are reasons that it does so (just as the encyclical *Veritatis Splendor* does so to a much greater degree)[12]—it will justifiably encounter strong opposition. One must not, however, confuse a valid reservation against Neo-scholastic systematics with a critique (which is not tenable in its generality) of systematic theology as such. Systematic theology is essential for the actualization of the faith if one does not wish to remain caught in a fundamentalist orientation to Scripture. It should be noted that every fundamentalism also pursues its own systematics, even if it is not immediately apparent.

However, here the truly fundamental question arises as to how texts can function as 'holy' texts, as 'holy' Scripture, within a systematic reflection that

---

[11] Cf. E. Schulz, "Katechismus der Katholischen Kirche (KKK): Theologische Intention—Didaktische Anlage—Religionspädagogische Relevanz," in: E. Schulz (ed.), *Ein Katechismus für die Welt: Informationen und Anfragen* (Düsseldorf, 1994), pp. 9-70, 49.

[12] Cf. M. Vidal, "Die Enzyklika 'Veritatis splendor' und der Weltkatechismus: Die Restauration des Neuthomismus in der katholischen Morallehre," in: D. Mieth (ed.), *Moraltheologie im Abseits? Antwort auf die Enzyklika 'Veritatis splendor'* (Freiburg/Basel/Vienna, 1994), pp. 244-70; cf. also the critical discussion by H. Halter, "Es gibt drei göttliche Tugenden...," in *Schweizerische Kirchenzeitung* 38 (1993): 506-13.

is orientated first and foremost toward problems, and thus is not guided by the requirement of conformity to a textual authority but by the ideals of insight and understanding, or in short, by the search for truth. I have my doubts whether those who demand a scripturally-oriented theology are always aware of the complexity of this task. It is not for nothing that many exegetes recoil from a so-called 'biblical theology'.[13] This occurs for various reasons.

One important reason lies in the fact that in the first instance one can at most arrive at theologies of this or that biblical writing by this or that author. In order to arrive at *the* biblical theology one would have to synthesize that which in Scripture itself emerges as a plurality of voices. What Scripture offers are variations on a theme that is not given as such but can only be retraced or fathomed through the variations. A biblically-oriented theology can attempt to reconstruct this theme, but then only in the form of a permanently present retention of those variations, which will bring us to a clear relativization of our expectations on the role of Scripture in a systematic theology. The more biblical a theological systematics is, the more modest its general statements will be. In principle such a theology will have to remain more fundamental; for the rest, it will respect the colourfulness of the Scriptures and of the experiences of faith of people contained therein and *not* attempt to view them under one denominator. Systematic theology on the basis of the Bible is the systematization of a process and of a history. The only thing that it can do is to try to discover continuities and continuous lines in a permanent process of change.[14] The Scripture illustrates a process of faith—not a doctrine of faith.

But this process goes further—and here is a second reason for the tension between Scripture and moral theology. The multiple statements of faith in Scripture must not only be mutually connected with each other, but should also be charted once again in their meaning for us. The interest (*erkenntnisleitende Interesse*) of a systematic theology begins with the meaning of Scripture for today, for us. Through this the biblical word, or rather, the biblical *words*, are once again placed in new contexts and frameworks, and again the question is posed as to where exactly one must seek the continuing meaning of holy Scripture in changed circumstances. Nor does this complicated relation make it impossible to come to well-reasoned assessments regarding an acceptable or no

---

[13] Cf. P. Walter, E. Haag, and K. Kertelge, "Biblische Theologie," in *LThK* II (1994): 426-35.

[14] In my opinion, noteworthy examples of a survey that is conscious of the problem of biblical ethos with regard to historical development, variety, *and* continuity are the contributions by R. Oberforcher, "Alttestamentliche Ethik," in: H. Rotter and G. Virt, (eds), *Neues Lexikon der christlichen Moral* (Innsbruck/Vienna, 1990), pp. 24-37, and J. Kremer, "Neutestamentliche Ethik," in: *Neues Lexikon der christlichen Moral*, pp. 549-57.

longer acceptable processing of the biblical givens in one's own thinking, and thereby on the use, whether responsible or not, of holy Scripture in current theological reflection—at least where this use of the Bible is directed by the intention of linking up with the biblical tradition and to stand within this tradition.

Having looked at these considerations we will now examine our question of how the Catechism deals with Scripture. I will treat the following points in succession:
- A few observations on the general use of Scripture in the Catechism;
- Some comments on the use of Scripture in the section on fundamental morality;
- Catholic morality—'remotely' biblical.

A Few Observations on the General Use of Scripture in the Catechism

For those who read the Catechism, the work presents itself as a text that, on the one hand, is characterized by a relatively strict construction that is argumentative and logical. On the other hand, it has a style which older people may recognize from the classic Sunday sermons and which has a very long tradition. Personally, I had already recognized it while writing my thesis on St. Cyprian, bishop of Carthage in the third century. The arguments are interspersed with biblical quotations from the Old and New Testaments. Literally, in paraphrase or by allusion, they form together with the other text a whole and can thus fulfil various 'functions'—for example, as the starting point or end of an argument, as the basis or rounding off of an argument, as a body of authority, or rhetorical decoration.

In this way the individual story of the speaker or writer and Scripture become one complete argument in which Scripture substantially 'carries', situates, rounds off, enriches, and decorates the new text,[15] but (and this is the other side of the coin) also, conversely, in which the new text conditions the understanding of the Scriptural texts and gives them a certain direction.

In a comparison of the Catechism of 1992 with the *Catechismus Romanus* (CR) of 1566, Jan van Laarhoven points out that the CR had already interwoven large numbers of quotations from the Old and New Testaments:

> The Catechism has gone even further in this: the 550 pages of text are literally strewn with biblical citations and references: 290 quotations from the Old Testament and 1316 from the New Testament, plus 577 and 2007 references, re-

---

[15] For an example of the various possibilities, cf. the close analysis of Thomas Aquinas's use of the Scriptures in W.G.B.M Valkenberg, *Did Not Our Heart Burn? The Place and Function of Holy Scripture in the Theology of St. Thomas Aquinas* (Utrecht, 1990).

spectively. Should a person who is a total stranger to Christianity page through this book, he would have to state that there is only one authoritative book for the Catechism.[16]

I should like to relativize this last remark somewhat. For the sake of completeness we must observe that the text also quotes extensively from other works, which in a way is partially comparable with the CR (for example, the church fathers, the ecumenical councils), but is also partially unique in that it uses specific sources. After all, the role of Vatican II (531 quotations, 276 references) is specific, as well as the great number of quotations from papal and curial documents. "... the current pope is honoured with 51 quotes and 85 references, i.e., therefore more than all of the 'ecclesiastical writers' referred to from the Middle Ages and the newer period together."[17]

Naturally, in the context of the Christian faith, none of the other quotations have the dignity that our faith attributes to holy Scripture. Nevertheless, the nonscriptural quotations, particularly the papal and conciliar texts, are not there simply for decoration. On the basis of the relationship between tradition and Scripture and the role of the *Magisterium* of the church in the authentic interpretation of tradition and Scripture (the *depositum fidei*) (Catechism 80 ff), biblical texts and ecclesiastical authoritative statements can be combined into an almost inseparable whole, which leads to an accumulation of authority in which the one authority stands surety, as it were, for the lacunas and imperfections of the other, and vice versa.

The problem that arises here—the possible immunization of authoritative statements against every critique due to their placement in the prolongation of Scripture (and tradition)—is a separate subject that is not part of the discussion here. We will restrict ourselves to the use of Scripture.

To summarize the answer concisely, O.H. Pesch states: "For a biblical scholar or one who is familiar with the problems of the Bible, reading the Catechism is agony."[18] In a critique on the first critiques of the Catechism, which often also focused on the use of the Bible, J. Eberle admits that one could expect a more extensive exegetical commentary in the Catechism. "However, that

---

[16] J. van Laarhoven, "Twee katechismussen: De catechismus Romanus en de Katechismus van de Katholieke Kerk," in *TvT* 33 (1993): 371-89, 378.

[17] J. van Laarhoven, "Twee katechismussen," pp. 378 f.

[18] Quoted by H. Vorgrimler, "'Der Katechismus der Katholischen Kirche,' A: in der Perspektive systematischer Theologie: Einblicke in eine Diskussion," in: *Theol. Rev.* 91 (1995): 3-8, 5.

the Catechism is said in principle to lack a sound exegesis is indefensible."[19] The examples that he gives, however, can clarify where exactly the difference is to be sought. The actual question is whether systematic theology can develop 'freely' with regard to exegesis, or whether it must regard exegesis much more as at least place where it can be tested critically.

One may assume that when the Catechism quotes Scripture it does so because of that which the text *itself* in all known interactions between text and interpreter *has to say* to us. Why else would quotations, themselves emphatically marked, be produced if not to call upon, by means of quotation, the authority of that quotation, which is that of holy Scripture, for its own statements? If this is so, the respect for the text of Scripture (the Word of God in *this* human word) desires to be taken seriously in all its dimensions (and this requires a very developed exegesis), so that Scripture is not put to a task to which it is not equal. The issue here is not whether a text has, in addition to the (traditionally viewed) 'literary' meaning, other 'spiritual' meanings as well (although someone like, for example, Thomas Aquinas warned against seeking the latter outside the first).[20] The point is rather that one should respect the literal meaning and not suggest something other than that which is present in the text. One may certainly not do this on the basis of criteria that are completely outside of the text itself and have their own contextual situation, such as, for example, finding a foundation in the biblical text for a dogmatic statement or a moral norm at any price.

Allow me to use two examples from Eberle's article. As a 'proof' for the biblical foundation of the statement that Jesus "institutes apostles as priests of the New Covenant" (Catechism, 611) at the Last Supper, 1 Corinthians 11:25 is not clear, even though the Council of Trent, session XXII, can. 2 saw it as such. Here, for dogmatic reasons, a biblical text becomes extra freight. The consideration of exegetical insights also seems half-hearted when, in relation to

---

[19] J. Eberle, "Zur bisherigen öffentlichen Diskussion um den neuen Weltkatechismus," in: *Internationale Zeitschrift Communio* 22 (1993): 553-63, 557.

[20] For example, *ST* I.1.10 *ad* 1: All that is essential for salvation can be found in the literal text: "since nothing necessary to faith is contained under the spiritual sense which is not elsewhere put forward by the Scripture in its literal sense;" cf. *Quodl.* VII.6.1. On Thomas' use of Scripture in general: O.H. Pesch, "Das Gesetz," *DThA* 13 (Heidelberg, 1977): 682-716; B. Bujo, *Moralautonomie und Normenfindung bei Thomas von Aquin: Unter Einbeziehung der neutestamentlichen Kommentare* (Paderborn, 1979), pp.76 ff.; W.G.B.M. Valkenberg, *Did Not Our Heart Burn?* On the shift in the evaluation of *sensus litteralis* and *sensus spiritualis*, the 'literal' and the 'spiritual' exegesis in the Catechism, cf. H. Verweyen, *Der Weltkatechismus*, pp.46 ff., 95 f. That the latter, in minimalizing the literary meaning for this purpose, would be important to the theological quality is, according to Verweyen, contrary to both the *Dei Verbum* and Pius XII. But it is suggested by the repeated polemics of, among others, Cardinal Ratzinger against the (intentions of) modern exegesis and exegetes (pp.131 ff.)

the story of the Fall, the Catechism (390) refers to the "figurative language," but on the other hand maintains that it "affirms a primeval event, a deed that took place *at the beginning of the history of man.*" That which is conceded with the left hand is immediately removed by the right hand. The text is also an example of the thoughtless use of Vatican II, shifting its meaning: "at the beginning of the history" (with reference to *Gaudium et Spes* 13, 1) is not the correct rendition of the more dynamic "*inde ab exordio historiae*", which means 'from the beginning' and not 'at the beginning'.[21]

The Catechism's occupation with the Bible does have a long tradition, but this does not excuse it, for in the meantime so many insights have arisen concerning intellectual honesty with regard to exegesis that the use of Scripture in many places in the Catechism must be viewed as a falling behind that which may now be regarded as normal.[22] Such falling behind is difficult to digest.

H. Verweyen[23] has indicated that an exegesis in the form of processing loose fragments (*Steinbruchexegese*) was common in the churches already in the early period. Jesus' words were quoted to include them in one's own interpretation, taking little account of the biblical context. It is only with the encyclical *Divino afflante Spiritu* by Pius XII (1943) that one begins to see (at least in Catholic theology) the factors that determine the biblical texts in their uniqueness, their individuality, such as time, context, literary genre, theological intentions of the various authors (writings), etc. Up until that time, according to Verweyen, the use of the Bible appears to have been random (*Querbeetlektüre*), with a preference for certain writings: Matthew and John, who were witnesses and, moreover, offered a 'high' Christology, as well as Acts as the beginning of a triumphant church. On the basis of a few catechisms Verweyen illustrates how, in the last forty years, the results of historical-critical exegesis slowly also began to determine the method of quotation; the quest for the historical Jesus (and thereby the significance of the gospel of Mark) received more attention in particular.

Against this background, it is remarkable that a quest for the 'earthly Jesus' did not take place in the Catechism. Instead, the Catechism reverts to presenting

---

[21] Cf. H.-J. Klauck, "Der Katechismus der Katholischen Kirche: Rückfragen aus exegetischer Sicht," in: E. Schulz (ed.), *Ein Katechismus für die Welt,* pp. 71-82, 79 f.; also see J. Ratzinger's commentary on the conciliar text in *LThK*, supplementary vol. III, pp. 319ff.

[22] That which may be regarded as 'normal' can be found in an excellent document published in 1993 (thus unfortunately after the Catechism) by the Pontifical Bible Commission, "The Interpretation of the Bible in the Church," in: *Origins*, Vol. 23 (6 January 1994), no. 29, pp. 498-524.

[23] H. Verweyen, *Der Weltkatechismus*, pp. 14ff.

an image of Jesus through the collection of fragmented passages of the Gospel, without taking into account literary coherence and the evangelists' intentions. "The theology of the writers of the Catechism prevails over that of the New Testament authors, who function here only as suppliers of proofs."[24] In contrast, precisely for theological reasons it is the unique theological profile (brought to light particularly through historical-critical methods and here especially the history of redaction) of the various biblical authors that is important: it is *within* this and not outside of it that God and his revelation is put into words.

What Verweyen has explained with fundamental and dogmatic-theological sections of the Catechism in mind is also confirmed by other theologians. In none of the authors provided can there be any doubt concerning the view that the Catechism must ultimately go back to the most important sources of belief, including the writings of the Old and New Testaments in particular. It is also acknowledged that this occurs profusely in the Catechism. But the problem is the way in which and the method by which it occurs. R. Heinzmann comments on this:

> To a large extent the text of the Catechism is read as a collection of quotations with some linking words in between. The quantity of the texts quoted is insufficient. What is lacking, and this is of utmost importance, is an organic unfolding of problems and answers from the sources in such a way that the criteria allow insight according to which quotations are selected. Now, however, one suspects that the propositions arose first and that subsequently places of proof were found.[25]

He sees a particular deficiency in the fact "that the texts are strung together without further qualifying their theological weight and their theological degree of obligation."[26]

The latter is also the impression of H.-J. Klauck, who observes that the Bible is dominantly paraphrased: "There are Scriptural texts quoted literally or freely rendered in different words. An actual explanation or interpretation rarely occurs directly, but constantly occurs implicitly by the way in which the texts are presented."[27] Klauck feels that this gives the average reader the impression

---

[24] H. Verweyen, *Der Weltkatechismus*, pp. 22 f.

[25] R. Heinzmann, "Was ist der Mensch? Anfragen an das Menschenbild des Katechismus der Katholischen Kirche," in: E. Schulz (ed.), *Ein Katechismus für die Welt*, pp. 83-99, 84 f.

[26] R. Heinzmann, "Was ist der Mensch?" p. 85.

[27] H.-J. Klauck, "Der Katechismus der Katholischen Kirche," pp. 78 f.

that that which is quoted is to be understood literally and strictly historically. Heinzmann writes:

> Something like biblical hermeneutics does not exist. ... That is why biblical argumentation is often inadequate and meaningless. Many passages give the impression they have been collected on the basis of associations with key words. Texts from the various books of the Old and New Testaments are quoted alongside one another, as if they arose from the same context. And within the New Testament one cannot speak of any differentiation whatsoever.[28]

Where the intention and contents of the writings themselves are not offered, however, any reference to Scripture becomes arbitrary. Heinzmann arrives at the severe verdict: "The way practised here of Scriptural proof is sometimes in close proximity to Scriptural fundamentalism."[29]

From a more ecumenically-oriented approach, O.H. Pesch has raised the question of the processing of Scripture. For him it is a serious question of how the Catechism "allows the normative witness of the holy Scripture to be *normative in actuality.*" He sees "valid doubt... as to whether Scripture is actually listened to or whether [the Catechism] does not rather express a prior dogmatic statement in fragments of biblical quotations which on the basis of the words used are particularly suitable."[30]

When the Catechism's methodological deficiencies in the use of Scripture are discussed so pointedly within various disciplines, then it is not simply a matter of splitting hairs by theologians who are never satisfied. Rather, it concerns a central moment of the inculturation[31] of the Christian faith in the view of life and the intellectual climate of today. The omnipresent awareness of the historical dimension of existence and, more particularly, the central place that disciplines such as semantics and semiology have taken in the whole of our science and cul-

---

[28] R. Heinzmann, "Was ist der Mensch?", p.85.

[29] R. Heinzmann, "Was ist der Mensch?", p.85.

[30] O.H. Pesch, "Der neue Katechismus und die Ökumene," in: E. Schulz (ed.), *Ein Katechismus für die Welt*, pp.141-65, 151. The question must arise as to how far this causes the Catechism itself to become an example of the "collection" of "discontinuous parts" of a dissected Bible which J. Cardinal Ratzinger believes materialistic and feminist exegesis must be charged with (J. Card. Ratzinger, "Schriftauslegung im Widerstreit. Zur Frage nach Grundlagen und Weg der Exegese heute," in: J. Card. Ratzinger (ed.), *Schriftauslegung im Widerstreit (Quaestiones disputatae 117)* (Freiburg, 1989), pp.15-44, 18-19).

[31] It is very much worth one's while to read the comments on the inculturation of the Scripture in the Pontifical Biblical Commission's "The Interpretation of the Bible in the Church," p.521.

ture are not taken seriously. But, as P. Hünermann correctly posits, for a contemporary understanding of faith it is inevitable that one deals with the witnesses of faith in a way suited to the current state of knowledge and thought, and this concerns Scripture (also) in a historical-critical way.[32]

In my opinion the reservation regarding critical exegesis could be motivated by the fear that it would endanger the truth, whereas historical thinking wishes to arrive at the truth honestly and more purely. With this the problem lies in the conflict between a view of truth in which truth appears only in history and a view in which truth (sometimes, ultimately) can be thought to be outside the historical context.[33] However one should wish to solve this problem, one conclusion, I think, is unavoidable in any case: *the* truth cannot be found at the price of lack of interest in or dishonesty with regard to historical insights ("truths"). This obtains to a special degree with regard to morality. From a moral point of view, truth and goodness mean nothing if they are not illuminated in one's own insights, and can affect one's conscience only in that way.

Some Comments on the Use of Scripture in the Section on Fundamental Morality

On the use of Scripture in the section on morality J. Gründel comments: "In the section on morality of the Catechism, the otherwise biblically inspired language of this Catechism has more the character of the old handbooks on moral theology, which assess specific ways of conduct casuistically."[34] With a Reformed sensitivity, M. Kiessig (who, from an ecumenical point of view, also produces a more positive evaluation for the extended use of Scripture) emphasizes this point for the section on morality: he feels the explanations concerning morality are "very philosophical."[35]

---

[32] P. Hünermann, "Die Feier des christlichen Mysteriums. Zum zweiten Teil des 'Katechismus der Katholischen Kirche'," in: E. Schulz (ed.), *Ein Katechismus für die Welt*, pp. 100-15, 107.

[33] Also cf. J. van Laarhoven, "Twee katechismussen," pp. 386 f. This consideration deserves emphatic attention, also in relation to the encyclical *Veritatis Splendor* and the view of 'truth' that it offers. Cf., for example, P. Jonkers, "Wat is waarheid? Cultuurfilosofische beschouwingen over vrijheid en waarheid," in: H.W.M. Rikhof and F.J.H. Vosman (eds), *De schittering van de waarheid: Theologische reflecties bij de encykliek* Veritatis Splendor (Zoetermeer, 1994), pp. 122-37.

[34] J. Gründel, "Der Weltkatechismus: Hilfe oder Hindernis für die Glaubensverkündigung?" in: E. Schulz (ed.), *Ein Katechismus für die Welt*, pp. 116-40, 119.

[35] M. Kiessig, "Der Katechismus der Katholischen Kirche," C: aus evangelischer Sicht (see note 18), pp. 11-19, 13.

Here, with regard to the section on morality, we are still confronted with an old complaint: the reproach that the Catechism is too philosophical, or, more precisely, Neo-scholastic. According to the impression of these authors, the large number of biblical quotations has apparently not affected this very much. This brings us to a twofold question: what is the status of the use of the Bible in the Catechism's section on fundamental morality? And in how far is it possible for one to search for the causes of that use of the Bible in the (traditional) model of morality which the Catechism has chosen? Finally, there is, of course, the question as to how we must proceed with the problematic relation of morality and the Bible.

What is the Status of the Use of the Bible in the Catechism's Section on Fundamental Morality?

The general assessment is that the Catechism's text is interwoven with Scriptural quotations but that these hardly play a supporting role in a number of sections and that, where they do appear to play a role, this sometimes occurs very superficially. The classical treatises on morality in particular appear to be formulated in a more 'biblical' way. More recent themes, such as that of the sociality of people (1877-1948: "The Human Community") and the questions that arise from this concerning one's participation in social life as well as the consequences for justice and human rights draw on other sources, in particular the social doctrine of the church. For that matter, the less Scriptural foundation also obtains for the statements on the authority of the Magisterium and the precepts of the church (2030-2043)—which gives one cause to think. Here it is the ecclesiastical documents, particularly Vatican II and the Codex Iuris Canonici, that are referred to.[36] The places where the Bible is quoted often leads to critique. I believe this is due in part to exegetical carelessness; but the main cause seems to me to lie in the Catechism's traditional model of morality. By way of example I will give a few particularly clear cases.

---

[36] In a quick count of quotes and references, the following appear to be at the top of the list: the New Testament 205 times, *Gaudium et Spes* 43 times (plus 17 other texts of Vatican II), the Old Testament 27 times, Augustine 23 times, CIC/CCEO 18 times, John Paul II 17 times, Thomas Aquinas 15 times. Of course, this is not the whole story, if one knows, for example, that it is the part in question that owes much to Thomas Aquinas, i.e. as he is conveyed through Thomism, with regard to structure (cf. M. Vidal, "Die Enzyklika 'Veritatis splendor' und der Weltkatechismus"). This indicates indirectly once again that quotations as such do not say much about the internal structure of an explanation.

a) Sometimes the use of Scripture must prove that concepts of moral theology, on which the Catechism apparently wishes to lay emphasis, are brought out by Scripture itself. It can be illustrated again and again that this involves concepts that are derived from another context, for example, from later scholastic systems. In number 1736 the quotations concerning Eve, Cain, and David are expressions of the accountability of individual sins, but yet have nothing to do with the specific formulation that "every act *directly willed* is imputable to its author." The distinction between *mortal* and venial sin, to which number 1854 refers, is not as such evident in Scripture (1 John 5:16-17).[37] With respect to number 1858, what a *grave matter* entails is important in a certain system of categories of sin, but is not a topic that is already clarified in the Ten Commandments. It is significant that sometimes important texts are *not* cited with respect to a theme. It was noted that, in the framework of the doctrine of justification, Romans 3:28 ("For we maintain that a man is justified by faith apart from observing the law"), and on the erring conscience, Romans 14:23 ("... everything that does not come from faith is sin"), are missing.[38]

b) Of more weight than the function of proof in such conceptual (re)constructions, however, are the more general statements on the connection between nature, experience, reason/revelation/Magisterium in moral issues and the presumed role of Scripture in the whole of the tradition of faith implied therein. Here it concerns the question of the relation between the various *loci theologici*, of which for morality the trio of *fontes theologiae moralis* (the sources of moral theology)—that is, the revelation (Scripture/tradition), natural reason, and the Magisterium—are traditionally central. The authors of the Catechism were apparently not aware of the problems connected with the interpretation of this system of mutually supporting authorities.

c) Scriptural texts as such are included in the argumentation. However, this does not mean that Scripture is to be seen as a quarry for proofs but rather as the "inexhaustible source of all theology," as K. Rahner expresses it (who nevertheless has spoken of Scripture as *"norma normans non normata,"* as, one might translate, the ultimate measure).[39] But we have learned from the exegete that this norm is not easy to apply because in itself it already contains a pluriform theology.

---

[37] Cf. H.-J. Klauck, "Der Katechismus der Katholischen Kirche," pp. 75 f.

[38] Cf. W. Schöpsdau, "Moral und Sitte," in: *MD* 6 (1993): 115-18.

[39] K. Rahner, "Schriftbeweis (II)," in: *LThK* 9, pp. 486 f.: "Theology must always and everywhere justify itself to Scripture."

The Catechism does not promote this multi-dimensionality of Scripture. This is particularly noticeable in some themes that receive attention in contemporary moral theology: for example, the Bible gives us two versions of the Beatitudes that are quite different from each other. Yet only the spiritualizing and moralizing version of the Beatitudes in Matthew are given, while the more "earthly" version in Luke is not mentioned (1716 f.).[40] A Christological view of the ethics of Jesus prevails over a 'Jesuan'[41] ethic.

With reference to 1962, that the moral prescripts of the Old Law are summarized in the Ten Commandments is an old catechismal conviction, but it is incorrect, at least according to more recent exegesis; the Old Testament has a number of very important moral precepts that are not covered by the Decalogue, such as how widows, aliens, and orphans are to be treated. The quote from Augustine—"God wrote on the tables of the Law what men did not read in their hearts" (1962)—is, of course, strange, given that shortly before this one has just read that the Decalogue reflects something of the natural reason given to people in creation (1955).

The ideas on the relationship of the Old Law and the New Law (1961-1974) are, of course, of far-reaching significance: how must the relation between the Old and the New Testaments be viewed, and what does the former still mean for Christians? Here the Catechism remains in the traditional line of the theme of promise/fulfilment. The Old Testament's actual meaning only becomes clearly visible in the New Testament. Whether intentional or not, this threatens to promote a different evaluation of the parts of holy Scripture. This does not do justice to more recent considerations of the "continuity" of the Torah and to understanding Jesus' preaching as an explanation of that which is the will of God and the law in the name of God for him, which he himself, rooted in the traditions of his people, interprets faithfully.

The so-called 'newness' of the New Testament is not entirely new in relation to Jewish views. For example, one can hardly defend the image that the New Law is a *lex amoris* (law of love), whereas the Old Law would have been a *lex timoris* (law of fear) (1972). The liberation from the "ritual and juridical observances" through the "New Law" (1972) has been amply counterbalanced by ecclesiastical rubrics and the Canons.

---

[40] H.-J. Klauck, "Der Katechismus der Katholischen Kirche," p.76. He observes something similar with regard to the Lord's Prayer (p.72).

[41] The difference between a Christological ethics and a 'Jesuan' ethics wishes to point out that the words and views of Jesus himself are explained, elaborated on further, and in that sense also changed in the early believing communities. Cf., for example, the divergent views on divorce in the various writings of the New Testament.

d) Questions are also raised by the use made of the Bible for confirmation of the Catechism's views on the relation between reason and revelation as a source of moral knowledge, or on the role of the ecclesiastical authority with respect to morality. Thus the view that "a good and pure conscience is enlightened by true faith" (1794) is argued biblically: "for charity proceeds at the same time 'from a pure heart and a good conscience and sincere faith'" (1 Timothy 1:5). What is this quotation doing here? And what is to be done with the conscience of people who do not adhere to 'the true faith'? Compare also 1896 in this context: "There is no solution to the social question apart from the Gospel." Even though this is a quote from *Centesimus Annus* (no. 3), what about the justice of people who must manage without the Gospel?

e) The significance that is assigned to (ecclesiastical and worldly) authority (1899) is remarkable, but not really surprising: Romans 13:1-2 and 1 Peter 2:13-17 are quoted in a extremely *authority-friendly* context without any further conditions. For that matter, authority is also the first fact in the analysis of society, thematized even before the common good (1897-1904, 1905-1912). This certainly distorts essential relationships somewhat.

The end of the section on fundamental morality is of particular significance. It is rounded off with a section called "The Church, Mother and Teacher" (2030 ff.). This is a chapter that is relatively new within the doctrine of morality; I think it originated in this century or, at the earliest, in the previous century. At least it does not belong to the chapters of the classical handbook tradition of the contra-Reformation as such.

As has been repeatedly stated, Scripture, tradition, and the ecclesiastical Magisterium are closely interwoven in the Catechism. One could almost say that the significance of Scripture for morality is, like the last brick, crowned by a chapter that could be entitled "On the Significance of the Magisterium for the Significance of Scripture." Here we also encounter the theme of infallibility (2034 f.) and, in direct connection with this, the authority of ecclesiastical Magisterium with respect to the natural law. What is striking is that a scriptural argumentation for this is barely present. Basically, there is a suggestion of it within the general mission to proclaim the gospel and the significance of morality for salvation (2036). One is immediately struck by the fact that the role of the church is concentrated on that of the Magisterium to which is said that the believers must be obedient, even in disciplinary matters (2037). Now something beautiful seems to happen. While the authority of the Magisterium must essentially be content with conciliar statements, the contribution of ordinary Christians, through their experience of life "in Christ" by the Spirit, is confirmed by a Scriptural quotation, 1 Corinthians 2:10-15. Immediately following, however, (using Romans 12:8, 11, although these verses do not serve the purpose of proof) the prerogative of ecclesiastical Magisterium is brought forward on the most sensitive point. "Personal conscience and reason should not be set in opposition to the moral law or the Magisterium of the Church" (2039).

At the end of this list as well as that of the section of fundamental morality itself a general impression is confirmed. The model of morality used by the Catechism is not really a *biblical* but an *authoritarian model*. We have encountered the central place of authority more often: for example, in the relationship of authority and conscience (1783, 1785, 1992), in the meaning of authority for the community, where it is the first element mentioned (1897), and in the first introduction of the law (1951, but cf. 1976). Scripture can be of good service here and is used where the opportunity arises. If that is not the case, other documents are presented.[42] It does not surprise me then that after having introduced the precepts of the church (2041-2043) the last number of the section on fundamental morality in the Catechism reads: "The infallibility of the Magisterium of the Pastors extends to all the elements of doctrine, including moral doctrine, without which the saving truths of the faith cannot be preserved, expounded, or observed" (2051). This last number is not argued on the basis of holy Scripture, since it is nowhere to be found in Scripture.

What is Wrong with the Catechism's Model of Morality?

It is apparent that the use of Scripture is strongly determined by the general ideas of what morality is, and in which it finds its basis and foundation—thus by the model of morality for which the Catechism has chosen. What is wrong with it? I can only give a short outline of the answer to this question. A number of aspects have already been discussed in the various contributions of this volume, and therefore I can restrict myself to a few observations.[43]

---

[42] Also cf., unlike the CR, "the concern about the hierarchy," which was noticed by J. van Laarhoven ("Twee katechismussen: De catechismus Romanus en de Katechismus van de Katholieke Kerk," pp. 380 ff.) in the chapter on the church, which, among other things, is also confirmed by an emphatic use of juridical canons (27 of the 57 quotations from the CIC, in addition to a number of references).

[43] These comments are made against the general background of the recent developments in the area of moral theology, the encyclical *Veritatis Splendor* as critique on those developments, as well as reactions to the encyclical. Whoever wishes to delve more deeply into this is referred to J. Selling and J. Jans (eds), *The Splendor of Accuracy: An Examination of the Assertions Made by* Veritatis Splendor (Kampen, 1994); D. Mieth (ed.), *Moraltheologie im Abseits? Antwort auf die Enzyklika "Veritatis splendor"* (Freiburg/Basel/Vienna, 1994); H.W.M. Rikhof and F.J.H. Vosman (eds), *De schittering van de waarheid: Theologische reflecties bij de encykliek* Veritatis splendor (Zoetermeer, 1994).

J. Gründel has pointed out that the Catechism never discusses maturity and autonomy, two concepts that are central to the modern mentality of freedom.[44] The arguments of authority and tradition prevail far above rational argumentation. Thus the impression arises "as though the Christian faith would be mediated only 'from above', therefore in a positivistic way, deductively, and purely authoritatively."[45] He sees indications of this in the deontological argumentation (that is to say, norms obtain absolutely, without exception), in the question of "acts bad in themselves," in the statements on conscience, the role of the Magisterium and the problem of dissenting from that Magisterium, and in a view of natural law that is no longer defensible.[46] For Gründel, however, it is a central point of insights of moral theology that it is no longer possible today to pose and pass on moral demands without adding a minimum of convincing reasoning.[47] The use of the Bible is also to be seen in this light.

Unfortunately the use of the Bible in the Catechism leads one to confirm rather than to relativize Gründel's evaluation. The desire expressed by the Second Vatican Council that the doctrine of morality be renewed under biblical influence and be able to be carried out by theology and the church with more power of conviction, was not realized in the Catechism in spite of all the quotations. The reason is relatively simple: it is not the Bible that has renewed moral doctrine but moral doctrine has simply taken the Bible into its service. The Bible must confirm the model of morality (derived from elsewhere) that is proclaimed; this model of morality determines the interpretation of the biblical quotations cited. Thus the Bible does not so much say what it says but, rather, what it ought to say.

Is the result of our consideration that the Catechism is indeed not truly biblical, but that a true biblical morality could be possible in another way? Yes and no; the answer depends on one's expectations of a 'biblical morality'. What are the possibilities of casting morality along biblical lines? A number of critical considerations will be presented in the last section of this contribution.

---

[44] J. Gründel, "Der Weltkatechismus," p.125.

[45] J. Gründel, "Der Weltkatechismus," pp.118-19.

[46] In the second section on special morality, interpreted on the basis of the Ten Commandments, one will have to determine to which degree the image sketched by Gründel continues to have an effect. Ultimately the spelling out of moral principles, with concrete acts in mind, occurs there; unfortunately, it is to be feared that what we actually find there will confirm Gründel's objections.

[47] J. Gründel, "Der Weltkatechismus," p.139.

Catholic Morality—'Remotely' Biblical

From its development into a separate discipline in medieval scholasticism Catholic moral theology was always of the conviction that, as the late moral theologian Franz Böckle put it, "the morality of revelation is the true morality of reason." Insofar as it appealed to the biblical tradition for interhuman behaviour, it never saw it as a contrast to general human reflection.[48] This idea was expressed in the type of ethics that Catholic moral theology has developed: Catholic moral theology has presented itself as an *ethics of the natural law*. In this it was led by an interest in the objective, which is also the universally valid dimensions of morality. The natural law means, among other things, that the knowledge of that morality is rationally possible through so-called natural reason and does not specifically presuppose faith. "Just reasoning can never occur too much in moral theology," according to the famous moral theologian Dominicus Prümmer O.P.[49]

Must we ascertain from this that Catholic morality has therefore, at least since the Middle Ages, deviated from the correct path by ignoring its theological roots? For is the system of morality as it is found in the handbooks of traditional Catholic moral theology not basically the same as that found in Thomas Aquinas, upon which those handbooks also call as a rule? Does Thomas Aquinas himself not minimalize the theological roots when he asks why a revealed divine law (*lex divina*) is necessary in addition to the natural law (*lex naturalis*)?

The answer that he gives to this question is ultimately disappointing for someone who thinks there must be a clear distinction between ordinary human rational morality and Christian morality. For what do faith and revelation add to a natural morality? They put it in a transcendent framework, thereby orienting it by reference to its beginning and end. Otherwise the function of revelation is to strengthen, guarantee, and round off natural rational morality.[50] Apparently

---

[48] F. Böckle, "Werte und Normbegründung," in: *Christlicher Glaube in moderner Gesellschaft* 12 (1981): 37-89, 46.

[49] "Recta ratio in Theologia morali numquam nimis adhibetur," in: *Manuale theologiae moralis*, vol. 1 (1961), no. 8.

[50] Cf. *ST* I-II.91.4: "for *four reasons*: ... since man is ordained *to an end of eternal happiness* which is inproportionate to man's natural faculty ...: *on account of the uncertainty of human judgment* ...: man is not competent to judge of *interior movements* ...; because ... human law cannot *punish or forbid all evil deeds*." The translation is taken from Thomas Aquinas, *Summa Theologica*, tr. Fathers of the Dominican Province (London, 1922).

With respect to moral precepts there is a similarity between the old law and the natural morality law (cf. I-II.100.1: "The moral precepts ... are about things pertaining of their very nature to good morals."); see also the examples that Thomas mentions for the

Thomas Aquinas' view of a theological ethics is different than that of those who see this theological character in a maximal application of biblical authority (as well as that of the Magisterium). From his characteristic belief in the interwovenness of nature and grace, creation and redemption, reason and faith Thomas has no difficulty in valuing nature, creation, and reason highly and, as a theologian, learning from them, also and particularly with regard to morality. The theological does not overwhelm or supplant the philosophical; faith "performs" with reason in the beautiful meaning that this word has with respect to music.

It could be that people later no longer had a feel for the delicate sounds that theology inserted into the whole, so that they, fascinated by a rationalist ideal of objectivity of a universally valid morality, thought they could ignore it. This could be demonstrated by a comparison between Thomas and the moral handbooks. In spite of a number of titles, which are also to be found in the Prima Secundae of Thomas' *Summa Theologiae* (*ST*) ("Human Acts," "Passions," "Virtues," "Sin," "Law"), these treatments give a different impression in Thomas. He is and continues to think in an obviously biblical atmosphere[51] —without thereby replacing the systematic categories by biblical ones.

It is obvious, for example (I will mention only a few things), the fact that the whole of moral reflection in the *ST* is placed within the theological framework between the doctrine of creation and Christology. And fundamental theology comes up again in *ST* I-II, between the theological question of the final end, i.e. the meaning of life, and the treatise of grace, through which God helps people on their way. A famous example is the reflection on the foundation of norms. In the teachings of the law, the *lex aeterna* (eternal law) and the positive revelation in the writings of the Old and New Testaments form the theological framework for the natural law and human norms. But even though this includes all of the normative considerations theologically and with regard to faith, it is Thomas who tells us that the process of the search for moral truth occurs in a rational procedure in which people take an active role. Through the human capacity for reason the *lex aeterna* becomes active as the moral responsibility and creativity, and revelation confirms in creatures that which can already be discovered rationally at the same time.

Thus, in addition to the (in my opinion demonstrably wrong) conclusion that Thomas minimalizes the theological perspective of ethics, another conclusion is also possible: perhaps we should not look for the theological in a quantitative addition but in a qualitative change. We must not look for it in a materially dif-

---

need of a divine instruction (*ST* I-II.100.1): they concern the first table of the decalogue. With respect to the new law, cf., for example, 108.2 *ad* 1: the old law needs supplementation with respect to faith, but not with respect to the virtues.

[51] Cf. M.-D. Chenu, *Introduction à l'étude de Saint Thomas D'Aquin*, 2nd ed. (Paris/Montreal), p.271 and *passim*.

ferent morality with other specific norms and virtues and with other rationalizations to establish and argue norms, but in a morality of a different kind of significance. For this 'other' morality it is significant, for example, that a virtuous life with its exploration of good and evil has something to do with God as the source and fulfilment of our existence, with the relationship between God and people, with God's revelation in the history of Israel, in Jesus Christ particularly, and with the Spirit of God who is with us. But what does not change in a 'Christian' ethic is the structure of ethics, that is to say, the ways in which we, through experience and reflection, must continue to search for that which is good every time. This issue continues in discussions in moral theology even today.

The Second Vatican Council has required moral theology to be renewed and to be nourished more strongly by holy Scripture. Nevertheless, this has not led Catholic moral theology to abandon its principally rational conception of morality. Even though the perspective of holy Scripture is given more attention in modern moral theology, this does not lead to a scriptural argumentation in an actual sense, at least not in questions of *normative* ethics, that section of ethics in which the question of good and evil or right and wrong becomes concretely elaborated. Here the moral theological argumentation remains 'rational,' even though it is not in the style of a Neo-scholastic ethics of natural law. I do think that the inspiring role of Scripture, particularly where it questions that which is all too obvious in social conventions, has become much stronger. Yet Scripture does not replace thinking. The reason for this lies in the fact that moral theology cannot be reduced to exegetical statements with regard to morality. The gospel does not have in mind a retrospective biblical proclamation, but is oriented toward the dynamics of living in periods and circumstances that are constantly new. "Moral theology cannot," says Böckle, "simply repetitively quote exegetical statements concerning morality, but must provide insight into its meaning and sense in the form of an argumentative theory and make them applicable to the situation."[52] Thus the normativity of the holy Scripture is not immediate, it is *a 'distant' normativity* that constantly requires a mediation for actuality.[53] This obtains even for the commandments and prohibitions found in the holy writings of the Old and New Testaments. As a rule they are not directly applied but interpreted as ideals, or models, or principles. The actualization of this cannot occur without continually dealing with the uniqueness of the time and situation. It is not until modern exegesis, which believes it can illustrate the cultural gen-

---

[52] F. Böckle, "Moraltheologie und Exegese heute," in: K. Kertelge (ed.), *Ethik im Neuen Testament* (Freiburg, 1984), pp. 197-210, 199-200.

[53] These comments can link with the very balanced judgement of the relation of exegesis and moral theology in the Pontifical Biblical Commission's "The Interpretation of the Bible in the Church," p. 519.

esis of the decalogue, that the Ten Commandments were seen as indicators and not as rigorous and concrete rules for behaviour. The words of Jesus himself and of the apostles are also applied with a certain flexibility to continually new questions (cf., for example, the very divergent ways in which appeals to the Sermon on the Mount is concretized: why is swearing allowed, but not divorce?)—which the church has never understood in a way that they would not be taken seriously.

For the rest the nuanced contact with the holy Scripture can be based on the Bible itself. On many issues the Bible allows developments and also the tense relationship between principles and concretizations to be seen in its various layers. The fact that, for Christians, holy Scripture consists of the Old and New Testaments together has probably played a particular role in this. This gave rise at a certain point for Christian self-awareness to the question of what could still be binding in the Old Testament norms.

Reflection on this has led to a very nuanced answer in which a distinction is made between norms that were intended for the concrete situation of the people of Israel (legal regulations, cultic adjustments) and norms that express moral requirements and through this may be viewed as universally valid. Scripture itself does not offer criteria for this. They were won from an essentially rational reflection on morality (along the lines of the natural law) and its normative implications. This has sometimes caused problems for authors when they must reconcile directives, that are given by God according to Scripture and therefore cannot be bad in themselves yet do conflict with moral convictions, with the conviction that it is that which is moral that reflects the will of God and that therefore God cannot require anything that is immoral.

An example of this is the divine directive in Exodus 11:2 and 12:35 f. to plunder the Egyptians of their gold and silver articles. Other examples are God's command to Abraham to kill Isaac and his command to Hosea to marry a prostitute.[54] It is not all that amazing that a medieval author like Thomas Aquinas, who could not yet read Scripture with the eyes of a modern exegete, had to seek a kind of positivistic solution to the problems posed by these examples (God determines who is the owner of something; He is Lord of life and death; He himself has erected the institution of marriage—and can therefore dispose of it). It is much more amazing that such arguments, which undermine the rational character of natural law ethics, in Thomas and also in the broad school of the Catholic moral tradition remain very marginal. Apparently Thomas, the professor of exegesis (for that is what he was in the first instance—*magister in sacra pa-*

---

[54] Cf., for example, Thomas Aquinas, *ST* I-II.100.8 *ad* 3.

gina),[55] was very sensitive to the peculiarity of moral questions, which had to be solved not through authoritative texts but through insight and argumentation.

In reaction to the deficiencies of an essentialist (and ultimately authoritarian) ethics of the natural law, moral theology has developed new models of thought in which the requirement of individual insight and of moral reasonableness once again play the role that they, from the viewpoint of morality, must play.[56] Along the lines of the ideal of the authentic natural law, a movement away from a view of norms resting on external authority toward an internal understanding of their significance and meaning is typical for these models. When Scripture (and the Magisterium with its statements) plays a role in this, then it is not by shortchanging the question of meaningfulness, or offering ready-made answers, or even avoiding the question. Scripture and the Magisterium can, as it were, offer themselves as co-seekers and leaders in the consideration of that question in order to try to contribute to the development of moral insights. This is at first glance a modest role but, in my opinion, the only way through which moral authority can arise.

The question remains, of course, as to where revelation must be placed in this framework. First of all, a fundamental theological reflection on what revelation is would be appropriate here, how it is intertwined in the history of culture, what the relationship is between revelation and Scripture, in which way we must read the moral convictions of Scripture for us, how we must understand the imitation of Christ, etc. But this is not the place to elaborate on this.

I will only recapitulate the answer of a few prominent theologians, who represent a large number of moral theologians, to the question of the specific aspect of faith concerning ethics. In my opinion it seems that these theologians, also and particularly when they are called 'autonomous', have in common the fact that they always understand morality *a priori* as a morality in the context of the Christian faith. They also usually share the assumption that there are no concrete norms that are specific for Christians, at least with regard to human interaction. The influence and meaning of faith do not play a role on this level but do so on a deeper level and in a more encompassing way.[57]

---

[55] Cf., for example, Chenu, *Introduction à l'étude de saint Thomas D'Aquin*, pp. 207ff.

[56] Cf. K.-W. Merks, "Autonomie," in: J.-P. Wils and D. Mieth, *Grundbegriffe der christlichen Ethik* (Paderborn, 1992), pp. 254-81.

[57] Thus A. Auer, for example, stresses an integrating, criticizing, and stimulating function of the Christian faith with regard to morality: placing morality in an encompassing religious orientation of existence; the breaching of narrowing convictions of social value on the basis of the concepts of humanity and God in the tradition of faith; searching for more humanity from experiences of faith. J. Fuchs speaks of a Christian inten-

In contrast to proposals that see God as an almighty monarch who is not accountable to anyone and of which the commandments and regulations obtain, as it were, on the sole basis of these divine directives, that which is normative and obligatory is seen as a matter that stands on its own and principially in itself provides insight, that must be able to be demonstrated as such and does not find its justification in a decree by God. This means that when a moral theologian wishes to do his/her work well, namely, to explain the meaning of faith for acts, he/she is always referred to the rational procedures that must determine ethical discourse. The specific is therefore not to replace that discourse but to situate it. Finally, morality is not a remote area in life but stands in relation to the whole of the being and meaning of human existence in this world.

Conclusion

I will now conclude. Christians, just like the people of Israel, have always been convinced that faith and actions, truth in God and justice toward one another go together. Without the appropriate behaviour faith is not real, it is not even actually faith. I myself think that this faith emphatically influences our ideas on justice as well. The question is how does it do so. Does faith yield other insight into that which is required morally? Do Christians have better insights because of their faith? Or are they perhaps better able to follow their—other, better —moral insights? There is reason to be wary of an answer to these questions that is too quickly positive.

What we have done up until now is simply cleaning up, disposing of the wrong views. A Christian morality cannot and may not be an authoritarian morality, but must fulfil the same requirements of justice that every morality must fulfil. We must defend this most emphatically, also against an concept of morality that is sometimes advanced within the church, i.e., that Christian morality were also based on an obedience other than an obedience to one's conscience. Christian inspiration may not replace the normal rational procedures of the formation of moral judgement and moral justification. It is from this that F. Böckle comes to the conclusion that that which is specifically Christian may not be seen as exclusive but rather must be described in terms of "appropriate for Chris-

---

tionality by which acts are seen at the same time in their meaning for the relationship of people with God. For F. Böckle it is important that God himself is seen as the supporting ground of being human and of the challenge to use freedom responsibly, and that people may therefore share responsibility for their moral world under orders of the Creator himself. In this way, in contrast to that which is sometimes thought, it is precisely through faith that the wrong absolutizations of human insights can be averted.

tians," "typical of Christians."[58] The Bible is, in the first instance, the passing on of how Christians—no, more broadly, how Jews and Christians —have experienced in their time and with their faith that which in the light of the faith must be a typical, appropriate behaviour in search of a responsible, righteous life.

This is what is passed on for our education, to inspire us to search for ourselves, for example, in what direction answers might be found for the problems of today as well. It is passed on to encourage us, to entrust ourselves to proven ways but also to go in new directions where that appears to be needed morally. The Bible must not be viewed as a law book but as a challenging witness of experiences of faith, whose authenticity is based on their degree of actuality and truth and not on a formal authority. Every use of Scripture that evokes a different impression does not augment but undermines the authority of the Scripture. A good way to prevent that is, namely, by reading holy Scripture itself. I do not think that the Catechism will object.

---

[58] F. Böckle, *Fundamentalmoral* (Munich, 1977), p.290: "The problem of Christian ethics is not the exclusivity of norms shaped by faith but rather their communicability." See also H. Halter, *Taufe und Ethos* (Freiburg, 1977), p.485: "Perhaps one can better speak in general of typically Christian rather than specifically Christian patterns of behaviour, i.e, convictions and the corresponding 'norms', for therewith the moment of exclusivity is omitted."

Index of Names

Albert the Great 45, 109
Ambrose 12, 29, 104
Aquinas, Thomas 2, 13, 25, 27, 29, 34, 43-47, 49, 50, 53, 80, 86, 88, 95, 101-03, 107, 122, 155, 156, 158, 172, 173, 185, 186, 193, 213, 224, 227, 229, 234, 240, 241, 243
Aristotle 27, 34-46, 53, 95, 101-04, 169, 174
Arquillière, H. 14
Athanasius 12
Auer, A. 69, 70, 244
Augustine 2, 12, 43, 62, 101, 102, 150, 160, 187, 234, 236

Bentham, J. 32
Bernard of Clairvaux 13
Bévenot, M. 201-03
Bloch, E. 24
Böckenförde, E.-W. 66-69
Böckle, F. 70, 125, 143, 240, 242, 245, 246
Boff, L. 138, 157, 158
Boyle, John P. 205
Bruguès, J.L. 20, 23
Bujo, B. 45, 229

Caparros, E. 212
Carro, V. 14, 19
Catharine of Siena, St. 173
Chenu, M.-D. 17, 156, 162, 241, 243
Churton, T. 13
Congar, Y. 19, 198, 199
Coriden, James A. 212
Curran, C.E. 86, 199, 204
Cyprian, St. 227

Damu, P. 30
De Castro, A. 19
De Echeverria, L. 212
De Riedmatten, H. 17
De Smedt, Mgr. 19
De Soto, D. 14
Demmer, K. 28, 55, 91
Dostoyevsky, F.M. 73
Dürig, W. 11

Eberle, J. 228, 229
Engelhardt, P. 29, 31-33, 118

Facio, B. 13
Fahey, M.A. 198
Ford, J.C. 205-07
Fransen, P. 200-02
Fuchs, J. 86, 244

Galvin, J.P. 198
Gasser, Bishop 204
Green, T.J. 212
Gregory XVI 15, 16, 65
Grisez, G. 205-07
Gruber, H.-G. 84, 85
Gründel, J. 58, 233, 239

Haag, E. 226
Halter, H. 225, 246
Hamer O.P., J. 19
Häring, B. 107, 130, 189
Hegel, G.W.F. 169
Heintschel, D.E. 212
Heinzmann, R. 231, 232
Hirschmann, S.J., Fr. 17
Honoré, G. 20
Honoré, J. 30
Horstmann, R.P. 11
Hughes, G.J. 28, 30, 31, 53

INDEX OF NAMES

Hughes, P. 200, 202
Hünermann, P. 233

Jans, J. 9, 74, 84, 88, 195, 206, 238
Janssens, L. 86, 88-90
John Paul II 1, 66, 69, 174, 175, 178, 195, 234
John XXIII 16, 17, 109, 162, 172, 175, 180
Jone, H. 223
Jonkers, P. 233

Kant, I. 14, 15, 32, 69-71, 160, 161
Keller S.J., A. 57, 58
Kertelge, K. 226, 242
Kiessig, M. 233
Klauck, H.-J. 230, 231, 235, 236
Knauer, P. 86, 88, 89
Kremer, J. 226
Krings, H. 64

Las Casas, B. de 13, 14
Lecler, J. 19
Leclercq, J. 223
Leo the Great 11
Leo XIII 15, 16, 67, 164, 214
Lévi-Strauss, C. 24
Locke, J. 15
Lombard 45

Mahoney, J. 108, 114, 188, 191, 193
Manetti, G. 13
Marcuse, H. 24
Marx, K. 39, 127, 169
McCormick, Richard A. 84-86, 199, 204
Merks, K.-W. 1, 10, 28, 130, 192, 222, 244
Metz, J.B. 66, 137, 138, 150, 164
Mieth, D. 7, 11, 71, 72, 75, 131, 195, 225, 238, 244
Mill, J.S. 32
Moeller, C. 17, 18
Moltmann, J. 63, 64
Murray, R. 198

Nietzsche, F.W. 126, 131, 132

Oberforcher, R. 226
Oraison, M. 223
Origen 12, 30

Parsons, T. 167
Paul, St. 1, 94, 106, 148-50, 153-55, 187, 208
Paul V 105
Paul VI 110, 162, 173, 175, 194, 206
Pavan, P. 18
Pelagius 62
Peperzak, A. 32, 33
Pesch, O.H. 152-154, 156, 186, 188, 190, 193, 228, 229, 232
Pico della Mirandola, G. 13
Pius IV 200
Pius IX 15, 16, 67
Pius V 12
Pius VI 15
Pius X 15
Pius XI 16, 173, 174, 176, 206, 214
Pius XII 16, 17, 66, 109, 130, 229, 230
Prümmer, D. 240

Rahner, K. 61, 69, 137, 216, 235
Ratzinger, J. 20, 184, 229, 230, 232
Reese, T.J. 3, 30
Rikhof, H.W.M. 75, 233, 238
Rotter, H. 226
Rousseau, J.J. 15
Ruh, U. 21

Sangnier, M. 15
Schillebeeckx, E. 137, 152, 153, 158, 159, 164, 207, 210
Schnackenberg, R. 204
Schoonenberg, P. 29, 61, 137, 156, 157
Schöpsdau, W. 235
Schüller, B. 36, 84, 86, 91
Schulz, E. 225, 230-33
Schüssler Fiorenza, F. 198

Selling, J.A. 9, 76, 88, 89, 194, 195, 213, 220, 238
Sertillanges O.P, A.-G. 222
Skinner, B.F. 60
Slater, T. 223
Sobrino, J. 163
Sokolowski, R. 41, 47, 55
Spaemann, R. 25, 36
Sullivan, F.A. 202, 204, 205

Thorn, J. 212
Tönnies, F. 167

Valkenberg, W.G.B.M. 227, 229
Van den Hoogen, T. 9, 147, 162

Van Laarhoven, J. 5, 227, 228, 233, 238
Vereecke, L. 8, 26
Verweyen, H. 222, 224, 229-31
Vidal, M. 7, 8, 26, 75, 225, 234
Von Nell-Breuning, O. 174
Vorgrimler, H. 228
Vosman, F.J.H. 1, 8, 25, 75, 233, 238

Walsh, M.J. 28, 198, 213
Walter, P. 131, 226
Wilkins, John 84, 195
Wils, J.-P. 11, 24, 34, 36, 244
Woldring, H. 45

Index of Subjects

Act/acts 2, 3, 7, 8, 17, 21, 23, 28, 30-32, 34-38, 44, 47, 48, 51, 52, 55, 58, 67, 74-91, 79-85, 87, 88, 95, 102, 104-06, 114-19, 139, 145, 147-50, 171, 175, 185, 190, 192, 194, 200, 208, 211, 218, 223-25, 230, 235, 239, 241, 245
   good act 81, 83
Action/actions 2, 9, 12, 25, 26, 29-44, 47-49, 51, 53-55, 58, 59, 61, 62, 65, 69, 74-92, 114, 118, 121-23, 132, 137, 144, 145, 151, 152, 155, 157, 159-62, 167, 169, 170, 172, 176-79, 183, 185, 186, 188, 194, 197, 203, 209, 223, 225, 245
Ambiguity 43, 69, 89, 100, 215
Anathema 144, 201
Animals 57, 167, 178
Augustinianism 14, 15, 45, 62, 118
Authority 1, 4, 9, 57, 66, 69-71, 84, 111, 118, 119, 121, 127, 153, 155, 166, 168, 172, 174, 175, 186, 188, 190, 191, 193-203, 206, 209, 210, 212-21, 226-29, 234, 237-39, 241, 244, 246
Autonomy 14, 18, 33, 60, 69-73, 127-29, 132, 212, 239

Beatitude 19, 25-32, 45, 55, 56, 116, 135, 148
Beatitudes 2, 8, 27-31, 33, 46, 52-55, 236
Benedictus 200
Biblical theology 226
Bonum commune 9, 179, 180
   common good 21, 44, 50, 58, 168-70, 173, 174, 178-81, 186, 188, 193, 237
Business 171

Casti Connubii 206
Catechismus Romanus/Roman Catechism 4, 5, 12, 29, 30, 52, 213, 227, 228, 238
Centesimus Annus 121, 174-76, 237
Charity 15, 135, 145, 160, 168, 173, 177, 237
Christocentrism 30, 48, 49
Circumstances 8, 26, 67, 75-77, 80-84, 86, 100, 118, 133, 148, 191, 209, 217, 219, 220, 226, 242
Codex Juris Canonici
   Canon 57 § 2 212
   Canon 747 § 1 211
   Canon 747 § 2 211
   Canon 833 210
   Code of Canon Law 211, 212
Collective 16, 22, 108, 134, 137, 145, 170, 172, 176, 177
Community 2, 7, 9, 16, 17, 20, 26, 30, 31, 33, 34, 40, 46, 48, 49, 51, 53, 63, 111, 125, 139, 153, 154, 158, 159, 161, 164-77, 179, 180, 181-83, 185-87, 191, 194, 197, 208, 209, 212, 219-21, 234, 238
Conscience 2, 7-9, 15-18, 20, 21, 26, 57, 65, 69, 74, 77, 86, 87, 91, 93, 101, 113-29, 148, 150, 171, 178, 184, 185, 188, 190, 191, 215, 216, 223, 224, 233, 235, 237-39, 245
Council of Trent (1545-1563) 4, 199
Culture 4-6, 8, 25, 33, 42, 43, 46,

Index of Subjects

111, 112, 127-29, 145, 148, 151, 159, 161, 172, 233, 244

Decalogue 3, 20, 57, 190-92, 213, 217, 224, 236, 241, 243
Defense 22, 119, 180
Dei Verbum 196, 197
Democracy 6, 65, 70, 122, 124, 125, 176
Denz-Schoen 207
Depositum fidei 196, 204, 228
Dignitatis Humanae 66, 68, 69
Didaché 94-95
Dignity 2-4, 7, 8, 11-24, 46, 48, 58, 60, 113, 115-17, 119, 120, 124, 142, 148, 152, 166, 167, 170, 171, 173, 175-77, 181, 183, 184, 191, 195, 228
Disciplina 201-03, 207, 208, 210, 217
Doctrina 202, 203, 207, 208, 210, 217
   doctrina de fide 202, 203, 207
   doctrina de fide vel moribus 202, 203, 207
Doctrine
   social 164, 165, 234
Dogmatic Constitution on Divine Revelation 197

End 2, 8, 15, 17, 19, 20, 25, 26, 28, 29, 31, 32, 34-36, 38, 39, 42-44, 47, 48, 51, 58, 76-81, 83, 87-91, 94, 100, 117, 123, 128, 134, 135, 136, 153, 154, 156, 159, 162, 176, 194, 199, 218, 223, 227, 237, 238, 240, 241
   telos 34-36, 42
Enlightenment 4, 6, 9, 14, 26, 59, 65, 131, 161, 163, 193, 194, 199, 202
Ethics
   social 63, 123, 164-66, 170, 171, 178, 181
Eudaimonia 36, 42, 45, 46

Evil 2, 8, 27, 32, 34, 38, 41-44, 47-49, 51-55, 57, 58, 60, 62, 67, 74, 76, 77, 79-92, 95, 99-101, 104, 121, 128, 130, 134, 137, 139, 140, 142-44, 148, 162, 169, 173, 175, 183-85, 187, 190, 192, 209, 225, 240, 242
   ontic 86, 89, 90
Feminism 137, 139-41, 232
Fidei Depositum 1, 195, 211, 222
Fides et mores 200-03
Finis operantis 75, 86, 87
Finis operis 75, 86
Fontes moralitatis 75
Fontes theologiae moralis 235
Form and matter 88
Freedom 2, 8, 13-22, 35, 44, 49, 57-69, 71-73, 110, 113-24, 126, 127, 129, 132, 143, 144, 148, 151, 156-60, 169, 171, 174, 180, 186, 192, 215, 217, 239, 245
   religious 18, 19, 21, 66-68, 115-17, 215
   rights to 16, 21, 64, 171, 180
Friendship 31, 33, 40, 42-53, 55, 89, 103

Gaudium et Spes 16, 17, 20, 23, 36, 115, 120, 129, 162, 167, 212, 216
Good 2, 7-9, 19, 21, 22, 24-28, 31, 32, 34, 36-59, 61-63, 68, 74, 76-84, 86-91, 95, 100, 101, 104, 109, 110, 116, 117, 121, 128, 131, 134, 135, 139, 140, 144, 145, 148, 153, 159, 165, 166, 168, 169, 170, 173, 174, 176-89, 193, 209, 211, 215, 220, 225, 237, 238, 240, 242, 246
   bonum 9, 45, 46, 52, 54, 55, 81, 179, 180
Government 14, 21, 167, 174, 175, 180, 181, 189, 191, 202

Grace 2, 8, 9, 12-14, 21, 26, 28, 31, 44, 49, 51, 53, 59, 61, 62, 105, 107, 116, 140, 147-61, 165, 182-86, 192, 193, 195, 210, 219, 241

Happiness 2, 8, 20, 25-34, 38, 39, 42-48, 50, 52-54, 56, 89, 102, 103, 116, 123, 152, 153, 183, 240
Humanae Vitae 110, 194, 206, 216

Image of God 12, 14, 18-20, 23, 114-16, 119, 121, 124, 127, 128, 135, 166, 167, 183, 184
Inculturation 5, 232
Individual 6-8, 13, 16, 22, 32, 33, 37, 55, 63, 64, 69, 78, 100, 113, 116, 118, 119-25, 127, 136, 137, 139, 141, 143, 144, 159, 168, 170, 171, 173-81, 189, 194, 205, 213, 218, 221, 227, 235, 244
Infallibility 202-06, 205, 210, 212, 213, 237, 238
Intention 5, 8, 20, 26, 47, 75-84, 86-88, 90-92, 138, 157, 175, 183, 227, 232

Justice
    commutative 172
    distributive 172, 173
    social 21, 24, 171-74, 179, 180
Justification 154, 155, 160, 161, 235

Laborem Exercens 3, 8, 17, 20, 26, 29, 30, 36, 44, 85, 156, 175, 178
Law
    ecclesiastical 185
    eternal 13, 134, 187, 241
    moral 2, 9, 21, 59, 118, 135, 148, 149, 182-87, 189, 191, 192, 215, 238
    natural 7, 9, 13, 16, 18, 21,
        24, 58, 103, 164-66, 182, 187-93, 214, 215, 222, 223, 225, 237, 239-44
    New 2, 149, 150, 182, 188, 192, 193, 236, 241
    Old 149, 150, 182, 192, 236, 240, 241
Lawgiver 186-88, 193
Liberal 64, 128, 181
Liberalism 71, 170, 173, 181
Loci theologici 235
Love 17, 23, 40, 44, 45, 47, 49, 51, 52, 63, 78, 89, 96, 97, 101, 105, 106, 134, 135, 139, 141, 145, 148, 149, 152, 153, 156, 165, 168, 176, 177, 180, 183, 184, 192, 208, 213, 217, 218, 220, 236
Lumen Gentium 115, 116, 206, 207, 209, 211, 224

Magisterium/ 14, 15, 21, 59, 70, 93, 113, 127, 128, 165, 174, 186, 190, 191, 194, 196-99, 202, 204-207, 210, 211, 213-16, 222, 228, 234, 235, 237-39, 241, 244
    ordinary magisterium 205, 207, 210
Mater et Magistra 175, 178
Metaphysics 15, 19, 39, 53, 64, 158, 164
Modernity, Catholic Church and 6, 27, 34, 66
Moral methodology 195, 216
Morality 2, 3, 7-10, 17, 20, 25, 30, 36, 47, 53, 57, 68-72, 74-78, 80, 82, 83, 84-91, 93, 105, 116, 126, 128, 130, 131, 147, 159, 161, 164, 165, 182, 183, 185, 186, 189, 190, 193, 194, 196, 198, 199, 202, 204, 205, 211, 216-18, 220, 222-25, 227, 233-35, 237, 238, 239-45
Mores 200-05, 207-08

Index of Subjects

Neo-scholasticism 59, 70, 86, 156, 157, 225
Neo-Thomism 8, 26, 75, 121, 151

Object 8, 26, 66, 75-79, 81-87, 90-92, 135, 136, 141, 168, 187, 203-07, 209, 212, 246
Objectivism 83, 90
Obligations 171, 172, 181
Octogesima Adveniens 175

Pacem in Terris 17-19, 23, 120, 129, 162, 172, 175, 180
Participate/participation 39, 95, 166, 169, 171, 175, 176, 178, 179, 180, 181, 193
Peace 16, 52, 118, 165, 178-180
Person 8, 9, 11-13, 15-24, 31, 32, 36-37, 47, 55, 57-73, 86, 90, 114, 115, 117, 119-21, 125, 151, 165-68, 170-75, 177-81, 183, 223
Personality 24, 170
Political philosophy 122, 169
Polis 34, 35, 38-40
Populorum Progressio 173
Positivism 207
Postmodernity 59
Principium supernaturale 155
Proportionalism 86, 88

Quadragesimo Anno 173, 175, 176

Rationality/Reason 10, 12-14, 17, 21, 36, 48-50, 58, 69, 70, 71, 77, 88, 90, 104, 106, 113, 115, 150, 169, 187-89, 192, 202, 215, 217, 235-242, 245
Reformation 62, 102, 105, 106, 150, 160, 201, 213, 237
Relationships
  social 55
Responsibility 4, 5, 10, 17, 20, 21, 32, 57, 58, 61, 80, 85, 91, 92, 110, 114, 119, 123, 137-39, 142-44, 162, 167-69, 175-80, 197, 200, 222, 227, 241, 245, 246
Revelation 10, 49, 62, 103, 104, 127, 135, 154, 155, 159, 187, 188, 192, 196, 197, 201-08, 211, 212, 214, 215, 217, 218, 224, 231, 235, 237, 240-42, 244
Right 37, 38, 74, 75, 80, 81, 90, 91, 106, 116, 134, 165, 166, 189, 218, 242
Rights
  divine 14
  human (general) 14-18, 21, 33, 48, 58, 67, 68, 72, 116, 142, 161, 171, 172, 174, 179, 180, 189, 217, 211, 234
  natural 16, 18, 67, 189
  rights of the Church 161, 211
  rights of the state 14
  right to divorce 16, 21
  right to equality 15
  right to establish a family
  right to freedom 14, 15, 68
  right to life 16, 21, 22
  right to property 14, 16
  rights relating to conscience 116, 118
  right to self-determination 22
  right to self-government 14
  right to strike 171
  right to the truth 67
  social economic rights 171, 175, 178, 180

Scriptural quotations 227, 232, 234, 239
  Genesis 38:4-10 206
  Matthew 22:37-40 208
  Matthew 5-7 208
  Mark 12:39-31 208
  Luke 10:27 208
  Acts 1:8 211
  1 Corinthians 6 208
  1 Corinthians 9:16 211
  1 Timothy 3:15 211

Index of Subjects

Scripture 2, 10, 28, 53, 135, 151, 158, 162, 195-98, 203, 204, 206-09, 222-30, 232, 233, 235-38, 242-44, 246
  Literal sense of 229
  Spiritual sense of 229
Sexuality 96-98, 100, 103, 104, 108-10, 112, 133, 136, 141, 142, 165, 208
Social thought 164, 165, 170, 171, 175, 176, 179
Socialism 174, 178, 212
Society 8, 12, 17-19, 21, 23, 24, 27, 29, 31, 33, 38-40, 46, 52, 56, 58, 59, 63-68, 70, 84, 95, 108, 111, 120, 124, 128, 139, 141, 151, 161, 166-83, 188, 191, 193, 237
Sollicitudo Rei Socialis 174, 178
Spirituality 12, 17, 23, 67, 97-100, 107, 115, 132, 144, 146, 161, 167, 168, 171, 173, 177, 181, 212, 222, 229
State 14, 64, 67, 68, 96, 104, 118, 122, 125, 128, 168, 169, 170, 174, 176, 179, 180, 189, 219
Subsidiarity, principle of 9, 171, 174, 175, 180

Teaching Office 196-98, 200, 209-11, 216-18
Technology 23, 41, 60, 89
Ten Commandments 3, 10, 20-22, 30, 62, 70, 125, 135, 145, 150, 165, 168, 176, 177, 190-92, 213, 235, 236, 239, 243
Theology
  natural 18, 103
Theory of action 9, 26, 74-81, 83-87, 89-92

Thomism 8, 15, 20, 25, 26, 41, 86, 90, 121, 128, 151, 172, 180, 234
Tradition 2, 5-8, 10, 12, 18, 24, 25, 27-32, 34, 36, 41, 43, 51, 56, 61, 68, 71, 86, 101, 108, 110, 114, 118, 123, 134-36, 140, 141, 151, 152, 159, 165, 181, 188, 190, 195-99, 203, 207, 211, 214, 219, 220, 222, 224, 227, 228, 230, 235, 237, 239, 240, 243, 244

United Nations 16, 17, 172
Universal Declaration of the Rights of Man 16

Values
  premoral 89, 90
  premoral disvalues 89, 90
Vatican Council I (1870) 199-204, 206, 207, 212, 217
Vatican Council II 1, 4, 9, 23, 66-69, 108, 110, 114, 115, 118-20, 124, 125, 127, 162, 164, 166, 183, 185, 198, 206, 207, 210, 213, 215, 219, 222, 224, 228, 230, 234, 239, 242
Veritatis Splendor 4, 7, 28, 42, 72, 75, 76, 84, 88, 121, 126, 129, 192, 195, 216, 225, 233, 234, 238
Virtue 20, 36, 37, 40, 55, 89, 90, 101-05, 114, 121-23, 129, 179, 213
Women's studies 137, 139-42, 144
Wrong 71, 81, 83, 90, 91, 102, 131, 135, 141, 175, 186, 190, 192, 193, 213, 218, 238, 241, 242, 245

Personalia

THEO BEEMER (1927), doctorate in theology, professor emeritus in moral theology and medical ethics at the Catholic University of Nijmegen.
Fields of interest: general moral theology, Thomas Aquinas.

ANNELIES VAN HEIJST (1955), doctorate in theology, lecturer in theological women's studies at the Theological Faculty at Tilburg.
Fields of interest: care ethics in a theological perspective, historical research in Catholicism and femaleness.

TOINE VAN DEN HOOGEN (1947), doctorate in dogmatics, professor of systematic theology at the Catholic University of Nijmegen.
Fields of interest: religion and culture, economy and labour, fundamental theology and its relation to these fields.

RINUS HOUDIJK (1936), master's in moral theology, lecturer in moral theology at the Catholic University of Nijmegen.
Fields of interest: moral theology and modernity with the key concepts of autonomy and solidarity.

JAN HULSHOF, s.m. (1941), doctorate in systematic theology, Prior of the Dutch Province of the Congregation of Marist Fathers.
Fields of interest: ecclesiastical questions of policy, Catholic tradition in connection with human rights.

FRED VAN IERSEL (1954), doctorate in practical theology, special professor at the Theological Faculty at Tilburg for military pastoral care.
Fields of interest: theology of peace.

JAN JANS (1954), doctorate in moral theology, lecturer in moral theology at the Theological Faculty at Tilburg.
Fields of interest: fundamental ethics and concepts of God, medical ethics from the viewpoint of social ethics.

RONALD JEURISSEN (1958), doctorate in theology, lecturer in ethics Catholic University of Brabant.
Fields of interest: corporate ethics and economical ethics, Christian social way of thinking, peace issues.

KARL-WILHELM MERKS (1939), doctorate in moral theology, professor of moral theology at the Theological Faculty at Tilburg.
Fields of interest: fundamental morality, political ethics, Thomas Aquinas.

JOSEPH A. SELLING (1945), doctorate in theology, professor of moral theology at the Catholic University at Leuven.
Fields of interest: fundamental moral theology, ethics of marriage and sexuality.

PATRICK VANDERMEERSCH (1946), Master's in theology, doctorate in philosophy, professor of religious psychology at Rijksuniversiteit Groningen.
Fields of interest: the psychology of faith and of philosophy in relation to secularization.

FRANS VOSMAN (1952), doctorate in moral theology, lecturer in moral theology at the Catholic Theological University at Utrecht.
Fields of interest: medical ethics viewed from the Catholic tradition, moral theology in connection with the body.